PIERRE BOULEZ

ORGANISED DELIRIUM

Caroline Potter

THE BOYDELL PRESS

First published 2024
The Boydell Press, Woodbridge

ISBN 978 1 83765 085 9

The Boydell Press is an imprint of Boydell & Brewer Ltd
PO Box 9, Woodbridge, Suffolk IP12 3DF, UK
and of Boydell & Brewer Inc.
668 Mt Hope Avenue, Rochester, NY 14620–2731, USA
website: www.boydellandbrewer.com

The publisher has no responsibility for the continued existence or accuracy
of URLs for external or third-party internet websites referred to in this book,
and does not guarantee that any content on such websites is, or will remain,
accurate or appropriate

A CIP catalogue record for this book is available
from the British Library

This publication is printed on acid-free paper

CONTENTS

ILLUSTRATIONS

Figures

Tables

Music examples

The author and publisher are grateful to all the institutions and individuals listed for permission to reproduce the materials in which they hold copyright. Every effort has been made to trace the copyright holders; apologies are offered for any omission, and the publisher will be pleased to add any necessary acknowledgement in subsequent editions.

ACKNOWLEDGEMENTS

I AM GRATEFUL TO THE many friends and colleagues who helped me develop my ideas, whether by kindly forwarding articles or through in-depth conversations or chance remarks that proved extraordinarily fruitful. In particular, I would like to thank Julian Anderson, Paul Archbold, Sébastien Arfouilloux, Peter Asimov, Jean-Efflam Bavouzet, Edward Campbell, Robin Hartwell, Christine Jolivet-Erlih, Federico Lazzaro, Roger Nichols, Robert Orledge, Ian Pace, Caroline Rae, John Rea, Robert Sholl, Michael Worton and the late Alastair Brotchie, Jane Manning and Ornella Volta. I am especially grateful to Peter O'Hagan for reading the entire manuscript and making many useful suggestions.

I especially wish to acknowledge the organisations that awarded me funding to pursue the research that led to this book. The British Academy/Leverhulme Trust awarded me a small research grant, supported by the Modern Humanities Research Association, to study archive and manuscript material in Paris and Switzerland. In 2020–1 I was the beneficiary of an Edison Research Fellowship awarded by the British Library which supported my sound archive research, and I would like to thank Jonathan Summers and Vedita Ramdoss for their assistance in navigating the catalogue and digitising relevant resources. The Paul Sacher Stiftung in Basel enabled me to benefit from its unrivalled Boulez collection and superb working conditions, and I would especially like to thank Angela Ida De Benedictis, Marianne Diessner, Michèle Noirjean and Felix Meyer.

At different stages in the writing of this book I held visiting research positions at the Institute of Modern Languages Research, University of London, and the Royal Birmingham Conservatoire; I am grateful to both institutions for their support and especially to Catherine Davies and Christopher Dingle for facilitating these positions.

Thanks to all staff at Boydell Press, especially Michael Middeke, Crispin Peet, Christy Beale, Julia Cook and Elizabeth Howard, for their support for my work.

For permission to reproduce copyright material I wish to thank Alain Galliari (Succession Boulez); Therese Muxeneder (Arnold Schönberg Center); Marianne Diessner (Paul Sacher Stiftung); Claudia Patsch (Universal Edition); Hector Lemoine (Editions Henry Lemoine); Nickie Osborne and Andrea Natale (Hal Leonard Ltd.).

INTRODUCTION:
ORGANISED DELIRIUM

PIERRE BOULEZ'S CREATIVE OUTPUT has usually been studied from a music analytical perspective in the context of serialism, but I contend that the French literary and broader intellectual context of his formative years was equally, if not more, important to his musical evolution. This study will uncover the crucial impact of this context on Boulez's emergence as a composer, enhancing our understanding of his work by connecting it with significant trends in contemporary French culture and refocusing Boulez studies away from detailed musical analysis and towards a more visceral, emotional response to his work.

The composer gives us some pointers in his important article 'Propositions' (1948), written the same year as his Second Piano Sonata and published in *Polyphonie*. The principal topic of this article is rhythm in music, and it ends:

> I have a personal reason for giving such an important place to the phenomenon of rhythm. I think that music should be a collective hysteria and magic, violently modern – along the lines of Antonin Artaud and not in the sense of a simple ethnographic reconstruction in the image of civilisations more or less remote from us.[1]

Rhythm, therefore, has magical properties, and it is impossible to read this passage without considering the central impact of Artaud on the young Boulez. 'Hysteria and magic' are perhaps not the words that immediately spring to mind with Boulez, given the popular view of him as a cerebral musical mathematician, but the overwhelming emotional impact of his early work is quite the opposite of dry and calculated. And the image of Boulez the mathematician is also misleading and perhaps relates more to his biography, specifically his school studies in advanced

---

[1] Pierre Boulez, 'Propositions', *Polyphonie*, no. 2 (1948): pp. 65–72, at p. 72: 'J'ai enfin une raison personnelle pour donner une place si importante au phénomène rythmique. Je pense que la musique doit être envoûtement et hystérie collectifs, violemment actuels – suivant la direction d'Antonin Artaud, et non pas une simple reconstitution ethnographique à l'image de civilisations plus ou moins éloignées de nous.' The article was translated by Stephen Walsh in Pierre Boulez, *Stocktakings from an Apprenticeship* (Oxford: Clarendon Press, 1991), pp. 47–54, and I have modified these translations throughout this book. All translations are my own unless stated otherwise.

mathematics. Boulez's fixation with numbers in music – not only the number twelve associated with serialism – is not mathematical: rather, it is magical.

Boulez is a divisive figure whose reputation as the 'angry young man' of European modern music followed him for the rest of his long life. He was angry because music mattered hugely to him. Of course, this anger sprang from his rejection of the conservative French musical culture of his youth, from a desire to wipe the slate clean after the horrors of World War II, and surely also from his rejection of senior male role models, including his father who wanted him to train as an engineer. The manuscripts of his early compositions bear witness to his changing affinities, with dedications and epigraphs vigorously crossed out and replaced with ones more in tune with his latest sympathies. But, more profoundly, the violence and anger has striking parallels in Parisian artistic culture of the 1930s and 40s, and specifically from artists broadly connected with surrealism. The general assumption is that Boulez's music represented a post-war modernist break with what had gone before, but his aesthetic links with surrealism show that continuing threads from pre-war culture are fundamental to his work.

Paul Griffiths writes: '[Boulez] composed, in his early twenties, music that paralleled the violence and ecstasy in the recent writings of Antonin Artaud – music of "fury and mystery", to quote the title of a collection of poems by another writer Boulez strongly admired: René Char. He worked with the passion of someone entering a void.'[2] Violence, ecstasy, *fureur et mystère*: these extreme emotions characterise the aesthetics of an uncompromising, fiercely intelligent young composer who emerged startlingly quickly in the 1940s. His teacher, Olivier Messiaen, talked to Claude Samuel about the nineteen-year-old Boulez: 'he was very angry, as you know. He was like a lion that had been flayed alive, he was terrible!'[3]

Boulez had an extraordinary formative period, travelling from his first significant attempts at composition in 1944 via *Notations* (1945) and the first version of *Le Visage nuptial* (1946) to the overwhelming and fiendishly complex Second Piano Sonata (1948) in less than five years. And the music he composed in these few years was the source for much of his subsequent work: many later pieces are derived from

2   Paul Griffiths, *The Sea on Fire: Jean Barraqué* (Rochester: University of Rochester Press, 2003), p. 20.
3   Claude Samuel, interview (1988) with Olivier Messiaen, *Messiaen Edition*, 18 CD box set, Warner Classics 2564 62162-2 (2005); trans. Stuart Walters in CD booklet, pp. 109–35.

material, or even from themes (the seven-note theme of *Notations* 7, for instance) composed in this period.

From the late 1940s, Boulez also emerged as a polemical writer on music. Some of these early articles (including 'Propositions') use examples from his own works, though often he tends to discuss specific technical features without attributing them to a named piece. While he was outspoken, he also covered his tracks very well. A significant early article, 'Trajectoires: Ravel, Stravinsky, Schoenberg' (1949), is ostensibly about the composers named in the title, but although Boulez does not mention his work at all, it is clear that his own music is the true topic. Boulez's reputation as a polemicist has detracted attention from his music, though one suspects that many have not read articles such as 'Schoenberg est mort' (Schoenberg is dead; 1952) beyond the title.

Writing in 1965, Robert Henderson noted:

> Both in his theoretical writings, and in the numerous press interviews published in France, Pierre Boulez has consistently drawn attention to the fact that many of his more deeply rooted ideas have arisen 'more from reflections about literature than about music', that in his more recent work, in particular, 'musical considerations have counted less than the literary contacts I have happened to have'.[4]

Henderson's short article focuses on *Le Soleil des eaux*, a setting of René Char that started life as music for a radio play, and Char was without question the most important literary influence on Boulez during his formative years.

Boulez's affinity with literature has been widely acknowledged, most notably in English-language academe by Mary Breatnach, Peter Stacey and especially Edward Campbell.[5] Campbell's principal focus is on the relationship of philosophy to Boulez's music and ideas, though he is one of few authors to raise the possibility that other intellectual currents in France such as surrealism and the Bourbaki group of mathematicians may also have been important to him. On surrealism, Campbell writes, 'Boulez's relationship with surrealism is rather intriguing in its ambivalence and it may best be described as constellatory.'[6] By this, he means that Boulez had a number of contacts, either personally or in correspondence, with figures associated with the surrealist movement, such as the Belgian composer and writer André Souris, 'a

---

[4] Robert Henderson, 'Le Soleil des eaux', *Musical Times*, vol. 106 no. 1471 (September 1965): pp. 673–4, at p. 673.

[5] Mary Breatnach, *Boulez and Mallarmé* (Aldershot: Scolar, 1996); Peter F. Stacey, *Boulez and the Modern Concept* (Aldershot: Scolar, 1987); Edward Campbell, *Boulez, Music and Philosophy* (Cambridge: Cambridge University Press, 2010).

[6] Campbell, *Boulez, Music and Philosophy*, p. 28.

key figure in Boulez's early development'[7] who programmed Boulez's Sonatine for flute and piano in Brussels in 1947. Campbell concludes that Boulez was close to 'Breton's surrealism in his negational thinking and use of binary oppositions, his early aggressiveness and his interest in non-European cultures. While Breton was not alone in having these qualities and interests, and no causal relationship is suggested, we can simply note these intersections and pass on.'[8] Rather than 'pass on', I propose to investigate these important currents as they relate to Boulez and show that they had a crucial impact on his music. (I also disagree that 'binary opposition' is the right term for surrealist paradoxes such as 'explosante-fixe': the point is that apparent opposites are collapsed and brought together.) For example, his connections with Belgian surrealism – not just with Souris – were a good deal more extensive than has previously been acknowledged. Boulez was introduced to Souris by his fellow student Serge Nigg (1924–2008), and in a letter to Souris he wrote, '[Nigg] told me that besides being interested in atonal music, you are also involved with surrealism and you are one of the heads of this movement in Belgium, which was an excellent surprise to me.'[9]

Detailed exploration of the nature of the connections between Boulez's music and other artistic trends is surprisingly scanty. The distinguished Norwegian Boulez scholar Erling Guldbrandsen recognises this lack:

> If Boulez has been, at best, ambivalent in his rhetoric, widespread structural analyses of his music have been, at worst, methodologically one-eyed. To be sure, Boulez's many sources of inspiration – from literature and the arts, aesthetics, listening to earlier composers and rehearsing and conducting their scores together with musicians and ensembles – have been frequently though loosely mentioned, but their concrete impact has rarely been positioned right at the heart of his compositional method.[10]

[7] Campbell, *Boulez, Music and Philosophy*, p. 27.
[8] Campbell, *Boulez, Music and Philosophy*, p. 34.
[9] François Meïmoun, *La Construction du langage musical de Pierre Boulez: la Première Sonate pour piano*, thesis submitted to EHESS, Paris, 2018, p. 146 note 771, and published as a book the following year (Paris: Aedam Musicae, 2019), p. 147 note 103: 'il m'a dit qu'en dehors de musique atonale vous vous occupiez aussi du surréalisme et que vous êtes une des têtes de ce mouvement en Belgique, ce qui m'a fait une excellente surprise'. The letter dates from before 21 January 1947.
[10] Erling Guldbrandsen, 'Unpredictability and free choice in the composition of *Pli selon pli*', in Edward Campbell and Peter O'Hagan (eds.), *Pierre Boulez Studies* (Cambridge: Cambridge University Press, 2016), pp. 193–220, at p. 210.

I wish to respond to Guldbrandsen by exploring Boulez's literary and artistic as well as musical sources of inspiration and showing their vital impact on his formative years.

At the Paris Conservatoire, where Boulez enrolled during World War II, he was quickly recognised as a brilliant student. His secondary school education had been traditional and academic, culminating in mathematics-focused studies in Lyon, and while he was an able piano student who dabbled in composition, nothing pointed to him being an exceptional musical talent. But his discovery of the ondes Martenot at a rehearsal for the premiere of Messiaen's *Trois petites liturgies de la Présence Divine* (1943–4) led him to learn the instrument with its inventor and ultimately to find work as a professional performer on the instrument. This skill also resulted in an introduction to the actors Jean-Louis Barrault and Madeleine Renaud.

The Renaud–Barrault theatre company changed Boulez's life both intellectually and professionally. The actors founded their own theatrical company in 1946, and their first production was a version of *Hamlet* in André Gide's translation. Arthur Honegger composed incidental music for this production, for an ensemble of brass, percussion and ondes Martenot. As performers of the latter instrument were and are rare, Honegger's wife, Andrée Vaurabourg-Honegger, recommended her private student in counterpoint, Pierre Boulez, for the job. Vaurabourg wrote to Boulez on 5 October 1946: 'My husband and I await you next Tuesday [...], we would like to see you, listen to your [First Piano] sonata, and show you the incidental music for *Hamlet*.'[11] In fact, Barrault did not only employ him for this job; he and his wife ultimately offered Boulez the role of musical director of the company, despite his lack of experience.[12] Boulez's apprenticeship with the Renaud–Barrault company – much of it focused on music by composers with whom he had little or no sympathy – took him around the world and ultimately led to a major international conducting career with a repertoire that extended well beyond his own music and that of his contemporaries.

In 1953, the actors also founded a journal, the *Cahiers Renaud-Barrault*, to which Boulez contributed on several occasions. Barrault himself wrote of his first impressions of Boulez in the journal's

[11] Letter in the Boulez collection, Paul Sacher Stiftung, Basel: 'Mon mari et moi nous vous attendons mardi prochain [...], nous aimerions vous voir, entendre votre sonate, et vous montrer la musique de scène de *Hamlet*.'

[12] David Le Marrec, 'Boulez après les Folies Bergère: Agamemnon de Pierre Boulez', 24 April 2015, http://operacritiques.free.fr/css/index.php?2015/04/24/2666-in-edit-agamemnon-de-pierre-boulez-l-orestie-eschyle-jean-louis-barrault-ma-deleine-renaud-1955-bordeaux-marigny [accessed June 2023].

tenth anniversary number: 'Then, he lived with his claws out, skinned. He didn't spare anyone, or hardly anyone. He was trenchant, aggressive, sometimes he irritated; he must have been uncomfortable in his skin.'[13] How striking that Barrault uses the same metaphor as Messiaen: the extreme vulnerability and hypersensitivity of the skinned animal.

As an apprentice composer, Boulez absorbed an enormous amount of technical musical knowledge in a short space of time, studying harmony with Georges Dandelot and then Messiaen at the Conservatoire, earning first prizes in successive years – an exceptional feat. He also studied counterpoint privately with Andrée Vaurabourg-Honegger, but his most important apprenticeship was spent in other private classes, those of Messiaen and René Leibowitz. The latter promoted the music of the Second Viennese School in Paris, and while Boulez fell under the spell of Schoenberg in the first instance, and later Webern, his view of Leibowitz soon soured and the rift between them never healed; in 2002, many years after Leibowitz's death, Boulez was still criticising 'his narrowness of spirit and aridity of invention.'[14]

Boulez's studies outside the walls of the Conservatoire with Messiaen and Leibowitz have received a good deal of attention, but for any student, peer relationships are at least as important as the teacher–pupil dyad, perhaps especially in the French system where group tuition is the norm. Messiaen's private lesson group, which became known as 'Les Flèches' (The Arrows), included Yvonne Loriod, Yvette Grimaud and Serge Nigg as well as Boulez, and this close-knit group occasionally performed as well as studied together. Most of the group also worked with Leibowitz, and Boulez shared many common interests with Grimaud, a pianist of crucial importance in his formative years as she premiered his *Trois Psalmodies*, *Notations* and first two piano sonatas. Five years Boulez's senior, Grimaud was then also a composer who used microtones in her work; she learned to play the ondes Martenot when the instrument was still very new (she met Maurice Martenot before 1938), and her wide musical interests extended to non-Western musics. All of these interests were passed on to Boulez. While her music is now almost completely forgotten and it is hard to source recorded piano

13 Jean-Louis Barrault, 'Travailler avec Boulez', *Cahiers Renaud-Barrault, no.* 41 (December 1963); reprinted in *Résonance*, no. 8 (March 1995), http://articles. ircam.fr/textes/Barrault95a/index.html [accessed June 2023]: 'A cette époque, il vivait "toutes griffes dehors", "à l'écorché". Il n'épargnait personne, ou presque. Il était mordant, agressif, irritant parfois; sa peau devait lui faire mal.'
14 Interview with Claude Samuel published in Pierre Boulez and Claude Samuel, *Éclats 2002* (Paris: Mémoire du livre, 2002), p. 24: 'son étroitesse d'esprit et sa sécheresse d'invention.'

performances by her, there is plenty of evidence showing that Grimaud had a considerable impact on Boulez's musical development. Loriod was also an early performer of Boulez's piano music (and active as a composer when she was a student), and Nigg was close to Boulez when they were in the same classes; Boulez's twelve *Notations* are dedicated to him. In fact, contemporary reviews and critiques show that Nigg, not Boulez, was considered the most important young Messiaen pupil in the mid–late 1940s. Nigg's music was performed in public far more than Boulez's in this period, and his combative opinions on contemporary musical life appeared in print before anything penned by Boulez was published.

Much previous work on Boulez has focused on the importance of serialism in the development of his musical language. This emphasis on serialism has resulted in a long series of books with music analysis at their heart, from Lev Koblyakov's remarkably detailed *Pierre Boulez: A World of Harmony* (1990), written before Boulez's extensive sketches became available for study, to more recent work by scholars including Jonathan Goldman, Pascal Decroupet and Peter O'Hagan. Recent research in this area draws on the extensive Boulez manuscript collection at the Paul Sacher Stiftung in Basel, Switzerland; by uncovering Boulez's compositional process via the study of sketches, scholars have expanded our understanding of Boulez as creator through their detailed examination of this material. The best work of this type uses sketch study as a means to an end, for instance O'Hagan's work, which draws on sketches to enhance our understanding of his piano music from both listener and performer perspectives.[15]

However, both music analysis and manuscript study leave other questions unaddressed. One of the first books devoted to Boulez, a series of interviews and commentaries by Antoine Goléa published in 1958, acknowledged the emotional power of his early work:

> The truth is that it seems to me impossible to resist being bewitched by Boulez's music, by its explosive force, its relentlessness, its violence, its rage which is sometimes desperate, sometimes triumphant. The truth is that Boulez is an expressionist, the strongest and most implacable of them all, much more so than the German expressionists of the turn of the century.[16]

---

[15] Peter O'Hagan, *Pierre Boulez and the Piano* (Abingdon: Routledge, 2017).

[16] Antoine Goléa, *Rencontres avec Pierre Boulez* (Paris: Julliard, 1958), pp. 57–8: 'La vérité, c'est qu'il me paraît impossible de se soustraire à l'envoûtement de la musique de Boulez, à sa force explosive, à son acharnement, à sa violence, à sa rage tantôt désespérée, tantôt triomphante. La vérité, c'est que Boulez est un

Goléa does not mention Schoenberg here, but the term 'expressionist' can be assumed to be synonymous with the Schoenberg from around 1908 to the early 1910s, before the twelve-note series became his established method of construction. And from the start, Boulez always sought to go beyond previous composers, both technically and emotionally; there is no holding back in his early work. Where the Second Viennese School are concerned, it is Schoenberg, rather than Webern, who is the central musical influence on Boulez's first works, but we need to turn to France to explore his cultural context.

What is the cultural background – both musical and non-musical – to Boulez's work? Where does the extreme energy and visceral emotional impact of Boulez's music come from? This book will address these two fundamental issues, and I argue that surrealism is the key that allows us to unlock both questions. François Meïmoun's 2018 thesis on the background to and genesis of Boulez's First Piano Sonata, published in book form in 2019, is one of very few previous texts to acknowledge the key role of surrealism in the composer's formative years. Meïmoun believes that 'Boulez leaned briefly but effectively on surrealism to enable him to synthesise different sources of influence and help him to better define the music he wanted to compose: music of delirium and hysteria, that he wanted to inscribe in vast forms within which all of the musical parameters, considered in their own terms and reciprocally, are completely coherent on a small and large scale.'[17] Surrealism left an even stronger mark on Boulez that Meïmoun supposes.

It may seem surprising to place Boulez in the context of surrealism for three reasons. First, André Breton, the standard-bearer for surrealism from the origins of the movement in the early 1920s until his death in 1966, had no interest whatsoever in music. In *Le Surréalisme et la peinture* (1928), Breton insisted: 'allow me to give the plastic arts a value which I will always refuse to give to music. [...] May night continue to fall on the orchestra.'[18] After Breton's funeral, the artist André Masson

---

expressionniste, le plus fort, le plus implacable, bien plus fort et implacable que les expressionnistes allemands du début du siècle.'

[17] Meïmoun, *Construction du langage musical*, p. 175: 'Boulez s'appuie brièvement mais efficacement sur le surréalisme pour effectuer la synthèse des héritages et s'aider à mieux définir la musique qu'il veut composer, musique du délire et de l'hystérie qu'il veut inscrire dans de vastes formes maîtrisées à l'intérieur desquelles tous les paramètres musicaux, pensés pour eux-mêmes et en réciprocité, offrent une absolue cohérence du tout et des parties.'

[18] André Breton, *Le Surréalisme et la peinture* (1928; reprinted Paris: Gallimard, 1965), p. 1: '[...] qu'il me soit permis d'accorder à l'expression plastique une valeur que par contre je ne cesserai de refuser à l'expression musicale. [...] Que la nuit continue donc à tomber sur l'orchestre [...].'

told Ornella Volta that he and his fellow painter Max Ernst said, 'We won't have to listen to music in secret any more ...'[19] Indeed, the Masson name is now associated with music as well as the visual arts, because in an authentically surrealist coincidence, the artist's son Diego is a conductor specialising in contemporary music who worked on many occasions with Boulez.

But while Breton was the most prominent spokesman for surrealism – and he broke off relations with those who disagreed with him – his contemporaries showed that music can be surrealist. For instance, there was an important Belgian surrealist movement which emerged from the mid-1920s in parallel with its French counterpart but with subtly different foci, and the composers E.L.T. Mesens and André Souris were involved from the start in this Belgian circle. Beyond these 'official' groupings, composers were stimulated in their own ways by surrealism, both by setting surrealist poetry to music and by drawing on surrealist concepts in more general terms. As Boulez himself wrote in his article 'Poésie – centre et absence – musique': 'Music can be linked with poetry at a number of different levels of importance and intensity, from a mere title to intimate fusion and from the anecdotal to the essential.'[20] Recent years have seen increasing academic interest in the relationship between music and surrealism, pioneered by scholars such as Sébastien Arfouilloux.[21]

Second, Boulez himself acknowledged that the most important cultural figure in Paris during his student years was Jean-Paul Sartre (1905–80). By the 1940s, Sartre was already established as a philosopher, and his plays *Les Mouches* (1943) and *Huis clos* (1944) had brought his name and ideas to a wider public. Together with Simone de Beauvoir (1908–86), Sartre founded the journal *Les Temps modernes* in October 1945, which was quickly recognised as the pre-eminent Paris literary magazine. René Leibowitz occasionally contributed articles about the

[19] Ornella Volta, *Brèves Rencontres avec André Breton, avec vingt-deux photographies de Pablo Volta* (Paris: Éditions du Placard, 2003), n.p.: 'Nous n'aurons plus désormais à écouter la musique en cachette ...' I am grateful to Volta for introducing me to this very rare publication.

[20] Translated by Martin Cooper in Pierre Boulez, *Orientations*, ed. Jean-Jacques Nattiez (London: Faber, 1986), pp. 183–98, at p. 184. Pierre Boulez, *Points de repère*, ed. Jean-Jacques Nattiez, 2nd edition (Paris: Christian Bourgois, 1985), pp. 183–200, at p. 184: 'La musique se lie à la poésie à des niveaux bien différents, avec plus ou moins d'intensité, de présence: de la simple épigraphe à la fusion; de l'épisode anecdotique à la substance fondamentale.'

[21] Sébastien Arfouilloux, *Que la nuit tombe sur l'orchestre. Surréalisme et musique* (Paris: Fayard, 2009).

Second Viennese School to *Les Temps modernes*,[22] but Boulez otherwise had no connections with this circle and little or no interest in ideas associated with Sartre, such as existentialism or the notion that art should be politically engaged.

Third, Boulez's extensive published writings rarely mention surrealism, and it is obvious that Boulez's writings must be an important source when investigating the impact on him of the literary and intellectual environment of France of the 1930s and 40s. His writings are suffused with philosophical and literary allusions and quotations, though he did not always name the author, nor necessarily cite prose or poetry accurately (most of Boulez's published texts were written at speed and to commission, and I assume he sometimes quoted from memory). Robert Piencikowski, in his preface to Stephen Walsh's English translation of Boulez's *Relevés d'apprenti*, suggests that Boulez's polemical writing style is influenced by 'certain surrealist pamphlets of the 1920s',[23] presumably Breton's two *Manifestes du surréalisme* published in 1924 and 1929. Moving beyond this focus on Boulez's writing – which was always a secondary activity for him – I will explore how creative work (as well as theoretical and polemical writings) by authors such as André Breton might have affected Boulez as a creative artist.

The small number of references to surrealism in Boulez's published writings is perhaps not surprising; as David Walters writes in his thesis: '[Boulez's] tendency to hide his major sources of influence is a characteristic of his writings.'[24] But those references to surrealism and surrealist authors that do exist are strikingly significant. To give one example, the title of several related works he composed from the 1970s to the early 1990s, *...explosante-fixe...*, is a partial quotation of André Breton, and the union of the opposite qualities of explosion and stasis is a key concept in Boulez's music. In just two words, the Breton fragment crystallises what is at the core of Boulez the creative artist. Joan Peyser claims that for Boulez, this line was 'independently floating',[25] in other words divorced from its context, and significantly, in conversation with Peyser, Boulez misattributed this Breton quotation to *Nadja* (1928), not its correct source, *L'Amour fou* (1937). Connections between surrealism

---

[22] Boulez mentions this in an interview with David Walters; see Walters's PhD thesis 'The aesthetics of Pierre Boulez', Durham University, 2003, p. 44, available at Durham E-Theses Online, http://etheses.dur.ac.uk/3093/; the full interview appears as an appendix at pp. 402–16.

[23] Robert Piencikowski, preface to Boulez, *Stocktakings from an Apprenticeship*, p. xviii.

[24] Walters, 'The aesthetics of Pierre Boulez', p. 44.

[25] Joan Peyser, *Boulez: Composer, Conductor, Enigma* (London: Cassell, 1977), p. 238.

and Boulez's music can also be drawn on a conceptual level: central surrealist concepts such as the 'objet trouvé' (found object), 'hasard objectif' (objective chance), and the unification of apparent opposites all have musical equivalents.

Musical *objets trouvés* in Boulez can be purloined from other composers or from his own work. One particularly durable idea in his oeuvre is a seven-note theme he first used in the seventh piece of his *Notations* which is reemployed in multiple contexts, for instance in the series of works entitled *...explosante-fixe...*. Found objects with origins external to Boulez include a twelve-note series used in his first book of *Structures* for two pianos (1951–2) which is derived from Messiaen's piano study *Mode de valeurs et d'intensités* (1949); a low bass cluster identical to one used in Jolivet's 'La Princesse de Bali' from his *Mana* suite (1935) which appears in many of Boulez's early piano works; and the SACHER cipher, a musical spelling of Paul Sacher's surname first used by Boulez in *Messagesquisse* (1976–7) and subsequently in several pieces, including *Dérive* (1984).

Many critics and listeners have drawn attention to the paradox of Boulez's integral serialist works of the early 1950s, including *Structures 1a*. Integral serialist works are predetermined in the sense that all of their musical parameters – including pitch, rhythm, modes of attack and dynamics – are obtained from sequences of numbers which each relate to a particular pitch, rhythm or other parameter, though the final aural result could be described as random. Boulez himself recognised this coexistence of calculation and spontaneity, telling Michel Archimbaud of his reaction to two very different painters: 'Klee is a very calculating artist, whereas the spontaneous gesture is at the heart of Pollock, and I share both their qualities.'[26] This encounter of calculation and chance strongly parallels 'hasard objectif'. It is essential to emphasise that Boulez's interpretations of the term 'chance' differ from its commonplace English meanings, being instead related to surrealist aesthetic notions of automatism.

It must also be stressed that the cultural context of French surrealism in the 1930s and 40s was highly multidisciplinary and outward-looking. Surrealism, ethnography, esotericism and the emerging discipline of ethnomusicology were closely related, and this interdisciplinary cultural context will be outlined in Chapter 1. An interest in mysticism and the occult is a continuing thread in French culture from the late nineteenth century into the 1930s and, though it is more often associated with the

---

[26] Pierre Boulez, *Entretiens avec Michel Archimbaud*, Folio Essais (Paris: Gallimard, 2016), p. 175: 'Chez Klee, il y a un grand calcul des choses, tandis que Pollock est un geste spontané, et je suis partagé entre les deux.'

visual arts and literature than with music, Debussy and his close friend Satie met in the heady artistic environment of Montmartre in the 1880s, where this search for something beyond everyday experience was shared by artists of all types. Roy Howat has discussed the importance of this Montmartre scene to Debussy, showing that his employment of Golden Section structuring emerged from an artistic environment where scientific mysticism was a common interest. And Satie collaborated in the 1890s with the eccentric writers Jules Bois and Sâr Péladan and was involved in esoteric religious practices, which led to his foundation of the ultimate in sects, a church of which he was the sole member.

This artistic curiosity about esotericism was shared by the surrealists. For Breton, 'le point suprême' (the supreme point) is the point when contradictions cease to exist, when everything comes together. Michel Carrouges wrote that 'The notion of the supreme point is the fundamental touchstone of surrealist cosmology; it is the crucible of the real and the surreal and it comes from esotericism.'[27] This mystic union of opposites has important precursors in French literature, most notably Charles Baudelaire's concept of the double (*le dédoublement*) and Alfred Jarry's pataphysics, where the equivalence of opposites is a key concept. It is a notion highlighted near the beginning of Breton's Second Surrealist Manifesto:

> Everything leads us to believe that there is a certain point where life and death, the real and the imaginary, the past and the future, the communicable and the incommunicable, high and low cease to be perceived as contradictions. The fundamental aim of surrealist activity is the hope of determining this point.[28]

This reconciliation of apparently contradictory impulses – specifically, intellectual structuring and demonic fury – is also a crucial aspect of Boulez's earliest works. While the intellectual, constructivist side of Boulez has been extensively analysed, a more or less exclusive focus on this aspect of his composing ignores the equally important emotional dimension of his music.

---

[27] Michel Carrouges, *André Breton et les données fondamentales du surréalisme* (Paris: Gallimard, 1950), p. 22: 'La notion de point suprême est la pierre d'angle fondamentale de la cosmologie surréaliste, elle est le foyer vivant du réel et du surréel et elle vient de l'ésotérisme.'

[28] André Breton, *Deuxième manifeste du surréalisme* (1929; reprinted Paris: Gallimard, Folio edition, 1985), pp. 72–3: 'Tout porte à croire qu'il existe un certain point de l'esprit d'où la vie et la mort, le réel et l'imaginaire, le passé et le futur, le communicable et l'incommunicable, le haut et le bas cessent d'être perçus contradictoirement. Or, c'est en vain qu'on chercherait à l'activité surréaliste un autre mobile que l'espoir de détermination de ce point.'

Surrealism might have emerged in Paris, but it became both an international movement and one that was inseparable from contemporary trends in ethnography and sociology. Boulez's musical curiosity extended to non-European cultures, and this curiosity needs to be understood in the light of his broader intellectual environment. Drawing inspiration from non-Western music is hardly unusual for a French composer – Rameau, Bizet, Debussy and, closer to Boulez's time, Jolivet and Messiaen are cases in point – but unlike any of his predecessors, Boulez might have spent his career as an ethnomusicologist had fate not intervened. Boulez transcribed recordings in the Musée Guimet and was more broadly interested in non-European cultures, an interest that soon had an impact on his own music. Boulez's discovery of the musics of Asia and Africa was not simply an encounter with attractive and exotic sound resources, but one with cultures in which music had a central, sacred place. And while he was far from a 'keeper of the flame' for these non-Western musics – as a Western European composer, he could not be – Boulez identified with the seriousness of purpose of music that was a fundamental part of a living culture.

His friendship with the ethnomusicologist and author André Schaeffner dates from 1949, and Schaeffner kept him in touch with non-European musics; their published correspondence reveals that Boulez often asked Schaeffner's advice on particular instruments, and Maxime Joos goes as far as to say that 'Boulez found in Schaeffner the ethnomusicologist that he wanted to become.'[29] Later, Boulez dedicated a section of the first version of his piano piece *Incises* (1994) to the Franco-Israeli ethnomusicologist Simha Arom, an eminent specialist in music of the Central African Republic. The connections between music, surrealism, ethnology and ethnomusicology in this period are not linear but circular or indeed sideways.

Perhaps most importantly of all, the writer and performer Antonin Artaud was a crucial formative influence on Boulez who draws all these different strands together. Artaud was a member of the Paris surrealist circle from 1924 to 1926, a contributor to the review *La Révolution surréaliste* and editor of several numbers and director of the Bureau de Recherches Surréalistes (Bureau of Surrealist Research) before, like so many others, he broke with Breton. He was also an actor with a striking physical presence, and his live performances of his own work encompassed all manner of utterances. Artaud was close to Jean-Louis Barrault in the mid-1930s, a decade before Barrault met Boulez; the two actors

---

[29] Maxime Joos, 'Variations esthétiques (Schloezer, Boulez, Schaeffner)', *Revue de musicologie*, vol. 91 no. 2 (2005): pp. 401–24, at p. 402.

worked together in *Autour d'une mère* (1935, Barrault's final production with the theatrical troupe L'Atelier), and Barrault attended rehearsals of Artaud's ambitious production of *Les Cenci* (1935). Published correspondence shows that Artaud and Barrault were in contact during Artaud's journey to Mexico, but their relationship tailed off when Artaud returned to France and was interned in an asylum in Rodez.[30]

Artaud attended the Exposition Coloniale Internationale (International Colonial Exhibition) in Paris in 1931 (unlike contemporary members of the surrealist circle, who protested against this exhibition), and there he witnessed a Balinese theatrical performance including dance and a gamelan ensemble. Just as Debussy had been enthralled by a Balinese performance at the 1889 Paris Exposition Universelle, Artaud was hugely struck by this display, which fed into his theory of the Theatre of Cruelty. As an established opera conductor, Boulez referred many years later to Artaud's ideas when discussing Debussy's only completed opera *Pelléas et Mélisande* (1892–1902),[31] but more significantly, Artaud's writings and especially his performance style were vitally important to the development of his musical style from the mid-1940s. The impact of Artaud's verbal performance style, combined with Schoenbergian *Sprechstimme* (speech-song) techniques, strongly marked not only Boulez's two early Char settings, *Le Visage nuptial* and *Le Soleil des eaux*, but also the instrumental music of his formative years. These key writers in Boulez's development were both briefly associated with the Paris surrealist movement, but essentially they were fiercely independent artists who resisted labelling and pigeonholing. Boulez was much the same.

Towards the end of the fourth movement of Boulez's Second Piano Sonata, we read the striking performance instruction 'pulvériser le son' (pulverise the sound), a term which encapsulates the overwhelming violent passion of the work. While Boulez tends to be described as a cerebral composer, this work above all others shows that the intellectual, constructivist side of his work coexists with extreme visceral energy – with the 'collective hysteria and magic' mentioned in his article 'Propositions' which he specifically links with Antonin Artaud's work.

Artaud travelled to Mexico in 1936 on a lecture tour to promote surrealist writers, and during this visit he went on an expedition and

---

[30] See Antonin Artaud, *Lettres d'Antonin Artaud à Jean-Louis Barrault* (Paris: Bordas, 1952).

[31] Boulez described Golaud as 'this horrid man who wants to know everything' ('cet horrible monsieur qui veut tout savoir') in a letter to André Schaeffner written in November 1961. See Rosângela Pereira de Tugny (ed.), *Pierre Boulez, André Schaeffner: correspondance 1954–1970* (Paris: Fayard, 1998), p. 50.

participated in a voodoo ceremony which is narrated in 'D'un voyage au pays des Tarahumaras' (1937).[32] Surely Boulez's 'collective hysteria and magic' specifically references Artaud's involvement in collective rituals, and his opposition of Artaud's attempt at cultural immersion to 'a simple ethnographic reconstruction' is impossible to understand without exploring what Artaud's work meant to Boulez.

Boulez attended a reading by Artaud in July 1947, an event described by Peter O'Hagan as a 'decisive encounter in Boulez's development'.[33] The previous year, Artaud had left the asylum in Rodez where he had been interned for three years and returned to Paris, though he was in very poor mental and physical health; this reading was one of only two performances he gave before his death on 4 March 1948. Artaud's final performance, *Pour en finir avec le jugement de Dieu*, was recorded by Radio France on 22–9 November 1947, when Artaud's texts were read by the author and three others including Paule Thévenin. Like Breton, Thévenin had trained in psychiatry, and she is a particularly important figure in this story as she was a common friend of Boulez and Artaud and she introduced Boulez to the author's work. The Radio France recording of *Pour en finir avec le jugement de Dieu* was scheduled for broadcast on 2 February 1948, but the director of Radio France, Wladimir Porché, pulled the programme the day before because of concerns about blasphemy as well as the highly experimental nature of the performance.

Every account of Artaud's readings focuses on his distinct vocal performance style which encompassed sounds beyond speech, an issue Boulez addressed in an article which he significantly titled 'Son et verbe':

> I am not qualified to study Antonin Artaud's language thoroughly but I can locate in his writings the fundamental preoccupations of modern music; hearing him read his own texts, accompanying them with cries, noises, rhythms, has shown us how to create a fusion of sound and word, how to make the phoneme spurt out when the word can do no more; briefly, how to organise delirium.[34]

---

[32] First published in *Nouvelle revue française* (August 1937): pp. 232–47.

[33] O'Hagan, *Boulez and the Piano*, p. 74. Also see Brice Tissier, 'Pierre Boulez et le *Théâtre de la cruauté* d'Antonin Artaud: de *Pelléas* à *Rituel, in memoriam Bruno Maderna*', *Intersections*, vol. 28 no. 2 (2008): pp. 31–50.

[34] Translated by Walsh in Boulez, *Stocktakings from an Apprenticeship*, p. 43; originally published in *Cahiers Renaud-Barrault* and later in Pierre Boulez, *Relevés d'apprenti*, ed. Paule Thévenin (Paris: Seuil, 1966), pp. 57–62, at p. 62: 'Je ne suis pas qualifié pour approfondir le langage d'Antonin Artaud, mais je puis trouver dans ses écrits les préoccupations fondamentales de la musique actuelle; l'avoir entendu lire ses propres textes, les accompagnant de cris, de bruits, de rythmes, nous a indiqué comment faire gicler le phonème, lorsque le mot n'en peut plus, en bref, comment organiser le délire.' The article was later published

'How to organise delirium.' More than anything, this expression of Boulez shows the union of structure and chaos, of explosion and stasis, of serialism and surrealism at the heart of his aesthetic. These apparent opposites coexist in his music as 'both/and', not 'either/or'. The primary focus of this book is on the delirious, surreal, visceral side of Boulez's work, a fundamental aspect of his aesthetic that has been underplayed by previous authors and which is severely underestimated in the popular opinion of Boulez. But I would stress that this side exists with, not instead of, the analytical and constructivist side which has been emphasised by the vast majority of Boulez scholars.

At the end of his article 'Éventuellement' (1952), Boulez quotes Paul Verlaine: 'The heart, a viscera which replaces everything.'[35] This discussion of post-war developments in music that also looks to the future ends with an enigmatic reference not to the brain, but to organs representing emotion and gut feelings (the commonest English translation of 'viscère', 'intestine', does not adequately convey 'gut feeling'). This book's discussion of Boulez's music and aesthetic will give primary place to this visceral intensity of emotion. Jean-Louis Barrault said that he lacked formal musical education, but his reaction to Boulez's early work shows how deeply he understood this intensity: 'music makes my body vibrate. [...] whenever I've heard Boulez's music, I've felt violent impulses, passionate shivers, lyrical outbursts, suddenly held back by an extreme reserve, a marvellous chastity.'[36] The extremes of the emotional spectrum united: this perfectly encapsulates Boulez's aesthetic.

This study aims to show how Boulez's music is connected in a wide sense to contemporary arts and ideas, especially literature, and in particular how the turbulent, violent emotional world of his early works shows the impact of surrealist literature. Tracing this impact involves following multiple threads and exploring what Boulez might have taken from a source. Boulez was highly curious about other art forms, and he took what he required for his creative purposes; it mattered not at all to him if these sources were decontextualised and deformed as a result. To further complicate the picture, Robert Piencikowski has aptly noted

---

in expanded form in German under the title 'Son, verbe, synthèse' (*Melos*, vol. 25 no. 10 (1958), pp. 310–13), and translated by Martin Cooper in Boulez, *Orientations*, pp. 177–82.

[35] Boulez, *Relevés d'apprenti*, p. 182; the reference is to Verlaine's prose work of 1865, 'Les œuvres et les hommes par Barbey d'Aurevilly'. Walsh's translation ('Possibly'), is in Boulez, *Stocktakings from an Apprenticeship*, pp. 111–40.

[36] Barrault, 'Travailler avec Boulez': 'la musique me fait vibrer le corps. [...] chaque fois que j'ai entendu de la musique écrite par Boulez, j'ai ressenti des poussées violentes, des jaillissements passionnés, des éclatements lyriques, subitement retenus, retenus par une pudeur extrême, une chasteté merveilleuse.'

that, when many of Boulez's influential early articles were published in the 1950s, the compositions of his own which he cited remained unpublished and 'the [verbal] text, which was to have facilitated access to them, ended by diverting attention to itself'.[37] This book will start by charting the myriad literary and intellectual influences on Boulez, though its ultimate aim is to lead us back to the music. And few individuals have had as significant an impact on the twentieth-century musical world as Pierre Boulez. His friend the author Pierre Souvtchinsky wrote, 'There are not many who, between the ages of twenty-two and twenty-six, succeeded not only in making a mark on their art, but in changing its face and even its essence.'[38] How Boulez began changing music will be explored in this book.

---

[37] Boulez, *Stocktakings from an Apprenticeship*, p. xxiii.
[38] Cited in Joan Peyser, *To Boulez and Beyond: Music in Europe since the Rite of Spring*, revised edition (Lanham, MD: Scarecrow Press, 2007), p. 182.

1

SURREALISM IN THE 1930s AND 40s

S URREALISM IS ALL ABOUT liberation of the mind, freedom from constraints, accessing the irrational, privileging dreams, the fantastic, the marvellous, and embracing chance. André Breton is the author who is most closely associated with surrealism, as the author of the two most celebrated Surrealist Manifestos (1924, 1929) and self-appointed leader of the movement in Paris, but he drew on the ideas of many precursors, and the origins of the word 'surrealism' can be traced back to Guillaume Apollinaire (1890–1918).

In fact, the word first came to public attention in Apollinaire's programme note for a Ballets Russes premiere, Erik Satie's ballet *Parade* (1917), a collaboration with Picasso, Massine and Cocteau. This ballet was rooted in street and circus entertainment, though the American Girl character came straight out of the movies, and Picasso's oversized cardboard box costumes – a literal twist on cubism – gave it a strong contemporary edge. The Ballets Russes audience greeted the work with catcalls: they did not expect to see highly trained ballet dancers performing acrobatic moves and gestures such as using a typewriter, and the inclusion of shotgun and siren sounds in an entertainment context in 1917 was, to say the least, provocative. Writing in *Vanity Fair* that year, Satie himself ruefully described his music as 'a background to throw into relief the noises which [Cocteau] considers indispensable to the surrounding of each character with his own atmosphere'.[1]

While Cocteau described *Parade* as 'un ballet réaliste', Apollinaire described Satie's collaboration as follows:

> From this new alliance [...] there resulted in *Parade* a kind of sur-realism which I consider the departure point of a series of demonstrations of this new spirit which [...] promises to change arts and customs from top to bottom in an entirely vigorous way, because good sense wants them

---

[1] Cited in Robert Orledge, *Satie the Composer* (Cambridge: Cambridge University Press, 1990), p. 224.

to be at least on the same level as scientific and industrial progress. [...] Picasso's decor and cubist costumes demonstrate the realism of his art. This realism, or cubism, as you wish, is what has most deeply stirred the arts in these last ten years.[2]

Apollinaire's hyphenated neologism 'sur-réalisme' is something 'more than real', something that pushes boundaries and could even be termed a kind of research project. It is something that is unequivocally modern, a new way of seeing the world, which creates something new through an alliance of different art forms and the juxtaposition of different ideas. He underlined this coining of a new term in a note written in the same year on his own play *Les Mamelles de Tirésias*, which although written in 1903 was not premiered until 1917, the same year as *Parade*. The play was published in Pierre-Albert Birot's review *SIC*, and here Apollinaire replaced his original descriptors of the play 'surnaturaliste' and 'surnaturalisme' with 'surréaliste' and 'surréalisme'.[3]

Surrealism was born in Paris, and its early years were characterised by aesthetic disputes played out in public. The movement grew in part out of Dada: Tristan Tzara, the Dada pioneer, moved to Paris in 1919 and was a co-editor of the magazine *Littérature* with Breton, Philippe Soupault and Claude Rivière. Tzara also mounted performances in Paris galleries and venues such as the Théâtre de l'Œuvre, some of which included music; works by composers including Satie and the writer-composer Georges Ribemont-Dessaignes were performed. Tzara's quarrels with Breton came to a head with the so-called Congrès de Paris affair early in 1922, and the publication in April that year of the review *Le Cœur à barbe*. Satie published a short spoof autobiographical sketch in the review and was a willing participant in the polemics and personal slights which culminated in the Congrès de Paris affair and ultimately in the birth of surrealism. As with many aesthetic disputes in Paris in this

---

[2] Guillaume Apollinaire, '*Parade* et l'esprit nouveau', cited in Eveline Hurard-Viltard, *Le Groupe des Six* (Paris: Méridiens Klincksieck, 1987), pp. 298–9: 'De cette alliance nouvelle, [...] il est résulté, dans *Parade*, une sorte de sur-réalisme où je vois le point de départ d'une série de manifestations de cet Esprit Nouveau qui, trouvant aujourd'hui l'occasion de se montrer, ne manquera pas de séduire l'élite et se promet de modifier de fond en comble les arts et les mœurs dans l'allégresse universelle, car le bon sens veut qu'ils soient au moins à la hauteur des progrès scientifiques et industriels. [...] Les décors et les costumes cubistes de Picasso témoignent du réalisme de son art. Ce réalisme, ou cubisme, comme on voudra, est ce qui a le plus profondément agité les arts durant les dix dernières années.'

[3] Peter Read, *Apollinaire et Les Mamelles de Tirésias* (Rennes: Presses Universitaires de Rennes, 2000), p. 139.

period, André Breton was the instigator. Sébastien Arfouilloux noted that Breton

> took the initiative to organise a group representing the different artistic trends under the broad banner of 'l'esprit moderne'. He invited painters, writers and composers, notably Auric who acted as intermediary with Les Six. Tzara refused to participate in the group, considering that this mix of different trends would be 'harmful to the search for newness'. Breton reacted in a letter, accusing Tzara of being the 'promoter of a "movement" coming from Zurich'. This was a poor choice of expression considering the meeting was promoted as being an 'international congress'. Satie led the protest meeting on 17 February which called for a vote of no confidence in the steering committee and in Breton himself; this was so successful that the congress failed.[4]

Indeed, Satie had been a signatory (with Éluard, Ribemont-Dessaignes and Tzara) of the letter to Breton demanding a meeting at the Closerie des Lilas café on 17 February; this letter was published in *Comœdia* on 14 February 1922.[5] The upshot of these events was Breton's split from Dada and the birth of surrealism as a distinct movement.

Beyond this aesthetic infighting, many of the concepts of surrealism are rooted in other disciplines. The Swiss linguist Ferdinand de Saussure's *Cours de linguistique générale* (1916) emphasised the arbitrary meaning of the linguistic sign, stressing that meaning is ultimately a product of social convention. This undermining of sign relations was seized on by the surrealists; any 'truth' is not to be located on the surface. Both Apollinaire and Breton also drew, albeit loosely, on ideas from contemporary physics and mathematics, both the non-Euclidean term 'Fourth Dimension' and Einstein's notion that time is subjectively experienced, relevant to the observer, as expressed in his General Theory of Relativity (1915). As Breton described in *Le Surréalisme et la peinture*: 'just as

---

[4] Sébastien Arfouilloux, *Que la nuit tombe sur l'orchestre. Surréalisme et musique* (Paris: Fayard, 2009), p. 115: 'Breton a pris l'initiative d'organiser un congrès regroupant les différentes tendances de l'art dans le concept très large de "l'esprit moderne". Il s'adresse à des peintres, des écrivains et des musiciens, notamment Auric qui [...] joue le rôle de contact avec les Six. Tzara renonce à participer au congrès, considérant que le mélange de tendances très diverses sera "nuisible à cette recherche du nouveau". Breton réagit dans un communiqué traitant Tzara de "promoteur d'un 'mouvement' venu de Zurich". Les termes sont mal choisis pour une réunion dont on met en avant le caractère de "congrès international". Satie dirige la réunion de protestation du 17 février qui retire sa confiance au comité directeur en même temps qu'à Breton, si bien que le congrès échoue.'

[5] Michel Sanouillet, *Dada in Paris*, trans. Sharmila Ganguly (Cambridge, MA: MIT Press, 2012), p. 243. A copy of the letter is housed in the Bibliothèque Kandinsky, Centre Pompidou, Paris (Fonds Brancusi).

contemporary physics tends to be based on non-Euclidean systems, so the creation of 'surrealist objects' derives from the necessity to create, in Paul Éluard's terms, a true "physics of poetry".[6]

A plaque on the wall of 17 place du Panthéon in Paris states that 'In this building in spring 1919, André Breton and Philippe Soupault invented automatic writing and gave birth to surrealism by writing *Les Champs magnétiques*'.[7] This joint book (*Magnetic Fields*) was published the following year. The result of a spontaneous writing experiment where each author wrote as quickly as possible, its chapters ended at the point the author stopped writing at night, and a new chapter began the following morning. In his 1922 text 'Entrée des médiums' (The mediums enter), Breton referred to automatic writing as 'une dictée magique' (magic dictation) and coined the terms 'l'automatisme psychique' (psychic automatism) and 'le sommeil hypnotique' (hypnotic wakeful-ness).[8] Here, he explicitly links creativity to mysticism and magic and implicitly, through the title of the text, suggests that automatic writers are conduits to the beyond. The 'author', rather than being a conscious creator of a text, is an intermediary, the channel through whom ideas are transmitted.

Breton's definition of surrealism which appears in the Surrealist Manifesto of 1924 is 'pure psychic automatism, through which it is proposed to express, either verbally, in writing or in any other way, the true functioning of thought. Dictation of thought, in the absence of any control exercised by reason, outside any aesthetic or moral concerns.'[9] This passage appears after a discussion of Breton's and Soupault's first experiments with automatic writing. This first Surrealist Manifesto outlines Breton's hatred of realism and empiricism and love of what is marvellous: 'what is marvellous is always beautiful, any type of

6   André Breton, *Le Surréalisme et la peinture* (1928; reprinted Paris: Gallimard, 1965) p. 279: 'La création des "objets surréalistes" répond à la nécessité de fond-er, selon l'expression décisive de Paul Éluard, une véritable "physique de la poé-sie".

7   'Dans cet hôtel au cours du printemps 1919 André Breton et Philippe Soupault ont inventé l'écriture automatique et donné naissance au surréalisme en écrivant "Les champs magnétiques".

8   André Breton, 'Entrée des médiums', *Littérature*, 2ème série, no. 6 (November 1922): pp. 1–16, at pp. 2 and 3. Copies of the complete series of *Littérature* are available at the International Dada Archive: http://sdrc.lib.uiowa.edu/dada/lit-terature/index.htm.

9   André Breton, *Manifeste du surréalisme* (1924; reprinted Paris: Gallimard Es-sais edition, 1985), p. 36: 'Automatisme psychique pur, par lequel on se propose d'exprimer, soit verbalement, soit par écrit, soit de toute autre manière, le fonc-tionnement réel de la pensée. Dictée de la pensée, en l'absence de tout contrôle exercé par la raison, en dehors de toute préoccupation esthétique ou morale.'

marvellous is beautiful, only the marvellous is beautiful.'[10] And what Breton would term 'le merveilleux' (the marvellous) has its origins in Apollinaire's concept of 'surprise'.[11]

Willard Bohn points out that Breton chose the term 'surrealism' as a homage to Apollinaire, who died in 1918 aged only 38, never having recovered from a head wound he sustained during the war. But

> although Breton admittedly borrowed the term "surrealism" from Apollinaire, he did not borrow the concept behind it. [...]. For Apollinaire, the prefix *sur-* functions as an intensifier, increasing the intrinsic value of the reality it modifies. [...] For Breton, on the other hand, *sur-* serves as an extender, increasing the extrinsic area to which the concept of reality applies.

Bohn characterises these uses of the sur- prefix as analogous to *surhomme* (superman) for Apollinaire, and *surnaturel* (supernatural) for Breton.[12]

How can artists enter a state of 'pure psychic automatism'? One of the first proto-surrealist experiments was hosted by André Breton and his then wife Simone Kahn, who invited fellow poets including René Crevel, Max Morise and Robert Desnos to their home on 25 September 1922. Crevel, who had been 'initiated by a spiritualist', instigated a séance and he was the first to enter a trance-like state, soon followed by Desnos.[13] Others involved in subsequent séances included Max Ernst, Paul and Gala Éluard, Benjamin Péret, Roger Vitrac, Man Ray and Giorgio de Chirico. While Breton himself never entered a trance state, he published an account of the evenings in 'Entrée des médiums'. He soon put a stop to the séances when they 'became increasingly dark in tone and even violent. [...] When, at a certain point, Breton discovered several members of the group in a side room preparing to hang themselves on Crevel's instigation, it became clear that things were getting out of hand.'[14]

Tessel Bauduin, in her excellent book on surrealism and the occult, locates the source of these surrealist experiments in contemporary psychiatry and spiritualism. Breton had himself studied medicine and once had an ambition to be a psychiatrist; he was an intern in several

[10] Breton, *Manifeste du surréalisme*, pp. 34–5: 'le merveilleux est toujours beau, n'importe quel merveilleux est beau, il n'y a que le merveilleux qui soit beau.'
[11] See Willard Bohn, 'From surrealism to surrealism: Apollinaire and Breton', *The Journal of Aesthetics and Art Criticism*, vol. 36 no. 2 (1977): pp. 197–210.
[12] Bohn, 'From surrealism to surrealism', p. 205.
[13] See Tessel M. Bauduin, *Surrealism and the Occult: Occultism and Western Esotericism in the Work and Movement of André Breton* (Amsterdam: Amsterdam University Press, 2014), pp. 35 and 37.
[14] Bauduin, *Surrealism and the Occult*, p. 35.

hospitals and met Freud in Vienna in 1921, and although he never qualified, his interest in the study of mental illness found expression in his literary activity. 'Psychic automatism' is one of the key phrases in the first Surrealist Manifesto, and Bauduin writes that this phrase

> serves a double function in Surrealism: it is both a mental state and a means of expression. The surrealists had appropriated automatism from the medical science of their day, specifically from dynamic psychiatry, the precursor to modern psychiatry. There automatism served two functions as well, first being employed as a therapeutic practice, and secondly as a tool for studying particular states of consciousness. [...] Psychic automatism is the surrealist poetic response to the discovery and investigation of the unconscious in the nineteenth century, and an attempt to appropriate it for revolutionary art.[15]

Another central surrealist concept is surprise, which can be provoked by unexpected juxtapositions that stimulate new thoughts, emotions and ideas. This concept has an important precursor in the emblematic association of an umbrella and a sewing machine on a dissecting table in the novel *Les Chants de Maldoror* (1868–9) by Isidore Ducasse (known as the Comte de Lautréamont). Lautréamont's well-known juxtaposition is very frequently evoked by later artists, not least Boulez, who alluded to Lautréamont in his inaugural lecture for the Collège de France:

> Invention must not be satisfied solely with the encounter of different material, even if it can draw benefit from the fortuitousness of this encounter and, in exceptional circumstances, magnify this chance element. To return to the celebrated comparison, the encounter of the umbrella and the sewing machine could not by itself create a significant event – the dissection table is also necessary ... Put differently, musical invention must essentially provoke the creation of the musical material that is necessary for its purposes; this provocation will give the necessary stimulus to technology which will enable a functional response to one's desires and imagination.[16]

---

[15] Bauduin, *Surrealism and the Occult*, p. 36.
[16] Pierre Boulez, 'Invention/recherche' (originally a lecture delivered at the Collège de France on 10 December 1976), in *Leçons de musique (Points de repère III)*, ed. Jean-Jacques Nattiez (Paris: Christian Bourgois, 2005), pp. 56–67, at pp. 62–3: 'L'invention ne doit pas se contenter d'un matériau de rencontre, même si elle peut profiter des hasards de cette rencontre et les magnifier en des circonstances exceptionnelles. Pour revenir à la célèbre comparaison, la rencontre du parapluie et de la machine à coudre ne saurait à elle seule créer l'événement, il y faut la table de dissection ... En d'autres termes, l'invention musicale doit essentiellement provoquer la création du matériau musical dont elle estime avoir

In this lecture, Boulez touches on several key surrealist concepts: imagination, surprise, fortuitous encounters, chance. Boulez's frequent evocation of chance (in French, either the noun 'le hasard' or the adjective 'aléatoire') needs to be understood in the context of the surrealist notions of surprise and the marvellous. Even closer to Breton specifically is Boulez's musing on the topic of future creative thought towards the end of this lecture: 'l'effort sera collectif ou ne sera pas ...' (effort will be collective or it will not be),[17] an obvious borrowing and adaptation of the final sentence of Breton's novella *Nadja* (1928): 'la beauté sera convulsive ou ne sera pas' (beauty will be convulsive or will not be). This short phrase, and Breton's later expansion of it, had many ramifications in Boulez's work.

While Bauduin is right to stress that 'throughout his career Breton insisted upon his refusal to believe in communication with spirits',[18] esotericism and magic are also central to the surrealist worldview, particularly from the 1930s. To give an example directly connected to Breton, his text on automatic writing 'Le Message automatique' was published in the review *Minotaure* in 1933.[19] Like many texts in this lavishly illustrated publication, Breton's words appear interspersed with images of many kinds, including a reproduction from the esoteric writer Jules Bois's book *Le Satanisme et la magie* (1895); examples of automatic writing and drawing; even what is labelled a 'texte martien' (text in 'Martian language') dictated to the medium Hélène Smith in 1897 during a séance. The diverse articles and images in *Minotaure* together provide a complete portrait of contemporary surrealism, from psychoanalytical studies of delirium to images provoking new ideas through incongruous juxtapositions. Surrealist discourse on automatically generated art thus embraced everything from medical case studies to the borderline crackpot, and this breadth of preoccupation reflects intellectual trends in contemporary France.

The psychoanalyst René Allendy (1889–1942) organised a series of lectures at the Sorbonne in 1933 on magic ('la pensée magique'), and it is probable that writers and artists in surrealist circles either attended the lectures or read the published versions.[20] The principal focus of these

besoin; par ses initiatives, elle donnera l'impulsion nécessaire à la technologie pour répondre fonctionnellement à ses désirs, à son imagination.'

[17] Boulez, 'Invention/recherche', p. 66.

[18] Bauduin, *Surrealism and the Occult*, p. 37.

[19] André Breton, 'Le Message automatique', *Minotaure*, no. 3–4 (December 1933): pp. 55–65.

[20] See the special number 'La Pensée magique' of *Revue française de la psychanalyse*, vol. 7 no. 1 (1934).

lectures was on so-called 'primitive' peoples, and the speakers often drew on well-known authorities such as the British anthropologist James Frazer (1854–1941; his best-known work, *Golden Bough* (1890), had been translated into French and was known to Breton) and the French anthropologist and philosopher Lucien Lévy-Bruhl (1857–1939).[21] Bauduin stresses that 'surrealists, anthropologists and psychoanalysts shared the idea that the magical worldview was still part of contemporary culture out in the colonies, but had become peripheral and outdated in the West after the triumph of the rational worldview'.[22] Allendy's psychoanalytical clients included the authors Anaïs Nin and Antonin Artaud and the painter Paul Klee,[23] and he was acquainted with the composer André Jolivet, who shared his preoccupation with magic and whom he invited to give a talk, 'Génèse d'un renouveau musical' (Genesis of musical renewal), at the Sorbonne in January 1937.

The connection between Allendy and Jolivet is just one of many intriguing links between French music and surrealist thought in the 1930s and 40s, arising within a cultural context where surrealism, ethnography and the emerging discipline of ethnomusicology were closely related. French surrealism was a pluridisciplinary environment that embraced wide-ranging artistic and intellectual interests. Often these coexisted in one publication or artwork, as in the reviews *Documents* and *Minotaure* which brought together different art forms. And Breton himself frequently combined photography, autobiography and fiction in a single publication; he also had a strong interest in ethnography and amassed an impressive collection of non-Western and esoteric objects.

This interconnection of surrealism and ethnology was a significant driving force in French culture of the interwar years. The Institut d'Ethnologie was founded in 1925, a year after the publication of the first Surrealist Manifesto, and many of the same people were involved in *Documents*, the Musée de l'Homme (which was founded in 1937) and the Collège de Sociologie. For instance, the ethnomusicologist André Schaeffner – later a friend of Boulez – studied with the distinguished sociologist Marcel Mauss and worked at the Musée de l'Homme alongside people including Georges-Henri Rivière, one of the founders of *Documents* who is described by James Clifford as 'a music student

---

[21] Bauduin, *Surrealism and the Occult*, p. 120.
[22] Bauduin, *Surrealism and the Occult*, p. 120.
[23] See Julian Anderson, 'Jolivet and the *style incantatoire*: aspects of a hybrid tradition', in Caroline Rae (ed.), *André Jolivet: Music, Art and Literature* (Abingdon: Routledge, 2019), pp. 15–40, at p. 31. I am very grateful to Anderson and Rae for sending me a copy of this chapter in advance of its publication.

and amateur of jazz who would become France's most energetic ethnographic museologist.'[24]

The short-lived Collège de Sociologie (1937–9) was a discussion group which got together regularly, usually at a member's Paris flat, to exchange ideas. Many of the group's texts were later published in reviews such as *Acéphale*. This diverse group of writers and ethnologists 'were preoccupied with those ritual moments where experiences outside the normal flow of existence could find collective expression, moments when cultural order was both transgressed and rejuvenated.'[25] Georges Bataille's concept of 'sociologie sacrée' was one definition of their activity (and James Clifford notes that in France, ethnology and sociology were not sharply distinguished).

Alastair Brotchie, who has edited texts by the Collège, asks what the organisation was:

> An initial and somewhat unexpected answer might be that it was a religious organisation aiming to reactivate the sacred in society. [...] for Bataille these words, society, the sacred, and religion, had very different meanings from their use in common parlance [...]. Many of them derived originally from the writings of Durkheim, before acquiring slightly differing inflections in the thought of Bataille and the other participants.[26]

The book *The Sacred Conspiracy* publishes many documents connected with Acéphale, a secret society founded by Bataille that shared many members with the Collège de Sociologie, and June 1936 marked the first issue of the group's review *Acéphale*. A key member of both organisations was Michel Leiris, a frequent collaborator for *Documents* who later worked at the Musée de l'Homme, and the image on the cover of the review, a naked headless man with a skull covering his genitalia, was designed by André Masson. Interviewed by Paule Thévenin – a close friend of Boulez – about Acéphale, Masson said: 'We are not for a religious world but we are for a world in which the sacred exists. [...] The sacred is not necessarily divine [...] in this sense there is something better, even in surrealism.'[27]

---

[24] James Clifford, 'On ethnographic surrealism', *Comparative Studies in Society and History*, vol. 23 no. 4 (October 1981): pp. 539–64, at pp. 546–7.

[25] Clifford, 'On ethnographic surrealism', p. 559.

[26] Georges Bataille, *The Sacred Conspiracy*, ed. Alastair Brotchie and Marina Galletti (London: Atlas Press, 2018), p. 63.

[27] Interview 'Acéphale or the initiatory illusion', first published in *Les Cahiers obliques* in 1980 and translated into English by Rainer J. Hanshe, available at http://blacksunlit.com/2016/10/acephale-or-the-initiatory-illusion-paule-thevenin-and-andre-masson-translated-from-french-by-rainer-j-hanshe/ [accessed June 2023].

One common preoccupation of these different movements was myth, which Bataille defines in his essay *L'Apprenti sorcier* (1938):

> Myth alone enters the bodies of those it binds together and asks of them the same expectation. It is the quickening of every dance; it brings existence to its boiling point; it communicates the tragic emotion that makes its sacred intimacy accessible. For myth is not only the divine figure of destiny and the world in which this figure moves: it cannot be separated from the community to which it belongs and which ritually takes possession of its kingdom. [...] Myth ritually lived reveals true being, no less [...].[28]

This pithy statement shows the strong connection between the Collège de Sociologie and its Acéphale offshoot on the one hand, and also the broader Parisian cultural concern with ethnography. Specifically, Artaud's and Jolivet's conceptions of *mana* in theatrical and musical contexts are close to Bataille's definition of myth as 'the quickening of every dance'. This diverse cultural and intellectual environment generated ideas that were to have a crucial influence on Boulez in his formative years.

Breton as novelist: *Nadja, Les Vases communicants, L'Amour fou*

Breton's importance in cultural history should not be limited to his authorship of the two Surrealist Manifestos, and his creative work, not the manifestos, had a more significant impact on Boulez's creativity. His first three novels *Nadja* (1928), *Les Vases communicants* (Communicating vessels; 1932) and *L'Amour fou* (Mad love; 1934–6, published 1937) are interconnected, sharing themes and even specific phrases and imagery. *Nadja* is semi-autobiographical, a story about a disturbed young woman with whom the author had a brief affair, and in Breton's words 'the tone adopted for the story is that of a medical study, partly neuropsychiatric'.[29] Like Thévenin, Breton originally trained as a doctor and was particularly fascinated by psychiatry. The protagonists

---

[28] Bataille, *The Sacred Conspiracy*, p. 303. Original French (Georges Bataille, *Œuvres complètes*, vol. 1, Paris: Gallimard, 1988, pp. 535–6): 'Le mythe seul entre dans les corps de ceux qu'il lie et leur demande la même attente. Il est la précipitation de chaque danse; il porte l'existence "à son point d'ébullition": il lui communique l'émotion tragique qui rend son intimité sacrée accessible. Car le mythe n'est pas seulement la figure divine de la destinée et le monde où cette figure se déplace: il ne peut pas être séparé de la communauté dont il est la chose et qui prend possession, rituellement, de son empire. [...] Le mythe rituellement vécu ne révèle rien de moins que l'être véritable [...].'

[29] André Breton, *Nadja* (1928; revised edition Paris: Gallimard, 1964), p. 6: 'le ton adopté pour le récit se calque sur celui de l'observation médicale, entre toutes neuropsychiatrique [...].'

wander around Paris locations and the story is illustrated with photographs, with the aim of eliminating verbal description (an issue Breton raised in the first Surrealist Manifesto). Another art form is therefore essential to the unfolding of the work; images can 'say' more than words and specifically more than poetic description. Desire, obsession and, most importantly, accidents or coincidences that turn out to be not accidents at all, are at the heart of the story. All these topics are treated explicitly as objects of philosophical speculation in the three Breton stories being addressed here. In these stories, Breton demonstrates his concepts of 'hasard objectif' (objective chance) and 'la beauté convulsive' (convulsive beauty) in theory and in practice. Both concepts are cognates of that key surrealist principle, the marvellous.

What does 'chance' mean for Breton? The term is, for him, related to surrealist aesthetic notions of automatism. This concept has been linked by several literary scholars to Baudelaire's theory of *correspondances* – where the senses are mingled – and to Proust's theory of involuntary memory. Chance, for these authors, is a mediator: an idea or memory can spontaneously be triggered by an object or gesture. Boulez himself, in his article 'Alea', gives his surrealist-inflected interpretation of the term 'aléatoire': 'opposing accidental chance, we find chance by automatism, whether consciously pure or with some idea of controlled alternatives.'[30]

The literary scholar Alison James writes: 'The surrealists seek access to the secrets of the unconscious and liberation from rational constraints in the surprising coincidences of daily life – a quest explicitly theorized by André Breton in terms of "hasard objectif" (objective chance; defined, paradoxically, as a manifestation of necessity).'[31] Breton explores this concept, typically, across several works, most notably in *Nadja*, *Les Vases communicants* and *L'Amour fou*. For instance, in *L'Amour fou*, Breton refers to the same Giacometti statue that appears in a photo in *Nadja*, which he describes as a 'work in progress' by the artist. Breton feels the need to explain this repeated image: 'who cares about this repetition of the background, excused by the deep and constant transformation of the location.'[32] This is part of the paradox of 'objective

---

[30] Translated by Walsh in Boulez, *Stocktakings from an Apprenticeship*, p. 29; article 'Alea' at pp. 26–38.

[31] Alison James, *Constraining Chance: Georges Perec and the Oulipo* (Evanston, IL, Northwestern University Press, 2009), p. 11. See André Breton, *Les Vases communicants* (1933; Paris, Gallimard, 1955), p. 110 ('la parole d'Engels'): 'La causalité ne peut être comprise qu'en liaison avec la catégorie du hasard objectif, forme de manifestation de la nécessité?'

[32] Breton, *L'Amour fou* (Paris, Gallimard, 1937), p. 39: 'tant pis pour cette répétition du décor, qu'excuse la transformation profonde, constante, du lieu.'

chance': was his meeting with Nadja truly a random encounter in the street, or something that was somehow predestined? As Hal Foster puts it, in Breton's three principal novels 'objects are "rare", places "strange", meetings "sudden", yet all are haunted by repetition'.[33]

An especially rich example of verbal connections, uncanny coincidences and autobiographical material appears in *L'Amour fou*. Here, Breton refers (p. 79) to 'un poème automatique', a poem he composed in 1923 during his 'automatic writing' period. He goes on to analyse this poem, 'Le Tournesol' (pp. 80–1), which is dedicated to Pierre Reverdy (its title, 'The sunflower', recalls a Man Ray photo of this flower which appeared a few pages earlier in his story, when Breton transitions from a passage about 'le tour St-Jacques' (St Jacques tower in central Paris) to 'un tournesol', by means of their common first letters). To his astonishment, the poem anticipates many events that happened to him in 1934, and on p. 95 of the novel he talks of these 'bouleversantes concordances' (overwhelming concordances) with René Char and Paul Éluard.

The 'surrealist attitude' has sensation and change at its heart. Indeed, Breton wrote in *L'Amour fou*, citing the physicist Gustave Juvet: 'It's in the surprise created by a new image or new association of images where the most important aspect of progress in the physical sciences can be found, because it is astonishment which excites the rather cold sense of logic, and obliges us to establish new connections.'[34] This was paralleled by Boulez in his Collège de France lecture cited above: the artist needs not only a surprise encounter (for instance Lautréamont's sewing machine and umbrella), but the creative imagination which can make something out of the incongruity.

Alison James emphasises that

> the surrealist concept of chance is double-edged. [...] When Breton defines surrealism as an 'automatisme psychique pur' (pure psychic automatism) that, in the absence of any intervention of reason, expresses 'le fonctionnement réel de la pensée' ['the real functioning of thought'; citing the first *Surrealist Manifesto*], it is clear that this inner reality is not considered wholly random. Indeed, from the surrealist point of view, rational, moral and aesthetic preoccupations represent a set of exterior accidents that obscure and disrupt the essential operation of the mind.

---

[33] Hal Foster, *Compulsive Beauty* (Cambridge, MA: MIT Press, 1993), p. 30.

[34] Breton, *L'Amour fou*, p. 122: 'c'est M. [Gustave] Juvet qui, dans *La Structure des nouvelles théories physiques*, écrit en 1933 "C'est dans la surprise créée par une nouvelle image ou par une nouvelle association d'images, qu'il faut voir le plus important élément du progrès des sciences physiques, puisque c'est l'étonnement qui excite la logique, toujours assez froide, et qui oblige à établir de nouvelles coordinations."'

This reversibility of chance and necessity is most evident in *L'amour fou*, where Breton develops the notion of 'objective chance'. [...]. Italo Calvino argues convincingly that Breton's formula 'did away with the irrationality of chance'. Objective chance, illuminated and motivated by surrealist logic, is no longer chance at all.[35]

This is a highly stimulating notion to apply to Boulez's serial compositional procedures. Viewed through this lens, serial musical processes are paradoxically a way not only of creating or ensuring order, but also of creating the new and unforeseeable – of controlling chance and, in Boulez's words, organising delirium. Boulez might have written to Cage in December 1951 'I am a little afraid of what is called "automatic writing", for most of the time it is chiefly a lack of control',[36] but it seems that for him, at that time, serialism was the perfect medium for expressing his paradoxical need for control and automatism, for what Breton would have termed 'objective chance'.

One obvious connection between Breton's stories – one that was particularly resonant for Boulez – is the recycling of the last phrase of *Nadja* in *L'Amour fou*, 'La beauté sera CONVULSIVE ou ne sera pas' (Beauty will be CONVULSIVE or it will not be). Indeed, a first version of *L'Amour fou* was published in *Minotaure* in 1934 under the title 'La Beauté convulsive'. And at the end of the first part of *L'Amour fou* we read this extension of the final words of *Nadja*: 'La beauté convulsive sera érotique-voilée, explosante-fixe, magique-circonstancielle ou ne sera pas' (Convulsive beauty will be erotic-veiled, exploding-fixed, magic-circumstantial or it will not be).[37] This concept of 'convulsive beauty' is elucidated by Breton in the section leading up to the threefold statement:

> I admit without the least confusion, my deep lack of sensitivity in the presence of natural phenomena and artworks which, from the start, do not provoke in me a physical trouble characterised by the sensation of a shudder in the temples which might lead to a true shudder. I have never

---

[35] James, *Constraining Chance*, p. 112. She cites Italo Calvino's book *The Uses of Literature* (New York: Harcourt Brace Jovanovich, 1986), p. 47.

[36] Jean-Jacques Nattiez (ed.) and Robert Samuels (trans.), *The Boulez–Cage Correspondence* (Cambridge: Cambridge University Press, 1993), p. 113. The first French publication of this correspondence is Jean-Jacques Nattiez (ed.), *Pierre Boulez/John Cage: correspondance* (Paris: Christian Bourgois, 1991): 'Je suis un peu effrayé parce qu'on appelle l'"écriture automatique", car la plupart du temps, c'est surtout un manque de contrôle' (pp. 181–2).

[37] Breton' *L'Amour fou*, p. 26.

been able to stop drawing a connection between this sensation and erotic sensations, and can only distinguish the two in matters of degree.[38]

Convulsive beauty is a physical shock, an instant unmediated reaction which has the power to unite supposed opposites. Making a further connection with a writer who is one of the most important antecedents of surrealism, Breton states that Lautréamont's descriptions that start with the words 'beautiful like' ('beaux comme') are 'the true manifesto of convulsive poetry'.[39] Convulsive beauty provokes profound sensations instantaneously which 'could not come to us via ordinary logical paths',[40] akin to automatic writing, a spontaneous act of creativity.

In the published text of *L'Amour fou* there appears a photo by Man Ray captioned 'explosante-fixe':[41] a female dancer wearing a full skirt and sleeves, perhaps a flamenco dancer and perhaps in a trance, captured in a freeze frame with her arms, sleeves and skirt suspended in mid-whirling motion. This fleeting instant captured on film exemplifies 'la beauté convulsive'. In the original *Minotaure* publication of the story,[42] the other two elements of Breton's definition of convulsive beauty are also presented to the reader in the form of an image. A whole-page photo by Man Ray is captioned 'érotique-voilée': here, a naked woman stands by a large black wheel. Her left forearm is raised, revealing that her hand and forearm are covered in black paint. She is partly veiled in shadow by the wheel, and paint conceals some of her flesh. Finally, a Brassaï photo is titled 'magique-circonstantielle'. This features a central kernel which is obviously vegetable in origin and from which spindly structures jut out, though it also looks like a heart with branching veins.

---

[38] Breton' *L'Amour fou*, pp. 12–13: 'J'avoue sans la moindre confusion mon insensibilité profonde en présence des spectacles naturels et des œuvres d'art qui, d'emblée, ne me procurent pas un trouble physique caractérisé par la sensation d'une aigrette de vent aux tempes susceptible d'entraîner un véritable frisson. Je n'ai jamais pu m'empêcher d'établir une relation entre cette sensation et celle du plaisir érotique et ne découvre entre elles que des différences de degré.'

[39] Breton, *L'Amour fou*, p. 14: 'Les "beaux comme" de Lautréamont constituent le manifeste même de la poésie convulsive.'

[40] Breton, *L'Amour fou*, pp. 18–21: 'Une telle beauté [la beauté convulsive] ne pourra se dégager que du sentiment poignant de la chose révélée, que de la certitude intégrale procurée par l'irruption d'une solution qui, en raison de sa nature même, ne pouvait nous parvenir par les voies logiques ordinaires.'

[41] Breton, *L'Amour fou*, p. 16.

[42] André Breton, 'La Beauté sera convulsive', *Minotaure*, no. 5 (May 1934), pp. 8–16. The 'explosante-fixe' image appears on p. 8, 'érotique-voilée' on p. 15, and 'magique circonstantielle' on p. 16. The latter two images do not appear in the later Folio edition.

Images, it is suggested, are superior to words as conduits of convulsive beauty, provoking as they do an instant, unmediated reaction. And moving beyond Breton, music has an even stronger power to convey convulsive beauty. Music can exist only in time and in sound; its action on our senses is literally 'moving'. Unlike Breton, André Souris understood the unique power of music; he believed that 'the language of music was more apt than any other to faithfully relay the deepest feelings' and that music was 'perhaps the medium most suited to surrealist expression'.[43]

Messiaen, surrealist poet

Olivier Messiaen, a composer who wrote almost all the texts he set to music, surely also stimulated Boulez's surrealist outlook. Messiaen's texts are strongly marked by surrealism, particularly those vocal works composed in the period when Boulez and others took private lessons with him: *Trois petites liturgies de la Présence Divine* (1943–4) and the song cycle *Harawi* (1945). Richard D. E. Burton writes of Messiaen's 'enthusiasm for the work of Paul Éluard' and notes echoes in Messiaen of 'the most famous single image in surrealist poetry, Éluard's "La terre est bleue comme une orange / Jamais une erreur les mots ne mentent pas" (from *L'amour la poésie*, 1929; 'The earth is blue like an orange / Never a mistake words do not lie).[44] The line 'Orange-bleu, force et joie' (Orange-blue, strength and joy) in the third of Messiaen's *Petites liturgies* would surely not have been written without Éluard's specific example. This is a colour combination favoured by the synaesthete Messiaen, who described his musical style as 'colour in motion, not at rest'.[45] In his preface to the second movement of *Quatuor pour la fin du Temps* (1941) 'Vocalise, pour l'Ange qui annonce la fin du Temps', Messiaen states that the piano plays 'gentle cascades of blue-orange chords'. Similarly, the seventh movement, 'Fouillis d'arc-en-ciel, pour l'Ange qui annonce la fin du Temps' (Jumble of rainbows, for the Angel who announces the end of Time), mentions 'ces coulées de lave bleu-orange' (these streams

---

[43] Robert Wangermée, *André Souris et le complexe d'Orphée: entre surréalisme et musique sérielle* (Liège: Mardaga, 1995), p. 6: 'la matière musicale était plus propre qu'aucune autre à épouser fidèlement les mouvements intérieurs [...] la musique constituait peut-être le moyen le plus conforme aux démonstrations surréalistes'.

[44] Richard D. E. Burton, *Olivier Messiaen: Texts, Contexts, and Intertexts (1937–1948)*, ed. Roger Nichols (New York: Oxford University Press, 2016), p. 112.

[45] Ernest de Gengenbach, 'Messiaen ou le surréel en musique', *Revue musicale de France* (15 April 1946): pp. 1–3 and 18, at p. 3: 'Je conçois mon style musical comme de la couleur en mouvement et non en repos'.

of blue-orange lava). Messiaen's vividly coloured aural imagination did not come from nowhere: he is certainly echoing Éluard.

Messiaen told an interviewer that his music of the late 1940s was 'more or less surrealist' and that in his own texts accompanying his works, 'he had endeavoured to pastiche the writings of André Breton, Paul Éluard and Pierre Reverdy'.[46] While on the surface, Messiaen's position as a Catholic composer distances him considerably from the surrealist movement, contemporary commentators already recognised that for this composer, being a Catholic and a surrealist was not irreconcilable. In 1946, Ernest de Gengenbach (1903–79), who had studied in a seminary with the intention of becoming a priest, published an article in *Revue musicale de France* titled 'Messiaen ou le surréel en musique', and the same author had in 1938 privately published a pamphlet entitled *Surréalisme et christianisme*. Gengenbach's leaving holy orders – provoked by a love affair – coincided with his meeting André Breton and embracing surrealism, and Breton himself wrote a preface to Gengenbach's prose poem *Satan à Paris* in 1927. Gengenbach's article on Messiaen explains how his music forms a specifically Christian parallel to surrealist concepts such as the marvellous, or what Messiaen terms 'le merveilleux surnaturel chrétien' (the Christian supernatural marvellous). Messiaen himself responded to Gengenbach's questioning:

> if you define surrealism as a mental vantage-point where visible natural realities and invisible supernatural realities are no longer in opposition to each other and where they cease to be perceived as contradictions, then I am a surrealist composer. The disciples of André Breton [...] wanted passionately to have, here on earth, a state of the beyond. All they need is to attain it through faith. In a present eternity, I glimpse infinite life beyond the categories of Time and Space.[47]

While this reconciliation of opposites ('le point suprême') was the surrealist tenet that was most relevant to Messiaen, his surrealism was distinct from Breton's as he envisioned this process in the light of his

---

[46] Cited in Robert Sholl, 'Love, mad love, and the *"point sublime"*: the surrealist poetics of Messiaen's *Harawi*', in Robert Sholl (ed.), *Messiaen Studies* (Cambridge: Cambridge University Press, 2007), pp. 34–62, at p. 35: 'plus ou moins surréaliste'.

[47] Gengenbach, 'Messiaen ou le surréel en musique', p. 3: 'si vous appelez surréalisme un point de l'esprit où les réalités visibles naturelles et les réalités invisibles surnaturelles ne s'opposent plus et cessent d'être perçues contradictoirement, alors je suis un compositeur surréaliste ... Les disciples d'André Breton [...] désirent violemment avoir, *dès ici-bas, l'au-delà de leurs jours* ... Il ne tient qu'à eux de l'avoir par le foi ... J'entrevois dès maintenant dans un présent d'éternité, la vie infinie hors des cadres du Temps et de l'Espace.'

Catholic faith, which was always the most fundamental aspect of his life and art.

More recent authors have also connected, in surrealist fashion, the apparent opposites of surrealism and Catholicism in relation to Messiaen. Burton focuses on a striking line in 'L'Amour de Piroutcha', the fifth song of *Harawi*: 'Coupe-moi la tête, doundou tchil' (Cut off my head, doundou tchil):

> For fairly obvious historical reasons, the French imagination is haunted by the theme of decapitation and the almost iconic image of the severed head [...] Not for the first time, there is a weird convergence between Messiaen's 'erotic Catholicism' and the decidedly godless, but still 'mystical', eroticism of Georges Bataille who, in 1936, launched a review named *Acéphale* ['Headless'].[48]

Messiaen himself acknowledged that *L'Île invisible*, a painting by the British surrealist Roland Penrose, inspired *Harawi* (the same painting had been reproduced in *Minotaure* in 1937 under the title 'Seeing is believing');[49] in this striking painting, a young woman's head seems to emerge, inverted, from a grey sky, and her blonde hair falls towards a rainbow-tinged landscape as a single hand reaches up towards her.

Messiaen was also drawn to the surrealist poet Pierre Reverdy, and he quotes a line from his 'La Jetée' (from the collection *Les Ardoises du toit*, 1918) at the start of *Technique de mon langage musical*: 'Les étoiles sont derrière le mur' (The stars are behind the wall). Reverdy wrote this poem – on the chasm between love and death and the capacity of faith to bridge the gap – three years before he formally became a Catholic, and he moved to a house near the Solesmes monastery in 1926.[50]

To sum up, Messiaen told Gengenbach: 'The impression of the surreal, ethereal, luminous, winged and stellar that emanates from my musical poems shows that in my work, the supernatural marvellous of Christian mysteries is married harmoniously to the natural marvellous.'[51] Again, we note the conflation of surreal/supernatural in Messiaen's unified conception. The interconnection of esotericism, magic and surrealism has already been noted, and Messiaen further extends the network by embracing 'the supernatural marvellous of Christian mysteries' under

---

[48] Burton, *Olivier Messiaen*, p. 186 footnote 47.
[49] Sholl, 'Love, mad love, and the *"point sublime"*', p. 55. The painting was reproduced in *Minotaure*, no. 10 (Winter 1937).
[50] Sholl, 'Love, mad love, and the *"point sublime"*', p. 57.
[51] Gengenbach, 'Messiaen ou le surréel en musique', p. 3: 'L'impression de surréel, éthéré, lumineux, ailé, stellaire, qui se dégage de mes poèmes musicaux, provient de ce que, dans mon œuvre, le merveilleux surnaturel des mystères chrétiens se marie harmonieusement avec le merveilleux naturel.'

this capacious umbrella. We might also note the surrealist unification of the opposites of Messiaen's light, bright and airy conception with the dark, obscure mysteries of the occult.

Ethnomusicology

The most obvious connection between ethnology and music is the discipline of ethnomusicology, which developed in Paris in the 1930s. Recordings of musics from French colonies, as well as live performances, were included in the Paris 1931 Exposition Coloniale, and Boulez transcribed some of these recordings when they became available for study some years later in the Musée Guimet. Reports of field trips appeared in both specialist publications and those aimed at audiences less directly connected with ethnography. André Schaeffner and Michel Leiris were both part of a French government mission that travelled from Dakar in Senegal to Djibouti in 1931, and both published articles that came out of this field trip in the first number of *Minotaure* in 1933. Leiris wrote on funeral rites of the Dogon in Mali, in an article illustrated with images of drummers, and Schaeffner's article, which includes music notation, focuses on music in Cameroon.[52] These articles appear somewhat incongruously alongside a promotional text by Breton about a new edition of Achim von Arnim's *Contes bizarres*, articles by Jacques Lacan, and even the first two pages of the manuscript of Kurt Weill's stage work *The Seven Deadly Sins*. *Minotaure* therefore brought ethnography to an audience that valued contemporary culture and the avant-garde, in a lavishly illustrated review with high production values.

Specialist music publications also showcased the work of ethnomusicologists. Schaeffner contributed an article 'Le Théâtre musical' to the first number of *Polyphonie*, dated 1947–8; one of Boulez's first important articles, on rhythm, was featured in its second issue. Schaeffner's article, using language which belongs to the period in which it was written and is now discredited, 'questions the historical tradition that opera is a specifically Western genre whose origins hark back to Florentine court festivals of the 16th century [...] he studies a series of processes, characteristics, even institutions that one might consider are unique to Western theatre, but which exist, whether in outline or in more or less complete form, with primitive peoples'.[53] Schaeffner was a pioneer in

---

52 André Schaeffner, 'Notes sur la musique des populations du Cameroun septentrional', pp. 65–70 and Michel Leiris, 'Danses funéraires Dogon', pp. 73–6; both published in *Minotaure*, no. 1 (1933).

53 Wangermée, *André Souris*, pp. 269–70: 'André Schaeffner [...] met en question la tradition historique selon laquelle l'opéra est un genre spécifiquement

the study of Asian and African instruments who founded the ethno-graphic instrument department at the Trocadéro in 1929, and indeed supplied many of these instruments from his own travels. This museum was re-established as the Musée de l'Homme in the wake of the 1937 Exposition Internationale.

Boulez's appreciation of non-European musics and instruments was certainly deepened by Schaeffner,[54] but his interest predates their meeting and is audible in his earliest works. Messiaen was a catalyst in this sense, as was Jolivet. Both these composers tapped into the interests in myth and ritual shared by ethnographers, sociologists and surrealists, and the incantatory aesthetic is central to Jolivet's music and indeed to much French music of the twentieth century and beyond, including Boulez.[55]

André Jolivet, magic and incantation

It is evident that French composers in the 1930s were uncomfortable with the exoticism prevalent in the nineteenth and early twentieth cen-turies, and Jolivet for one had the opportunity to hear traditional music in the field on visits to Algeria in 1932–3. Jane Fulcher alleges that the Exposition Coloniale 'jolted' French intellectuals generally 'out of their ethnocentrism',[56] leading to a new humanist attitude exhibited in music by the Jeune France group of composers. But Fulcher does not men-tion that this humanism was coupled with a strong interest in esoteric aspects of art. For Jolivet, according to his biographer Lucie Kayas: 'The discovery of ethnology as framed by philosophers was combined with childhood memories linked to non-European cultures and anchored in his studies of memory and the imaginary. Surrealism was the unifying stimulus in an aesthetic of the juxtaposition of opposites which also opened the way to an esoteric approach.'[57] Partly through his wife, who

---

occidental dont les origines remontent aux fêtes florentines de cour au XVIe siècle. [...] il étudie un ensemble de procédés, de caractéristiques, voire d'insti-tutions que l'on pourrait croire propres au théâtre occidental, mais qui existent, à l'état d'esquisses plus ou moins achevées, chez des populations primitives ou demi-civilisées.'

[54] Schaeffner wrote his most important book, *L'Origine des instruments de mu-sique*, in 1936.

[55] See Anderson, 'Jolivet and the *style incantatoire*'.

[56] Anderson, 'Jolivet and the *style incantatoire*', p. 17, citing Jane Fulcher, *The Com-poser as Intellectual: Music and Ideology in France 1914–1940* (Oxford: Oxford University Press, 2005), p. 289.

[57] Lucie Kayas, *André Jolivet* (Paris: Fayard, 2005), p. 148: 'La découverte de l'eth-nologie dans un cadre philosophique se mêle à ses souvenirs d'enfance liés aux cultures non européennes et ancré des connaissances d'ordre intellectuel dans

studied sociology at the Sorbonne, Jolivet developed an interest in that discipline, particularly in Émile Durkheim's work. And Breton brings the French sociologists Marcel Mauss and Durkheim into his argument in *L'Art magique*, where he writes that *mana* is 'the fundamental notion of magic, the one that is most revelatory about the roots of magic and religion and yet which seems to resist analysis and slide towards evanescence via its excessive shape-shifting.'[58]

There is a very strong emotional and visceral dimension to Boulez and Messiaen's enthusiasm for non-European musics. Boulez wrote of the experience being an 'indelible branding,'[59] while Messiaen, for once, allowed his music to speak largely for itself. Messiaen's two piano studies of the early 1950s, *Île de feu I* and *II*, are dedicated 'à la Papouasie' (to Papua New Guinea) and are overtly inspired by ritualistic drumming, but there are precedents in Messiaen's oeuvre for this style. 'Regard de l'esprit de joie', the tenth of his *Vingt regards sur l'enfant-Jésus* (1944), opens with a strikingly intense ritual stamping dance, hammering on the lower register of the piano and shrieking treble interjections. Unusually for Messiaen, this type of passage tends to be based on a single rhythmic value, stressing the reiterative qualities of the ritual dance.

But Jolivet, not Messiaen, is the contemporary French originator of this style, and the impact of Jolivet's music of the 1930s on both Messiaen and Boulez has been underestimated. Jolivet attended the Exposition Coloniale in Paris with Varèse in 1931, and the combination of non-Western cultures being brought to Paris and a strong humanist streak was irresistibly appealing to him. Since childhood, Jolivet had been aware on some level of non-Western culture, as his mother's cousin, Louis Tauxier, worked in a colonial civil service position linked to Africa. Jolivet remembered being fascinated by the huge map of Africa in Tauxier's home in Saint-Maur des Fossés and by the many objects he had brought home, including musical instruments. The composer recalled: 'For many years, I must have lived out imaginary music through these almost mute witnesses with which I felt a strong

---

le terrain de la mémoire et de l'imaginaire. Le surréalisme en assure le ferment unitaire dans une esthétique de juxtaposition des contraires, ouvrant en même temps la voie à une approche ésotérique.'

[58] André Breton, *L'Art magique*, Formes de l'art (Paris: Club Français du Livre, 1957), p. 9: 'La notion de "mana", dont ils font l'un et l'autre l'idée mère de la magie, celle qui pour eux rend le mieux compte à la fois des "faits-souches" de la magie et de la religion, lui parait mal résister à l'examen, glisser à l'évanescence de par sa plasticité excessive [...].'

[59] Originally written for a Domaine Musical programme of 15 April 1959 and published in Pierre Boulez, *Regards sur autrui*, ed. Jean-Jacques Nattiez and Sophie Galaise (Paris: Christian Bourgois, 2005), p. 552.

connection.'[60] However, the Exposition Coloniale was Jolivet's first opportunity to hear non-Western musics, and Deborah Mawer contends that 'The Exposition most likely influenced *Danses rituelles* and *Mana* – especially "La Princesse de Bali".'[61] Two years after the Exposition, in 1933, Jolivet travelled to Algeria to meet his future parents-in-law in Blida, where he also heard a performer on the nay which struck him deeply and had a strong impact on his *Cinq incantations* for flute (1936).

Jolivet was certainly interested in the sonority of non-Western instruments, but he was equally concerned with an 'aspiration to universality and the desire to make music accessible to the greatest number of people, to touch everyone directly.'[62] Rather than primarily seeking to imitate a particular non-Western music, he was therefore seeking the essence that, according to him, all musics have in common – the essence that speaks to everyone, whatever their cultural background. We are reminded of Bataille's definition of myth in *L'Apprenti sorcier* as 'the quickening of every dance; it brings existence to its boiling point; it communicates the tragic emotion that makes its sacred intimacy accessible. [...] Myth ritually lived reveals true being, no less.'[63] This is as close as one can possibly come in words to the essence that Jolivet is seeking, and his musical means for attaining this essence can be summarised as incantation.

Musically speaking, the incantatory style is linked to Varèse and, further back, to Stravinsky's rhythmic language and to Debussy's arabesque melodic lines which fall away or spiral out from a central pitch. Iteration and reiteration, using a narrow range of pitches and/or rhythms, is what creates a sense of incantation in musical terms. But it is also necessary to relate the concept of musical incantation to its broader cultural sources in order to pinpoint why it was so important to composers including

---

[60] Cited in Kayas, *André Jolivet*, pp. 132–3: 'Pendant bien des années, j'ai dû vivre sur ces <u>musiques imaginées</u> à partir de ces témoins quasi muets avec qui cependant je me sentais 'en correspondance.' See also Caroline Potter, 'The anxiety of exoticism: André Jolivet's relationship with non-Western musics', in Caroline Rae (ed.), *André Jolivet: Music, Art and Literature* (Abingdon: Routledge, 2019), pp. 159–72.

[61] Deborah Mawer, 'Jolivet's search for a new French voice: spiritual otherness in *Mana* (1935)', in Barbara L. Kelly (ed.), *French Music, Culture, and National Identity, 1870–1939* (Rochester, NY: University of Rochester Press, 2008), pp. 172–96, at p. 178.

[62] Emmanuel Hondré, 'Les Fondements d'un "primitivisme" musical chez André Jolivet (1935–1939)', in *André Jolivet: les objets de 'Mana'* (Paris: Cité de la Musique, 2003), p. 30: '[...] une aspiration à l'universalité et le désir de rendre cette musique accessible au plus grand nombre, à même de toucher tous les hommes'.

[63] See p. 28.

Jolivet and Boulez, especially as they were both more conscious of the cultural origins of this style than earlier composers were.

Jolivet linked the concept of incantation with non-European philosophy, spirituality and music, and a book by Jules Combarieu, *La Musique et la magie* (originally published in 1903), was a key influence in this context. Combarieu describes incantation as 'the essential source of art',[64] and Jolivet himself told Antoine Goléa:

> My spiritual leanings, which date from my early childhood, combined with the sociological studies I was pursuing at that time at the Sorbonne with my young wife, quite quickly led me down an esoteric path. Meetings with so-called primitive peoples, and a deep sense of the ordering of things, aided me to find my own sonic system. That explains to you why I was led to abandon both Schoenberg's strict system and Varèse's theories in favour of a return to the very sources of music. In a word, to magic.[65]

In what sense is 'magic' a quality of music, according to Jolivet? His call for 'a return to the very sources of music' and abandonment of Schoenberg's and Varèse's systems and theories is not a rejection of abstract constructivist principles, far from it. In his talk 'Genèse d'un renouveau musical' given at the Sorbonne at the invitation of René Allendy in 1937, Jolivet stated, 'It's not arithmetic that is the foundation of music, but *numbers*. And it's because it's based on number that music is a *magic art*.'[66] This important statement is directly applicable to Boulez, who, contrary to popular opinion, is not an arithmetical composer, but one whose music springs in part from the magic of numbers. Jolivet suggests that it is this basis in number that renders music an esoteric, spiritual art, not any particular association of music with religious worship.

Like Messiaen some years later, Jolivet explains contemporary harmony through the prism of the harmonic series which, as he

---

[64] Cited in Hondré, 'Les Fondements d'un "primitivisme" musical', p. 34: 'la source de l'art lui-même.'

[65] Cited in Kayas, *André Jolivet*, p. 132: 'Mes tendances spirituelles, qui dataient de ma plus jeune enfance, combinées aux études sociologiques que je poursuivais alors en Sorbonne avec ma jeune femme, m'ont assez vite mené à des préoccupations ésotériques. La fréquentation des peuples dits primitifs, le sentiment profond de l'ordonnancement numérique des choses m'ont aidé à établir mon ordre sonore. Cela vous explique que j'ai été amené à abandonner aussi bien le strict système de Schoenberg que les théories de Varèse au profit d'un retour aux sources mêmes de la musique. En un mot, à la magie.'

[66] Jolivet, 'Genèse d'un renouveau musical' (1937), published in Christine Jolivet-Erlih (ed.), *André Jolivet: écrits* (Paris: Delatour, 2006), vol. l, pp. 53–73, at p. 57: 'Ce n'est pas l'arithmétique qui est la base de la musique, mais les *nombres*. Et c'est parce qu'elle est basée sur les nombres que la musique est un *art magique*.'

demonstrates, includes an augmented fourth in the upper partials above a fundamental pitch.[67] He also justifies the contemporary use of microintervals by referring to the harmonic series, and specifically mentions new electronic instruments such as the ondes Martenot as instruments which can renew our harmonic language as 'they allow us to approach natural harmony as closely as possible'[68] – in other words, they can get closer to the overtones of the harmonic series than the equally tempered piano, which cannot play pitches in between its keys. This unexpected confluence of the ondes Martenot and non-Western music proved highly stimulating to Boulez and his fellow students.

It is perhaps surprising that only at the end of this talk does Jolivet explicitly refer to the incantatory in music, though this is central to his conception of magic in music. He states that Varèse believes his latest work *Écuatorial* (1934) is 'at the same time a clamour and an *incantation*'. Jolivet adds: 'When it is *incantatory*, art will cease to be *not of our time* – meaning without relation to the present, to everyday life – art will become a vital necessity, being based on life and not on intelligence.'[69] For Jolivet, incantation is not only a fundamental quality of his music, but one which guarantees the eternal value of an artistic work.

This incantatory, ritual dance aspect of Jolivet's music can be summarised, in stylistic terms, as music with a strong rhythmic aspect – usually irregular rhythm – which, melodically, reiterates around a small group of pitches. An extreme example is the opening of the first of his *Cinq danses rituelles*, 'Danse initiatique', which focuses exclusively on the G below middle C for several bars, accompanied by open diminished fourths or fifths in the bass. Linear, contrapuntal processes are rare in this musical style. Sometimes the melodic line erupts in a florid gesture, reminiscent of a Debussy arabesque, inevitably returning to its point of origin after the eruption. It is remarkable how often this type of florid arabesque gesture is present in Boulez's music, from the *Notations* until his very last works. True, Boulez's more contrapuntally detailed musical language is also apparent from the start, but the strong impact of Jolivet on his music is undeniable.

---

[67] Jolivet, 'Genèse d'un renouveau musical', in Jolivet-Erlih (ed.), *André Jolivet: écrits*, vol. l, p. 60.

[68] Jolivet-Erlih (ed.), *André Jolivet: écrits*, vol. l, p. 60: 'ce sont eux qui permettent de se rapprocher le plus possible d'une harmonie naturelle'.

[69] Jolivet-Erlih (ed.), *André Jolivet: écrits*, vol. l, p. 72: 'La dernière œuvre de Varèse [...] est, dit-il, en même temps une vocifération et une *incantation*. En étant incantatoire, l'art cessera d'être inactuel – dans le sens de: sans rapport à l'actualité, avec la vie de tous les jours – l'art deviendra une nécessité vitale, étant fondé sur la vie et non sur l'intelligence.' Emphases in original.

On one of the few occasions when Boulez was asked specifically about surrealist authors and artists, he suggested he was interested only in the first years of the movement, from the mid-1920s to the outbreak of World War II. He told David Walters:

> I remember very well, we were visiting in 1947 an exhibition of Surrealist Art, the first Breton organised after he came back from the States. I remember, I went to this exhibition with some friends and one of my friends said, 'after Stalingrad and Auschwitz, it's very difficult to look at this kind of exhibition because it's so superficial.' We did not know at all about Adorno at this time – that Adorno made the same reflections that 'you cannot write poetry after Auschwitz.' That was our reaction also. This kind of artistic divertimento, who thought that they were really very provocative – it had absolutely no meaning for us at this time.[70]

It was this 'divertimento' style that Boulez also detested in French composers of the older generation: Boulez had no time for the light and frivolous in music, and his reaction to the 1947 Paris surrealist exhibition shows that he found this tone completely distasteful in the post-World War II environment. Rather, in this period, the writers who interested Boulez were René Char, Henri Michaux and Antonin Artaud, whom he described to Walters as 'three people who were Surrealist in the 1920s or early 1930s but who after the war when they saw that [Breton exhibition] were totally out of the movement', while he considered Breton was 'totally out of touch with the epoch [...] Breton was never at all what he was before the war in the 1930s.'[71] It was this earlier Breton who, more significantly than is generally assumed, impacted Boulez's thought and music, together with his near-contemporaries Artaud and Char. However, Boulez's most direct personal association with surrealism came through the Belgian surrealist movement.

Belgian surrealists

A Belgian surrealist circle emerged in 1924 around the journal *Correspondance*, which was founded in November that year, initiated by Paul Nougé one month after the publication of Breton's first Surrealist Manifesto. A more formal group was founded in September 1926, including André Souris, E.L.T. Mesens, René Magritte, Nougé and Camille Goemans. One distinctive difference from the Paris circle was the involvement of musicians in the Belgian group: Mesens was a composer who was known as a supporter of Erik Satie, and Souris changed his musical style from a Debussy-influenced language to one more reminiscent of Satie under the impact of his Belgian colleagues.

Two of the principal differences between the Belgian and French surrealist circles were that the Belgians were interested neither in automatic writing nor in esotericism. Instead, in the words of Souris, they aimed to 'take commonplace expressions, not to move in a fantastical direction or towards dreams or the unconscious, but to try to give a new and poetic angle to found objects'.[72] So Nougé's poetry and Magritte's paintings were often based on pre-existing texts or images, given a new meaning by being placed in new contexts, and some of Souris's compositions use similar procedures. A notable example of this is Souris's *Trois inventions pour orgue* (1926), for which he took barrel organ perforated cards, cut them up and stuck them back together in a different order; the result when fed through the organ mechanism is far from popular fairground music, though the original sonority is retained. Souris also set texts by Nougé in his Satie-esque *Trois flonflons* (1925–8) and *Quelques airs de Clarisse Juranville* (1928), the latter text being allegedly by a primary school teacher and based on grammatical teaching material.

While Nougé was a poet, not a professional musician, he was a great music lover who first met Souris at a concert in Brussels in 1925 which included Schoenberg's *Pierrot lunaire* performed by Marya Freund and conducted by Darius Milhaud.[73] There were protests in the hall, the performance stopped, and Nougé cried out to the protesters, 'wait for me outside!' Souris's and Nougé's common interest in contemporary music drew them together, and many years later, Souris said he was especially impressed that for Nougé, art was about 'the destiny of mankind', not an amusement ('un divertissement'). Souris continued: 'In this perspective, I understood that it was necessary for everyone, at least for me, to start again from nothing, and to ask myself the question: What does artistic activity represent today for a man who intends to live deeply, looking out to the world?'[74] The parallel with Boulez's seriousness of purpose is

---

[72] Robert Wangermée, 'André Souris avant *Correspondance*', *Revue belge de musicologie*, vol. 42 (1988): pp. 285–298, at p. 297: 'prendre des lieux communs, non pour aller dans le fantastique, dans le rêve ou dans l'inconscient, mais pour tâcher de donner une affectation nouvelle et poétique a des objets tout faits, des objets qui existent.'

[73] André Souris, *La Lyre à double tranchant: écrits sur la musique et le surréalisme*, ed. Robert Wangermée (Liège: Mardaga, 2000), p. 169.

[74] Souris, *La Lyre à double tranchant*, p. 170: 'la destinée de l'homme intégral [...] Dans cette perspective, j'ai compris qu'il était nécessaire pour chacun, en tout cas pour moi, de recommencer à zéro, et de me poser la question: "Que

almost too obvious to be mentioned. In 1929, Nougé gave a talk that was published as *La Conférence de Charleroi* in 1946, one of the few texts by an artist intimately involved in surrealist circles to focus on music. His principal message was that music has nothing to do with entertainment or relaxation: it is dangerous.[75]

It is therefore not surprising to learn that Souris was one of Boulez's earliest supporters. They made contact via the intermediary of Serge Nigg, who studied with Messiaen and Leibowitz in the same classes as Boulez. In a letter from Boulez to Souris, which is not dated but which Robert Wangermée believes predates 21 January 1947, Boulez wrote:

> My friend Nigg, who sent you my manuscripts, speaks about you with a lot of admiration and sympathy. Because he told me that besides your interest in atonal music, you are also involved with surrealism and are one of the heads of this movement in Belgium, which was an excellent surprise to me.[76]

In fact, Souris had been excluded from the Belgian surrealist circle in a letter dated 17 January 1936, written by Mesens and signed by other members of the group; this text was published later that month under the title 'Le Domestique zélé'.[77] His principal offence was to have conducted a religious work at a concert in Brussels's Place Royale, an action Mesens considered incompatible with surrealism. However, Souris failed to attend the meeting to discuss his exclusion, and he did not lose touch with members of the group.

While Boulez was not personally connected with the Paris group surrounding Breton, he was involved with people in the Belgian circle, especially Souris. The other direct link between Boulez and the surrealist groups of the late 1940s is the Belgian poet and artist Christian Dotremont (1922–79). Born into an artistic family in Brussels, Dotremont came into contact with Magritte in 1940, having seen the review *L'Invention collective* in the window of the bookshop La Licorne on rue de la Madeleine in Brussels. Even at this very early stage, Dotremont

---

représente aujourd'hui l'activité artistique pour un homme qui a l'intention de vivre profondément et le regard ouvert sur le monde?"'

[75] Paul Nougé, *La Conférence de Charleroi* (Brussels: Le Miroir Infidèle, 1946); the talk on which the text is based was given on 20 January 1929.

[76] Letter housed in the Souris archive in Brussels and cited in Wangermée, *André Souris*, p. 273: 'Mon camarade Nigg qui vous a porté mes manuscrits m'a parlé de vous avec beaucoup d'admiration et de sympathie. Car il m'a dit qu'en dehors de musique atonale vous vous occupiez aussi du surréalisme et que vous êtes une des têtes de ce mouvement en Belgique, ce qui m'a fait une excellente surprise.'

[77] Wangermée, *André Souris*, p. 182.

was attracted to Magritte's questioning of the relationship between the word and the object, and he submitted a poem to the journal which was accepted for publication. He spent the 1940s between Paris and Brussels and was one of few intermediaries between the surrealist movements in those two cities.

Dotremont's acquaintance with Boulez dated from 1946, the year he co-founded both a group La Révolution Surréaliste and, with the poet Jean Seeger, a review, *Les deux sœurs*. The significance of the name of the review remains obscure, and like many similar small publications, it was short-lived, publishing only three numbers from 1946 to 1947. During this period – which coincided with Boulez's first version of *Le Visage nuptial*, his setting of five René Char poems – Char himself contributed a short prose poem, 'Élise', to the third number of *Les deux sœurs* and co-signed a text 'Au bar des deux frères' which was published in the second issue. Its final number began with a substantial article by Dotremont on surrealist revolution which heralded another review co-directed by Dotremont and Noël Arnaud, *La Révolution surréaliste*. Financial difficulties meant that its 1948 number was the only issue of this publication; while it shared a name with the pioneering Paris review which was first published in 1924, it had no connection to any of the original Paris authors. Dotremont's 'revolutionary surrealist' movement prized political engagement and published a tract 'Pas de quartiers dans la révolution!' expressing hostility to 'official' surrealism (fundamentally, to Breton) and specifically to the surrealist exhibition of 1947.[78]

François Meïmoun was the first to note that Boulez did not only read the group's publications; he also took part in 'lively' meetings of La Révolution Surréaliste, whose aims were, in Dotremont's words, to 'go beyond both the surrealist revolution and surrealism in service of revolution, in a perfect, unforced dialectic of surrealism and communism with neither subservient to the other'.[79] It is surprising to note that Boulez's closest connection to a contemporary surrealist movement came via someone engaged in political activity. A revolutionary in both art and politics, Dotremont joined the Belgian Communist Party in 1947, but Boulez, although or probably because he spent much of his career

---

[78] See the André Breton website: https://tinyurl.com/pbjwds74 [accessed June 2023].

[79] Karine Guihard, *Le Surréalisme révolutionnaire*, mémoire, DEA degree, Université de Nantes, 1998, p. 22, cited in Meïmoun, *Construction du langage musical*, p. 175: 'dépasser à la fois la révolution surréaliste et le surréalisme au service de la révolution en une dialectique parfaite du surréalisme et du communisme, sans rapport de force ou de soumission. Boulez assiste aux réunions chahutées des surréalistes révolutionnaires.'

engaging with politicians of all persuasions at the highest level, was not generally a party-political animal. After La Révolution Surréaliste fizzled out, Dotremont was best known for co-founding the CoBRA group (a group uniting Belgian, Dutch and Danish surrealists) in 1948, and for his logograms, a type of visual poetry. But while Dotremont was briefly important to Boulez as someone who could introduce him to ideas and artistic sympathisers, other writers had a much profounder impact on his music. Char is unquestionably the author who mattered most to him in the late 1940s, but another writer, whose words he never set, was fundamentally important to his aesthetic development: Antonin Artaud (1896–1948).

Antonin Artaud's Theatre of Cruelty

Artaud's collection of writings *Le Théâtre et son double* was published in 1938, though the various texts had been written between 1931 and 1936. The earliest of these was an article which was first published as a performance review in *Nouvelle revue française* in October 1931 about the Balinese theatre performance at the Exposition Coloniale Internationale. Each of France's colonies was represented at this exhibition, which combined cultural display and commercial advertisement and featured performances and recordings of traditional music from France's colonies and beyond. The exhibition provoked criticism from authors including André Gide, various surrealists and journalists writing for the Communist daily *L'Humanité* because of its colonial stance. Ultimately, the Exposition Coloniale led to the foundation of the Musée de l'Homme, which opened on 27 June 1938, a museum which has been described as 'a modern ethnographic museum based on the previously chaotic collections of the Trocadéro' and 'an act of defiance in the face of Nazi racial theories.'[80]

Putting contemporary critiques of the Exposition Coloniale aside, Artaud was particularly struck by a Balinese theatre performance, where he discovered a corporeal, non-naturalist stage production that aligned perfectly with his own views of what theatre should be. In his essay 'Sur le théâtre balinais' (1931), Artaud wrote: 'In this theatre, creation all arises from the stage, finds its expression and even its origin in a secret impulse which is Speech that comes before words.'[81] An actor

---

[80] Bataille, *The Sacred Conspiracy*, p. 250.
[81] Antonin Artaud, *Le Théâtre et son double* (1938; reprinted Paris: Gallimard, Folio edition, 1964), pp. 81–103, at p. 91: 'Dans ce théâtre toute création vient de la scène, trouve sa traduction et ses origines même dans une impulsion secrète qui est la Parole d'avant les mots.'

as well as an author, Artaud had at the heart of his theory and practice a bodily, visceral approach, and while his writings have been influential beyond the theatrical world, it was the live impact of his physical and vocal performance, not just his theoretical texts, that made an indelible impression on Boulez. Going beyond the centrality of written language to the Western theatre, for Artaud, performance should make an immediate emotional impact on everyone witnessing it (the term 'spectator' seems peculiarly inappropriate here: Artaud wanted audiences not just to look and listen, but to feel).

While Artaud was involved in Breton's surrealist project from the launch of the first Surrealist Manifesto, contributed frequently as author and editor of the review *La Révolution surréaliste* and was head of the Bureau du Surréalisme, fissures between the surrealist aesthetic and Artaud's soon became unbridgeable, and he was expelled by Breton from the movement. In a lecture given in Mexico 'Surréalisme et révolution' (1936) Artaud recalled his expulsion, dating it precisely to 10 December 1926: 'Doesn't Artaud care about the revolution? they asked. I don't care about your revolution, I care about mine, I replied, quitting surrealism since it too had become a political party.'[82] There were also creative divergences between Breton and Artaud; for Artaud, the key surrealist practice of automatic writing was anathema. And Barber suggests there were more profound differences in outlook between the two writers: 'With his ferocious invective against social and religious leaders, and writings about drug addiction and physical suffering, [Artaud] threatened the group's complacent tendency to move towards imagery of ideal communities and loving, subservient women.'[83]

During his involvement with the surrealist movement, Artaud was both active as a writer and studying acting with Charles Dullin, a training that encompassed physical theatre, gymnastics and vocal production. This expansion of the vocal possibilities of theatrical performance is central to Artaud's aesthetic, and for David Toop, Artaud's expanded vocal performance was a 'convoluted entwinement of poetics, theory and psychosis.'[84] Artaud founded the Théâtre Alfred Jarry with Roger Vitrac and Robert Aron in 1926, and also worked as a film actor and

[82] Antonin Artaud, 'Surréalisme et révolution' (1926), in Artaud, *Œuvres complètes*, vol. 8 (Paris: Gallimard, 1971), pp. 171–183, at p. 178: 'Est-ce qu'Artaud se fout de la révolution? me fut-il demandé. Je me fous de la vôtre, pas de la mienne, répondis-je en quittant le surréalisme, puisque le Surréalisme était lui aussi devenu un parti.'

[83] Stephen Barber, *Antonin Artaud: Blows and Bombs* (London: Faber, 1993), p. 23.

[84] David Toop, *Into the Maelstrom: Music, Improvisation and the Dream of Freedom before 1970* (London: Bloomsbury, 2016), p. 57.

scenario author, though only *La Coquille et le clergyman* (The seashell and the clergyman, 1928) was produced, a film which influenced both Salvador Dalí and Luis Buñuel and is often called the first surrealist film. Better-known films featuring Artaud as an actor include Abel Gance's epic *Napoléon* (1927) and Carl Theodor Dreyer's *La Passion de Jeanne d'Arc* (1928).

One of the most significant events of Artaud's life was his journey to Mexico in 1936, initially on a lecture tour to promote surrealist writers and study Mexican art and culture. In correspondence with the Ministers of Foreign Affairs and Education, Artaud states that his aim was to find in Mexico 'a perfect example of primitive civilization with a spirit of magic', and he proposed to interview 'healers and sorcerers on lost plateaux'.[85] The most important part of the journey was an expedition he made to the Sierra Madre to participate in an initiation rite which is narrated in 'D'un voyage au pays des Tarahumaras' (1937).[86] (The following year (1938), Breton described Mexico as 'the surrealist place par excellence'.[87]) His decision to visit the isolated Tarahumaras was made, according to Barber, because he believed them to be relatively 'uncontaminated by European civilisation. They were also one of the few surviving tribes to base their rituals of magic and religion (they believed in many gods) on the drug peyote.'[88] After his return to Europe, Artaud's mental instability and drug addiction ultimately led to his internment in 1943 in a psychiatric hospital in Rodez, a town near Toulouse; he was released in 1946, and placed by friends in a clinic in Ivry-sur-Seine, to the south of Paris.

Artaud was involved in several collaborations with composers which together form a frustrating story of interesting ideas that did not come to fruition. The largest of these was a project with Varèse, formulated and reformulated in the late 1920s and 1930s, which also has connections with Jolivet. Varèse planned a grand musical theatre production, first titled *L'Astronome* and later *The One All-Alone*, initially with a libretto by his wife Louise Varèse based on an Amerindian creation myth, featuring three invisible choruses and singing characters who are each doubled by a mime artist.[89] This extraordinarily

85 Cited in Uri Hertz, 'Artaud in Mexico', *Fragmentos*, no. 25 (2003): pp. 11–17, at p. 11.

86 First published in *Nouvelle revue française* (August 1937): pp. 232–47.

87 Cited in Melanie Nicholson, 'Surrealism's "found object": the enigmatic Mexico of Artaud and Breton', *Journal of European Studies*, vol. 43 no. 1 (2013): pp. 27–43, at p. 27.

88 Barber, *Antonin Artaud*, p. 82.

89 See Anne Jostkleigrewe, 'Reaching for the stars: from *The One All-Alone* to *Espace*', in Felix Meyer and Heidy Zimmerman (eds.), *Edgard Varèse: Composer,*

forward-looking concept is more reminiscent of Stockhausen than of Varèse's contemporaries; Varèse even incorporated the legend of Sirius, Stockhausen's spiritual home star, in a later iteration of the concept. Louise Varèse explained the significance of multiple representation for the protagonist:

> During action he is represented in three different ways: the figure of a man, as in the Prologue, whenever he is seen personally by one of the characters or when he is alone on the stage; a changing shadow during the ceremony of sacrifice, and a light when he is being worshipped as a God.[90]

However appealing Louise Varèse's libretto might have been, her husband's ideas moved from Amerindian creation myth to a dystopian future, and 'by mid-1929 at the latest he had found three writers willing to enter a joint working relationship with him: Alejo Carpentier, Robert Desnos, and Georges Ribemont-Dessaignes'.[91] The copious amount of sketch material surviving from these joint working sessions, heavily annotated by Varèse, suggests that the composer had very clear ideas about what he wanted from a text and found it challenging to leave space for collaborators to engage. It was at this stage, in mid-1933, that Artaud came on the scene. Impressed by Artaud's writings and ideas about extended vocal expression, Varèse thought he had found his ideal collaborator, but the composer returned to New York in September 1933, leaving Artaud to complete a draft libretto alone. (Let us briefly bring Boulez back into the picture at this point: an undated note addressed by Varèse to Boulez reads 'As promised, here's a photo with Artaud (1933). Best wishes, Varèse.'[92] As the Varèse letters to Boulez now housed in the Paul Sacher Stiftung date from 1952 to 1960, Boulez's request demonstrates a continuing interest in Artaud beyond his formative years.)

Artaud's text, under the title *Il n'y a plus de firmament* (There is no more heaven; 1931–2), is divided into five 'movements', though the fifth comprises only fragmentary ideas.[93] A hugely ambitious work, it has as its subject no less than the end of the world, a cataclysm that hints at the birth of a new, interplanetary world order, and Artaud responded

---

Sound Sculptor, Visionary (Woodbridge: Boydell Press, 2006), pp. 211–19, at p. 211.

[90] Louise Varèse, scenario typescript (1927) housed in the Paul Sacher Stiftung, Basel; cited in Jostkliegrewe, 'Reaching for the stars', p. 211.

[91] Jostkliegrewe, 'Reaching for the stars', p. 212.

[92] Paul Sacher Stiftung, Basel, Boulez collection, microfilm 25.1: 'Ainsi que promis – ci-joint photo avec Artaud. (1933). Amitiés, Varèse.'

[93] Antonin Artaud, *Il n'y a plus de firmament*, in *Œuvres complètes*, vol. 2 (Paris: Gallimard, 1961), pp. 91–110.

positively to Varèse's ideas of 'a layered spatial arrangement of light and colour to counterpoint Varèse's music'.[94] It oscillates between individual, personal reactions, such as a woman and child trying to understand what is going on, and violent earth-shaking scenes. Varèse and Artaud's aesthetics of violence and struggle at a cosmic level meet in this project; Artaud's scenario can be envisaged as a dystopian movie script, but it was never completed in its intended function as a libretto for Varèse. Barber explains that Artaud

> abandoned it at the end of the fourth movement with a fusion of 'violent percussions.' [...] in the early part of 1934, Artaud sent Varèse a typescript of part of the work he had done. By that time, Varèse was in a state of suicidal depression, which was to last for thirteen unproductive years.[95]

It is not well known that Artaud worked with Messiaen in 1932. Artaud had been asked to devise sound effects for Alfred Savoir's play *La Pâtissière du village*, and these effects were to be performed by Messiaen on the organ of the Théâtre Pigalle.[96] But creative differences between Artaud and Messiaen resulted in an unsatisfactory collaboration: Artaud wanted the sound effects to be realistic representations, while Messiaen's vision was of a musical, artistic imitation.

In the same year as this unhappy collaboration with Messiaen, Artaud met Jolivet. Varèse was a common friend and Jolivet's mentor, and for a time it seemed possible that Jolivet was going to take on some aspects of *The One All-Alone* project from Varèse. In this period,

> Jolivet participated in an event at the home of Lise and Paul Deharme [the surrealist and pioneering radio producer] for his future Theatre of Cruelty project. [...] At this time, Jolivet was sufficiently close to Artaud to visit him at his workshop on rue Victor-Considérant and envisage an artistic collaboration which would be like an extension of the writer's work for Varèse. A draft of a letter from Jolivet to Artaud, whose beginning has disappeared, shows their common interest in esotericism [...].[97]

This project, like so many others connected with Artaud, did not ultimately materialise, and nor did their plan to make a study of the

94   Barber, *Antonin Artaud*, p. 56, citing Artaud, *Il n'y a plus de firmament*.
95   Barber, *Antonin Artaud*, p. 56.
96   See Toop, *Into the Maelstrom*, p. 56.
97   Kayas, *André Jolivet*, p. 145: 'Jolivet participe à une séance chez Lise et Paul Deharme pour son future théâtre de la Cruauté. [...] A cette époque, Jolivet est suffisamment proche d'Artaud pour lui rendre visite à son atelier de la rue Victor-Considérant et envisager une collaboration artistique qui serait comme le prolongement du travail de l'écrivain pour Varèse. Un brouillon de lettre de Jolivet à Artaud, dont le début a disparu, montre leur attachement commun à l'ésotérisme [...].'

aesthetics of the cry. Looking back on their friendship, Jolivet recalled in an interview with Martine Cadieu in 1965:

> I was friendly with Artaud, you know, and before his illness, we worked together. He was to have written a libretto for Varèse. When he left France for America, Varèse charged me with stimulating Artaud. I owe this writer a lot, we used to share opinions about theatre. One of Artaud's central concepts was the cry ... We had 'yelling competitions', who could yell the loudest and longest! That left us in an altered state for our discussions ... [98]

This interview coincided with the premiere of Jolivet's ballet *Ariadne*, commissioned by Alvin Ailey, which was based on a text by Jolivet's elder son Pierre-Alain and inspired by Artaud's concept of the Theatre of Cruelty.

Jolivet's points of contact with Artaud were therefore multiple, and although their discussions about projects never resulted in a finished work, the impact of Artaud on Jolivet was considerable. In the 1930s, one of Jolivet's most creative decades, there are such strong connections between Jolivet's incantatory aesthetic, as heard in works such as the piano suite *Mana*, and Artaud that it is hard to believe he had not read Artaud's essay 'Le Théâtre et la culture'. Here, Artaud wrote: 'Unlike our idea of art, which is inert and disinterested, a genuine culture conceives of art as something magical and violently egotistical [...]. Because Mexicans capture *Manas*, the powers lying dormant in all forms [...] which only arise from a magical identity with these forms.'[99] Inevitably, one thinks of *Mana* as the title of Jolivet's piano suite and, on a more fundamental level, of Jolivet's aesthetic of music as magic. Compare Artaud's words with a passage from a lecture delivered by Jolivet at the Sorbonne on 20 February 1936: 'It's for us to recreate music based on universal laws. Give it back its incantatory sense and its magical qualities. Let's ensure it's no longer just a

---

[98] Interview 'L'homme a peur du silence' for *Les Nouvelles Littéraires* (23 December 1965), republished in Christine Jolivet-Erlih (ed.), *André Jolivet: écrits*, vol. 1, pp. 364–7, at p. 365: 'J'ai été lié d'amitié, vous le savez, avec Artaud et avant qu'il ne soit malade, nous avons travaillé ensemble ... Il devait écrire un livret pour Varèse. Varèse quittant la France pour l'Amérique m'avait chargé de stimuler Artaud ... Je dois beaucoup à cet écrivain, nous partagions nos vues sur le théâtre. Un des points chers à Artaud c'était le cri ... Nous faisions, lui et moi, des "concours de cris", à qui crierait le plus fort et le plus longtemps! Cela nous mettait d'ailleurs ensuite dans un état second pour discuter ...'
[99] Artaud, *Le Théâtre et son double*, p. 17: 'A notre idée inerte et désintéressée de l'art une culture authentique oppose une idée magique et violemment égoïste [...]. Car les Mexicains captent les Manas, les forces qui dorment en toute forme [...] qui sortent d'une identification magique avec ces formes',

game or just sensual pleasure – but a manifestation in sound which is directly connected to the universal cosmic system.'[100]

What was Artaud's impact on Boulez? Werner Strinz surmises that, given Boulez's connections with André Souris and composition of the first version of *Le Visage nuptial* in October–November 1946, 'It is highly likely that Antonin Artaud came into the world of Boulez's ideas well before he became musical director of the Renaud–Barrault company in October 1946.'[101] This is all the more probable given Boulez's broader familiarity with the surrealist movement. However, a deeper, personal connection came through their common friend Paule Thévenin (1918– 93), who 'met Artaud for the first time on 5 June 1946 at the asylum in Ivry-sur-Seine where he then lived; she asked him whether he would like to do a reading for the Club d'Essai literary radio programme.'[102] This request led to *Pour en finir avec le jugement de Dieu*. It must have been shortly after this meeting that, according to Dominique Jameux, Paule Thévenin 'made [Boulez] read Artaud.'[103] Thévenin originally studied psychiatry, and in that capacity she was charged to look after Artaud on his return from Rodez; ultimately she became both his literary executor and the editor of the first major collection of Boulez's writings, published in 1966 as *Relevés d'apprenti*.

Thévenin almost certainly introduced Boulez to Artaud at a private event in July 1947 at the Galerie Loeb where Artaud read some of his texts surrounded by an exhibition of his drawings. This was an intimate space; 'Boulez and his friends had to sit in front of the first row of chairs, and they found themselves almost "under" the voice of Artaud when he was reading.'[104] Being within spitting distance of Artaud, still

[100] André Jolivet, 'Conférence Gil-Marchex', in Jolivet-Erlih (ed.), *André Jolivet: écrits*, vol. 1, pp. 40–6, at p. 43: 'A nous de refonder la musique sur les lois de l'Univers. Rendons-lui son sens incantatoire et ses attributions magiques. Faisons-en sorte qu'elle ne soit plus seulement un jeu de l'esprit ou un plaisir des sens – mais une manifestation sonore en relation directe avec le système cosmique universel.'

[101] Werner Strinz, '"Il y a un couteau que je n'oublie pas": Antonin Artaud et Pierre Boulez', in Florence Fix, Pascal Lécroart and Frédérique Toudoire-Surlapierre (eds.), *Musique de scène, musique en scène* (Paris: L'Harmattan/Orizons, 2012), pp. 21–33, at p. 23: 'Il est fort probable qu'Antonin Artaud soit entré dans l'horizon d'idées de Pierre Boulez bien avant qu'il ne devienne directeur de la musique de scène de la Compagnie Renaud-Barrault en octobre 1946.'

[102] Barber, *Antonin Artaud*, p. 129.

[103] Dominique Jameux, *Boulez*, trans. Susan Bradshaw (London: Faber, 1991; French original, 1984), p. 32.

[104] Sarah Barbedette, 'Différentes façons d'être voyant', in Sarah Barbedette (ed.), *Pierre Boulez* [exhibition catalogue] (Paris: Actes Sud, 2015), pp. 23–37, at p. 25: 'Boulez et ses amis doivent s'asseoir devant le premier rang de chaises, et

a charismatic performer despite his much reduced physical condition, was an experience that Boulez never forgot. Towards the end of his life, he recalled:

> Artaud wrote fatrasies [a poetic style dating from the Middle Ages where sound is more important than the meaning of the words], improvisations on words like the lettrists did, but more impressive in his case. You had to hear them to judge their quality. If you read them on the page, they don't make much sense. The way he did them had a real sonic value. [...] It was truly the sound of the syllables and his way of pronouncing them which were interesting. One could imagine amplifying this with a choir, or a speaking choir. [...] it made an impression on me because what initially seemed to make no sense suddenly made sense very strongly.[105]

For Boulez, Artaud was not primarily a cultural theoretician, but a performing artist whose work only truly existed live. Few recordings survive of Artaud as performer of his own texts; he recorded *Aliénation et magie noire*, a highly personal text about his electroshock treatment, for the Club d'Essai experimental radio slot on 16 July 1946, and his most celebrated recording is *Pour en finir avec le jugement de Dieu*, recorded in November 1947. Featuring Artaud himself (his voice is in significantly worse condition compared to the previous year's recording), the well-known actors Maria Casarès (who read the second section, 'Tutuguri')[106] and Roger Blin (the third section, 'La Recherche de la fécalité'), and Thévenin herself reading the fourth section, 'La Question se pose de ...', *Pour en finir avec le jugement de Dieu* was scheduled for broadcast on 2 February 1948, but its blasphemous and anti-American passages resulted in it being pulled from the schedule. A protest from significant cultural figures of the time led to a private hearing of the recording for journalists, writers and artists.

---

c'est presque "sous" la voix d'Antonin Artaud qu'ils se trouvent lorsque celui-ci profère ses poèmes.'

[105] François Meïmoun, *Entrietien avec Pierre Boulez: la naissance d'un compositeur* (Paris: Aedam Musicae, 2010), pp. 57–9: '[Artaud] faisait ce qu'on appelle des fatrasies, des improvisations sur des mots comme les lettristes l'ont fait, mais c'était dans ce cas-là plus impressionnant. Il fallait les avoir entendues pour pouvoir les juger. Si on les lit seulement, on trouve que cela n'a pas grand sens. La façon dont il le faisait avait un véritable sens sonore. [...] C'était vraiment la sonorité des syllabes qui était intéressante et sa manière de les prononcer. On pouvait imaginer amplifier cela avec un chœur, ou avec un chœur parlé. [...] ça m'a marqué en raison du fait que ce qui n'avait initialement aucun sens prenait d'un coup un sens, et un sens très fort.'

[106] Colette Thomas dropped out at the last minute and, at Thévenin's suggestion, she was replaced by Casarès (Barber, *Antonin Artaud*, p. 152).

The recording of *Pour en finir avec le jugement de Dieu* captures something of the power of Artaud's verbal performance. He underlines the incantatory repetitions of his text, stressing the 'il faut' (must) in the first section, but from the perspective of a listener of Boulez's work, it is his extreme changes in vocal register that are most striking. His abrupt moves from his regular speaking voice to something strangulated and in a falsetto register at 'l'épreuve dite de la liqueur séminale ou du sperme' (the so-called test of seminal fluid or of sperm) underlines the shocking subject matter, about supposed compulsory sperm donation in American schools. Artaud is also far more likely than the other professional actors to push his voice to extremes, holding nothing back, seemingly unconcerned with potentially damaging his vocal cords. The text, likewise, shocks on many levels, at the same time anti-American, anti-military, blasphemous and scatological. After the text read by Thévenin, which gradually increases in volume until she is speaking loudly and forcefully, Artaud enters with yells, punctuated by regular percussion interjections, each phrase ending with a gong strike. The recording ends with an interview with Artaud in which he – retaining his performative character – answers questions about the text and performance. In the middle of this text the following exchange occurs:

> – You are delirious, Monsieur Artaud. You are mad.

> – I am not delirious. I am not mad. I'm telling you, microbes were reinvented in order to impose a new idea of god.[107]

Thévenin recalled the recording sessions:

> Several musical instruments were made available to Antonin Artaud: a xylophone, drums, timpani, gongs, on which he improvised music that accompanied his chanting. He also recorded cries of varying intensities and passages of glossolalia. After a number of experiments, a glossolalia dialogue between him and Roger Blin was also recorded.'[108]

The glossolalia (speaking in tongues) was part of the soundscape that preceded the fourth section, 'La Question se pose de ..', the vocal

---

[107] Artaud, *Pour en finir avec le jugement de Dieu* (1948): '– Vous délirez, monsieur Artaud. Vous êtes fou. / – Je ne délire pas. / Je ne suis pas fou. / Je vous dis qu'on a réinventé les microbes afin d'imposer une nouvelle idée de dieu.'

[108] Cited in Michel Pierssens, 'Écrire en langage: la linguistique d'Artaud', *Langages*, no. 91 (1988): pp. 111–17, at p. 116: 'Plusieurs instruments de musique avaient été mis à la disposition d'Antonin Artaud: xylophone, tambours, timbales, gongs, sur lesquels il improvisa la musique dont il accompagna ses chantonnements scandés. Il enregistra aussi des cris de diverses intensités et des passages de glossolalies. Après différents essais, un dialogue en glossolalies entre Roger Blin et lui fut aussi enregistré.'

sounds combining with timpani and a xylophone. Towards the end of this improvisation, the sound of someone spitting is clearly audible. The selected percussion instruments transcend the boundary between classical and traditional music, Western and non-Western music, and the vocal performance encompasses all manner of utterances and places glossolalia into a secular performance context. Sound effects realised in Pierre Schaeffer's studio completed the sound sources of the performance. On 4 March 1948, less than a month after the private performance of this recording, Artaud died: one of his last visitors was René Char, who together with his collaborator Georges Braque had a long meeting with Artaud at the hospice in Ivry a few days before his death.[109]

Boulez's involvement with the Renaud–Barrault theatre company from late 1946 also moved him close to Artaud's orbit. Barrault's own formative years in the early 1930s were marked by Artaud when the two actors worked at the Théâtre de l'Atelier, founded by the great French actor Charles Dullin. Later, Barrault was to have appeared in Artaud's 1935 play based on Shelley, *Les Cenci*, but he walked out following an argument with the actress Iya Abdy. Reviews were negative and the play closed after only seventeen performances.[110] This was not the only connection between Boulez's circle of professional contacts, *Les Cenci* and Artaud: what would now be termed the 'sound design' of the play, consisting of recorded sounds diffused through four loudspeakers, was created by Roger Désormière, who conducted the first performance of the initial concert version of Boulez's *Le Soleil des eaux*.[111] While Barrault and Artaud's relationship was never as close after the failure of *Les Cenci*, Barrault contributed to the cost of Artaud's Mexican trip, and Boulez himself said that 'when Artaud came back from the asylum, Barrault was instrumental in his reinstatement as a very

---

[109] Anne Reinbold, 'Chronologie', in René Char, *Œuvres complètes*, Bibliothèque de la Pléiade (Paris: Gallimard, 1983), pp. lxxxvi–lxxxvii: 'Mort, le 4 mars [1948] d'Antonin Artaud, à Ivry-sur-Seine. Georges Braque et René Char s'étaient longuement entretenus avec lui à l'hospice d'Ivry quelques jours auparavant.' Char's contemporaneous tribute to Artaud, beginning 'Je n'ai pas la voix pour faire ton éloge, grand frère', is published in this same volume (p. 712).

[110] Barber, *Antonin Artaud*, pp. 71, 72.

[111] Catherine Peillon, 'Signaux de la très riche vie acoustique', *La pensée de midi*, no. 8 (2002): pp. 137–42, at p. 139 (article available online at https://www.cairn.info/revue-la-pensee-de-midi-2002-2-page-137.htm). Also note Paule Thévenin's article originally published in *Roger Désormière et son temps* (1966) and now available on the Désormière website: https://sites.google.com/site/rogerdesormiere18981963/roger-desormiere-et-son-temps/paule-thevenin-les-cenci-d-antonin-artaud-d-apres-shelley [accessed June 2023].

influential actor'.[112] Interviewed by the *International Herald Tribune* in 1981, Barrault explained that

> he learned from the wayward genius Antonin Artaud 'the metaphysics of theater': how the actor, through his body and breathing, through the use of silence and of the present moment, becomes a sort of field of magnetic energy. It's reflected in one of Barrault's favorite mottos: 'To be passionate about everything and attached to nothing'.[113]

For Boulez, Artaud's aesthetic and performance style responded at the right moment to his own artistic concerns, and Artaud's links between theory and practice provided a model for the composer who would soon emerge as a polemicist as well as a creative artist. Thévenin's friendship with Boulez and Artaud and her eventual role as editor of both of them reinforced this connection still more. Boulez's interest in Artaud went far beyond an admiration for him as writer and performer, even beyond their shared fascination with non-European cultures. In the mid–late 1940s, Boulez found a musical equivalent of Artaud's uncompromising art, encompassing the extremes of vocal utterance and emotional directness, what Artaud himself referred to as thought inhabited by 'multiplicity, finesse, an intellectual eye on delirium, not haphazard prophecies'.[114] For Meïmoun, Artaud was 'a poet who was indifferent to the Western concert platform who created a profoundly musical language';[115] it was Boulez who actualised the musical potential of this language.

Boulez made a striking statement about the essential core of a creative life on one of the few occasions when he explicitly quoted Breton. At the end of his article 'Nécessité d'une orientation esthétique' (1963), he states, 'I am convinced that in every great composer (in every great creator) there is an "unshatterable kernel of darkness"! [...] I put my faith in this "kernel of darkness", which will endure after a momentary flash

[112] Interview with Peter O'Hagan, in Peter O'Hagan, *Pierre Boulez and the Piano* (Abingdon: Routledge, 2017), p. 328.

[113] Anonymous author, interview with Jean-Louis Barrault, *International Herald Tribune*, 4–5 April 1981; available online at https://www.itinerariesofahummingbird.com/jean-louis-barrault.html [accessed June 2023].

[114] Cited in Werner Strinz, '... l'œil intellectuel dans le délire ..', in Barbedette (ed.), *Pierre Boulez*, pp. 97–9. (Artaud, 'Manifeste en langage clair' in *Œuvres complètes*, Paris: Gallimard, 2004, p. 149: 'la multiplication, la finesse, l'œil intellectuel dans le délire, non la vaticination hasardée.')

[115] Meïmoun, *Construction du langage musical*, p. 173: 'Poète indifférent aux scènes de concert occidentales, Artaud crée une langue profondément musicale.'

has dispersed.'[116] Boulez has, however, completely decontextualised this quotation; Breton wrote this phrase not in the context of artistic creativity, but in the introduction to a 1933 translation of Achim von Arnim's *Contes bizarres*, referring to sexuality.[117] But the quotation struck Boulez so much that he used it again when discussing the creative process in a lecture given at the Collège de France in 1978:

> This initial moment of creation is that which remains wild, unexpected. Certainly, one can later relate it to some sort of intention, source or accident. But there remains this 'unshatterable kernel of darkness' of which Breton spoke. It is initially inexplicable and remains, at the end of the day, unexplained. It's the primordial gesture, the one which cannot be explained by the banal and so obvious term: personality.[118]

Returning to the original context of Breton's statement, one must speculate that this essential flash of inspiration at the heart of a work, this 'unshatterable kernel of darkness', was for Boulez connected with sexuality, or at least with something at the core of our humanity. For Breton, desire is the primary motivational force, the unshatterable core; also essential to his art is the coexistence of passion and precision, of explosion and proportion. In *L'Amour fou*, he praises images in Lautréamont which are 'blessed with a force of persuasion that is rigorously in proportion with the violence of the initial shock that produced them.'[119] And when Boulez's early work is examined, this inseparable union of intellect and passion is equally apparent.

---

[116] Pierre Boulez, based on Darmstadt lectures from 1963 and originally published in *Points de repère*, ed. Jean-Jacques Nattiez, 2nd edition (Paris, Christian Bourgois, 1985), pp. 54–77, at p. 77: 'Pour conclure, je voudrais reprendre, à propos de la personnalité du compositeur, une admirable expression d'André Breton [...]. Je suis sûr qu'il existe dans tout grand compositeur (tout grand créateur) un 'noyau infracassable de nuit'! [...] J'ai confiance en ce 'noyau de nuit', qui subsistera après l'éclat d'un moment dispersé.'

[117] The original context of Breton's expression is 'De nos jours, le monde sexuel, en dépit des sondages entre tous mémorables que, dans l'époque moderne, y auront opérés Sade et Freud, n'a pas, que je sache, cessé d'opposer à notre volonté de pénétration de l'univers son infracassable noyau de *nuit*.'

[118] Pierre Boulez, 'Idée, réalisation, métier', in *Leçons de musique*, pp. 71–110, at p. 92: 'Ce moment initial de l'invention est celui qui demeure sauvage, imprévu. On pourra certes, plus tard, le rattacher à quelque volonté, quelque descendance ou accident. Mais en soi, il reste ce 'noyau infracassable de nuit' dont parlait Breton. Il est d'abord inexplicable et reste, en fin de compte, inexpliqué. C'est le geste primordial, celui qui ne s'explique que par ce vocable si banal et si inévitable, la personnalité.'

[119] Breton, *L'Amour fou*, pp. 128–9: 'douées d'une force de persuasion rigoureusement proportionnée à la violence du choc initial qu'elles ont produit.'

2

'A FLAYED LION': BOULEZ AS STUDENT

BOULEZ WAS BROUGHT UP in Montbrison, a small town near Lyon, where he received his first musical education. There was no public concert life in the town, but he was part of a church choir – he described being in a choir as 'a very good educational experience' – and in 1991 he recalled that there were local chamber music groups that rehearsed weekly.[1] While studying a mathematics-based curriculum at secondary school in Lyon, he took private lessons in piano and harmony with Lionel de Pachmann, son of the celebrated pianist Vladimir de Pachmann. These lessons were based on the standard repertoire and classical musical language. Opportunities for Boulez to hear contemporary music while he was at school were very limited; in discussion with François Meïmoun he remembered hearing the violinist Jacques Thibaud playing Szymanowski's *Mythes* (1915) and being 'especially struck' by the first piece, 'La Fontaine d'Aréthuse', because 'its sonic universe cut across that of modern music of the time, when Honegger was the acme of modernity.'[2]

Honegger was the most prominent contemporary composer in France in the early 1940s, and in Lyon, Boulez remembered hearing André Cluytens, then musical director of the Opéra National de Lyon, conduct works by him. Boulez particularly recalled Honegger's *La Danse des morts*, which seemed to him 'fabulous, completely different from the

1   Interview on 23 April 1991, available at https://www.ina.fr/video/R15049180/
     pierre-boulez-et-son-education-musicale-video.html [accessed June 2023]: 'un
     très bon éducateur'.
2   François Meïmoun, interview with Pierre Boulez, https://www.musicologie.
     org/publirem/entretien_avec_pierre_boulez.html [accessed June 2023]: 'La
     première pièce du cycle, *La Fontaine d'Aréthuse*, m'avait beaucoup frappé. L'œu-
     vre tranchait avec le paysage sonore d'alors où la modernité était essentielle-
     ment incarnée par Arthur Honegger.'

[musical] universe with which I was familiar'.[3] *La Danse des morts* (1938), an oratorio inspired by Holbein's *Dance of Death*, features a melange of material including French revolutionary songs, the *Dies irae* plainsong and a preachy text by Paul Claudel which draws on Biblical extracts. Its punchy opening, graphically depicting fire and brimstone with multiple trombones and percussion instruments, is more reminiscent of Varèse than of most of Honegger's work, and its scoring for narrator, soloists, chorus and orchestra shows Honegger and Claudel grappling with a 'total theatre' concept, as in their earlier *Jeanne d'Arc au bûcher* (1935).

Only a few years later, Boulez would himself be performing work by Honegger and by Claudel in his role as musical director of the Renaud–Barrault theatre company. Boulez did not experiment with composition until 1942, when he was 17 years old: one of his first surviving attempts was a setting of Baudelaire, *Recueillement*, which he may not have known at the time had been set by Debussy fifty years earlier.

Boulez at the Paris Conservatoire

Boulez moved to Paris in September 1943 with the aim of entering the Paris Conservatoire. His first harmony teacher was Renée Jamet, who taught preliminary classes in composition and harmony at the Conservatoire and was married to the harpist Pierre Jamet; the Jamets had friends in common with Boulez's family.[4] Boulez also auditioned for the advanced piano class (*classe de piano supérieure*) on 13–14 October 1943 but was not successful.

However, he transferred to Georges Dandelot's preparatory harmony class on 17 January 1944.[5] Although Boulez had had little previous formal education in harmony compared with students who had gone through the junior or regional Conservatoire system, he was evidently a very fast learner. Dandelot reported in May 1944 that he was 'the best in the class … [he] has nothing further to learn at this level'.[6] In the Conservatoire system, students could be awarded one of four classifications at the end of the academic year – in descending order, *premier prix*, *deuxième*

---

[3] Interview cited in François Meïmoun, *Entrietien avec Pierre Boulez: la naissance d'un compositeur* (Paris: Aedam Musicae, 2010), p. 16: 'Cela m'avait semblé fabuleux, complètement différent de l'univers qui m'était familier.'

[4] See Wenonah Milton Govea, *Nineteenth- and Twentieth-Century Harpists: A Bio-Critical Sourcebook* (Westport: Greenwood Press, 1995), p. 137. Boulez remained close to the Jamets, and their daughter, Marie-Claire, became a distinguished harpist and member of his Ensemble InterContemporain.

[5] Peter O'Hagan, *Pierre Boulez and the Piano* (Abingdon: Routledge, 2017), p. 13.

[6] Cited in O'Hagan, *Pierre Boulez and the Piano*, p. 13: 'le meilleur de la classe [...] n'a plus rien à apprendre en 1er degré.'

prix, premier accessit and *deuxième accessit* – and students who did not get a *premier prix* (first prize) would typically stay in that class the following year. Boulez got a first prize in harmony after less than five months' study in Dandelot's class, an exceptional achievement.

In his first term at the Conservatoire, Boulez encountered two people who would, in different ways, have a significant impact on his early studies. In his harmony class, one of his fellow students was Annette Vaurabourg, the niece of Andrée Vaurabourg-Honegger, a pianist who had a considerable reputation as a counterpoint teacher and was married to Arthur Honegger. Peter O'Hagan surmises that the niece introduced Boulez to Andrée Vaurabourg, and he subsequently had private lessons in counterpoint with her. Boulez also met Messiaen at this time and identified that he was another teacher with whom he wished to study. He sought private lessons from Messiaen in order to prepare for entry to his class while he was still studying with Dandelot,[7] and he formally enrolled in Messiaen's harmony class on 23 January 1945.

Messiaen's first appointment at the Conservatoire was as a harmony teacher, following his return to Paris in 1941 from a prisoner of war camp. In 1947 he was appointed professor of analysis and aesthetics, though he was not officially named a composition professor until 1966. Messiaen was one of five teachers of the advanced harmony classes, and his Conservatoire harmony class, according to Christopher Brent Murray and Yves Balmer, 'remained well within the boundaries of Conservatoire traditions'.[8] Murray and Balmer studied Boulez's class notes, now housed in the Paul Sacher Stiftung, and they confirm that Messiaen used the harmony texts which were employed by other teachers at the Conservatoire. No doubt this was to ensure consistency, as all students studying a particular discipline at a given level took the same examination at the end of the year. Messiaen had, in fact, written his own textbook in 1939, *Vingt leçons d'harmonie. Dans le style de quelques auteurs importants de 'l'histoire harmonique' de la musique depuis Monteverdi jusqu'à Ravel* (Twenty harmony lessons in the style of several important authors from 'the history of harmony' from Monteverdi to Ravel), but evidence suggests that he did not use the more adventurous material in his Conservatoire class. Despite this, Boulez considered that Messiaen was

---

7 Jean Boivin, *La Classe de Messiaen* (Paris: Christian Bourgois, 1995), p. 34.
8 Christopher Brent Murray and Yves Balmer, 'Pierre Boulez and Olivier Messiaen's harmony class', in Paolo dal Molin (ed.), *Immagini di gioventù. Saggi sulla formazione e le prime opere di Pierre Boulez, Musicalia*, vol. 7 (2014): pp. 31–59, at p. 33.

the only truly creative professor in the *classes d'écriture* [technique classes] of that period. [...] He based his exercises, and we have the reflection of this in his book *La Technique de mon langage musical* [1944], on musical texts, which was not often the case with other professors. The other professors based their instruction on a sort of harmonic abstraction that had nothing to do with direct sources, while he gave us exercises where it we could develop our compositional and creative faculties. He always told us when he gave us homework – even a traditional type of homework like a harmonisation or figured bass – that we had to invent an idea or several ideas in order for the homework to make sense. [...] And in particular when he gave us homework that was to be realised in a certain style, he analysed pieces by a relevant composer, [...] and gave us a homework that he had composed himself.[9]

There is specific detail about the content of Messiaen's harmony classes in Boulez's exercise book; Murray and Balmer discovered that Boulez copied

a set of 71 harmony formulas attributed to Messiaen, written in a four-part texture appropriate for harmony lessons. The formulas' labels often make reference to the harmonic procedures they employ and the composer or work they are based upon. The formulas appear to have functioned as models of both particular procedures and the technique of adapting pre-existing musical passages from the repertoire into textures usable in the context of harmony lessons.[10]

These formulas 'betray a marked preference for the late nineteenth century French vocabulary that students needed to weather the concours [the end-of-year examination], most notably the vocabularies of Franck, Fauré, and French opera composers like Massenet, Delibes, Bizet and

---

9   Murray and Balmer, 'Pierre Boulez and Olivier Messiaen's harmony class', pp. 44–5; they cite a recorded interview Boulez gave Olivier Mille in 1996, translation modified. 'Je dois dire franchement, à mon avis, c'était le seul professeur vraiment créatif dans le domaine de l'écriture à cette époque-là. [...] [Il] s'est basé, on en a d'ailleurs le reflet dans son livre *La Technique de mon langage musical,* on voit très bien qu'il s'appuyait sur les textes, ce qui n'était pas le cas, souvent, des autres professeurs. Les autres professeurs s'appuyaient sur une espèce de l'abstraction de l'harmonie qui n'avait plus rien à voir avec des sources directes tandis que lui, au contraire, il nous donnait des devoirs [...] c'était des devoirs où le sens de la composition, de la création s'exerçait. Il nous disait toujours, quand il nous donnait un devoir, même un devoir disons traditionnel comme un chant donné ou une basse donnée, il nous disait toujours: il faut inventer une idée ou inventer des idées de façon à ce que votre devoir ait un sens. [...] Et en particulier il donnait des devoirs dans un certain style à faire, il analysait des pièces d'un compositeur, [...] et il donnait un devoir qu'il avait rédigé lui-même.'
10   Murray and Balmer, 'Pierre Boulez and Olivier Messiaen's harmony class', pp. 34–5.

Lalo'.[11] The intention was that the student should learn the formula – for instance, a harmonic progression such as a cadence – and be able to apply it in the correct context when required to harmonise a melody. Late nineteenth-century French composers were still the harmonic models for students at the Conservatoire in the 1940s; it appears that the curriculum for this discipline had not changed since Ravel left the institution in 1905, whatever the upheaval in contemporary musical language in the forty years from that date until Boulez's entry into Messiaen's class.

Although this shows that Messiaen adhered to the Conservatoire syllabus in his harmony teaching at that institution, it is curious that his students were not particularly successful in their final examinations. Boulez was a notable exception, as just as he had obtained a *premier prix* after one academic year with Dandelot, he was again awarded a *premier prix* from Messiaen's class at the first attempt following the end-of-year examination on 11 June 1945.[12] Murray and Balmer note that 'In five complete years of instruction, only three students from Messiaen's class received premiers prix: Sylvie Valès and Yvonne Loriod in 1943, and Pierre Boulez in 1945'.[13] Messiaen himself was awarded *premiers prix* in several different disciplines when he was a student at the Conservatoire, so he certainly knew what was required to succeed in the end-of-year examinations. But one wonders whether he, consciously or unconsciously, communicated his essential lack of sympathy with the Conservatoire's conservative approach to the teaching of harmony to his students.

Another peculiarity of the French conservatoire system was that students had to study harmony to an advanced level before being permitted to move on to study counterpoint. Henri Dutilleux, for one, never understood why this was the case, and he was fortunate that when he was a teenager in Douai, northern France, his local Conservatoire teacher Victor Gallois taught him harmony and counterpoint simultaneously. Boulez was typically trenchant when he described his opposition to this system:

> I thought it was stupid to wait, to have to first finish my studies in harmony in order to start counterpoint. It would have been a waste of time for me, and in my view a harmful dissociation of two disciplines that should be closely connected. For harmony and counterpoint are the two fundamental aspects of all polyphonic writing. They should be learned at the same time.[14]

---

[11] Murray and Balmer, 'Pierre Boulez and Olivier Messiaen's harmony class', p. 37.
[12] O'Hagan, *Pierre Boulez and the Piano*, p. 14.
[13] Murray and Balmer, 'Pierre Boulez and Olivier Messiaen's harmony class', p. 32.
[14] Antoine Goléa, *Rencontres avec Pierre Boulez* (Paris: Julliard, 1958), p. 13: 'Je trouvais stupide d'attendre, de finir d'abord mes études d'harmonie pour aborder

His decision to study counterpoint privately with Andrée Vaurabourg-Honegger (1894–1980) needs to be understood in this light. Vaurabourg originally trained as a pianist in Toulouse and transferred to the Paris Conservatoire, where she was awarded a first prize in counterpoint. As a pianist she was most associated with the works of her husband, whom she married in 1926. She remembered her former student: 'Pierre Boulez first came here on Wednesday 19 April 1944, at 3 pm. He continued to come weekly until 2 May 1946. He never missed a lesson and he was never late.'[15] In total, he attended forty-five individual lessons with Vaurabourg-Honegger. Her curriculum included two-part inventions and fugues in the style of Bach, Claude Le Jeune and Purcell, and Boulez also worked examples in the style of more contemporary composers including Fauré and Honegger. Susanne Gärtner writes, 'Vaurabourg quickly recognised the gifts of Pierre Boulez. She had never had a student whose abilities seemed so limitless and whose accuracy, memory and diligence were so phenomenal.'[16] For his part, Boulez said that 'with her, I very much enjoyed studying counterpoint' and that her teaching 'was certainly more academic that Messiaen's, but it was inspired academicism, if I may say. I remember she asked me to read and learn Bach's Chorales. I bought a copy and, indeed, I learned a lot about contrapuntal writing from this source.'[17] (It is interesting to note in passing that this text was used as a model of contrapuntal writing, not primarily as a harmony teaching aid as in many British educational institutions.) Boulez recognised that Vaurabourg was able to teach him something from the standard repertoire that he needed to know, and his unwavering respect for her is remarkable in the light of his contemporaneous disputes with other musicians.

---

le contrepoint. C'eût été une perte de temps pour moi, et une dissociation, que j'estime funeste, de deux disciplines qui doivent, au contraire rester étroitement liées. Car harmonie et contrepoint ne sont que les deux aspects fondamentaux de toute écriture polyphonique. Il faut y progresser en même temps.'

[15] Cited in Peter Heyworth, 'The first fifty years', in William Glock (ed.), *Pierre Boulez: A Symposium* (London: Eulenburg, 1986), p. 48.

[16] Susanne Gärtner, *Werkstatt-Spuren: Die Sonatine von Pierre Boulez* (Bern: Peter Lang, 2008), p. 38: 'Vaurabourg erkannte schnell die Begabung von Pierre Boulez. Nie sonst habe sie einen Schüler erlebt, dessen Fähigkeiten so grenzenlos schienen, und dessen Genauigkeit, Gedächtnis und Fleiss so phänomenal gewesen seien.'

[17] Pierre Boulez, interview with Sylvie de Nussac (1983); cited in Gärtner, *Die Sonatine von Pierre Boulez*, p. 38: 'avec elle j'ai beaucoup aimé l'étude du contrepoint. [...] [c']était certainement plus académique que celle de Messiaen mais d'un académisme inspiré, si je puis dire. Je me souviens qu'elle me demandait de lire et d'apprendre les *Chorals* de Bach. Je me les étais procurés et, en effet, j'ai ainsi beaucoup appris de l'écriture contrapuntique.'

Private lessons with Messiaen

But other lessons that Boulez took beyond the walls of the Conservatoire, first with Messiaen and later with René Leibowitz, would ultimately be more important to his development as a composer. 'The most delightful reference' to the young composer appears at the back of Messiaen's 1944 diary, where Boulez is described as someone who 'likes modern music, wants to take harmony lessons etc. with me'.[18] Messiaen's private classes often took place on Saturdays, initially at his own house, though they later moved to the more comfortable home of Guy Bernard-Delapierre, an Egyptologist and great lover of music who later became known as a film music composer. Boulez recalled that this impressive building, 24 rue Visconti in the sixth arrondissement of Paris, was 'where Racine died'.[19]

Messiaen's own memories of Boulez as a student reveal that their informal, chance conversations were at least as important as formal lessons. He recalled that at the Conservatoire, Boulez

> was only in my harmony class. What was either unlucky or lucky – I don't know which – was that he obtained his Premier Prix at the first attempt, so he only stayed a year. And afterwards I only saw him rarely. But even so, there's something more important than a class. He was living in the Rue Beautreillis at the time (that's in the fourth arrondissement) and my father lived on the Quai Henri-IV (which is also in the fourth arrondissement). So we used to take the metro together, me to have lunch with my father and he to go home. And we used to talk in the metro. And according to what he's told me since, these talks guided him much more than the class did. [...] We were exchanging points of view, that is. And he was very angry, as you know. He was like a lion that had been flayed alive. He was terrible! And so I tried to make him a little more moderate. But above all, I was trying to show him the fountain of youth at which he had to drink in order to get out of this fury.[20]

By 8 December 1943, Boulez was attending Messiaen's private lessons. Other members of this small group, which from the start included Serge Nigg and Yvonne Loriod (who were both also members of Messiaen's Conservatoire harmony class) and Yvette Grimaud, started going to

[18] Peter Hill and Nigel Simeone, *Messiaen* (New Haven: Yale University Press, 2005), p. 139.
[19] Interview with Richard Rodney Bennett, part of BBC Radio 3 programme on Messiaen and Leibowitz's pupils broadcast on 20 January 1986 and now housed in the British Library Sound Archive (B586/3).
[20] Olivier Messiaen, interview with Claude Samuel, *Messiaen Edition*, 18 CD box set, Warner Classics 2564 62162-2 (2005), trans. Stuart Walters: pp. 109–35, at p. 128.

these private lessons in November 1943.[21] The classes took place once a month, and by the following year, the class had become known as 'Les Flèches' (The Arrows), a nickname derived from a stylised rendering of Messiaen's initials: 'the "O" enclosed an "M" with arrow heads on the two upper tips.'[22]

What did this adventurous group of students study with Messiaen? Evidence suggests that most of the class focused on music analysis. Boulez told Richard Rodney Bennett that in the first lesson he attended, they studied Ravel's *Ma Mère l'Oye*. First, they read the tale, then played Ravel's piano duet and then studied his orchestration – a class that lasted six to seven hours that Boulez described as 'my first real lesson in composition and orchestration.'[23] Stravinsky's *Petrushka* was also on the programme, as were Debussy's *Jeux* (which was then very little known) and recent works by Bartók including his violin sonatas, string quartets and *Music for Strings, Percussion and Celesta* (1936).[24] This was a period when twentieth-century music was very rarely studied at the Conservatoire, and while music analysis is now a distinct class at this institution, it was not in Boulez's day. Henri Dutilleux often spoke to me of his regrets that contemporary music and music analysis were not on the curriculum when he attended the Conservatoire in the 1930s, and in Boulez's student days, even the study of Ravel's music would have been considered a daring choice for a Conservatoire class. Messiaen's own music was not formally studied, but Boulez was invited to a private performance of his *Visions de l'Amen* at Delapierre's home on 20 July 1944; Messiaen and Loriod were the two pianists.[25]

Many of the Messiaen private study group were excellent pianists, including Boulez, and Yvette Grimaud recalled that members of the class would often play score reductions at the piano: 'Yvonne Loriod and I were both very good sight-readers. Serge Nigg and I used to play the piano duet transcription of *The Rite of Spring* almost by heart!'[26] However, Boulez stated that Messiaen did not look at his students' compositions in this class, and certainly, he did not show his teacher any of his early works in progress.[27] And while Messiaen discussed

[21] Hill and Simeone, *Messiaen*, pp. 138–9.
[22] Hill and Simeone, *Messiaen*, p. 132.
[23] Boulez, interview with Bennett.
[24] Also see Hill and Simeone, *Messiaen*, p. 161.
[25] Invitation in Messiaen's hand, now housed in the Paul Sacher Stiftung, Pierre Boulez collection.
[26] Boivin, *La Classe de Messiaen*, p. 49: 'Yvonne Loriod et moi avions une grande rapidité de lecture. Serge Nigg et moi jouions presque par cœur *Le Sacre* à quatre mains!'
[27] Boulez, interview with Bennett.

Schoenberg's *Pierrot lunaire* and Berg's *Lyric Suite* with this group of students, none of them recall him talking about the twelve-tone method of composition.[28] The importance of these Messiaen private classes cannot be overstated: Boulez told Richard Rodney Bennett, 'It was for me really the great year of my development, because in one year, I went much quicker than ever before, and maybe ever after. When you discover a work like that, that's a violent opening to the world – it was very, very intense.'[29] Violence, intensity – these passionate and aggressive emotions are what Boulez recalled.

Of course, friendship and discussion with classmates are central to the experience of most students, and Boulez was no exception to this. The composer Serge Nigg (1924–2008) was, for a time, someone with whom he enjoyed exchanging ideas; Boulez's dedication of his twelve *Notations* for piano (1945) to Nigg testifies to the esteem he had for him. Nigg, who was of Scottish and Russian descent and only nine months older than Boulez, entered the Conservatoire in 1941 as one of Messiaen's first harmony students. He came to public attention before Boulez was at all known as a composer, and in the late 1940s he published polemical newspaper articles about contemporary music, again before Boulez.

It was also Nigg whose name was first cited in the international music press as a significant Messiaen pupil. In an article written in 1944 for the British contemporary music journal *Tempo*, Felix Aprahamian noted that

> His style is said to be harmonically richer and rhythmically more complex than that of Messiaen – which is difficult to credit. His piano sonata has received four performances in Paris. In his earliest work Nigg set to music André Gide's 'Perséphone', his treatment resembling in many ways Stravinsky's setting of the same text. [...] Nigg is now working on 'L'Europe ouverte', a symphonic poem in seven parts to last about half an hour. This is dedicated 'to the glory of the U.S.S.R.'[30]

Aprahamian's critique highlights one major difference between Nigg and Boulez: the former was politically active as a member of the Parti Communiste de France,[31] while Boulez's trenchant contributions to artistic politics were never coupled with party-political engagement.

---

[28] Boulez, interview with Bennett.
[29] Boulez, interview with Bennett.
[30] Rudolph Dunbar and Felix Aprahamian, 'The news from Paris', *Tempo*, no. 9 (December 1944): pp. 15–17, at p. 15.
[31] Leslie A. Sprout, 'The 1945 Stravinsky debates: Nigg, Messiaen, and the early Cold War in France', *Journal of Musicology*, vol. 26 no. 1 (2009): pp. 85–131, at p. 89.

At the same time, it is interesting to note in passing Nigg's precocious engagement with Gide's work, not least because Boulez included the same author's words as a preface to his *Trois Psalmodies* for piano (1945).

Yvonne Loriod (1925–2010), an exact contemporary of Boulez, was a pianist whom Messiaen described as 'unique, sublime and brilliant'[32] who, in the 1940s, was also a composer. Loriod was an early performer of Boulez's works including his Second Piano Sonata, as was Yvette Grimaud (1920–2012), who was even more important to Boulez in the 1940s. Grimaud premiered four of his piano works (and gave the first performance of Nigg's First Piano Sonata in 1943), but it is less well known that she was also a composer with exceptionally broad and adventurous interests. Maurice Martenot had introduced her to Messiaen in 1938: she was a regular attender at gatherings at Messiaen's home from this date, and her compositional output shows that she was an early adopter of the ondes Martenot, no doubt partly because she was drawn to music that does not conform to the standard chromatic scale. Music from non-European cultures was another enthusiasm of hers that proved long-lasting – she was to become a distinguished ethnomusicologist, a specialist in the music of sub-Saharan Africa and of Georgia – and she also championed and recorded work by the Russian émigré composer who developed his own notation, Nicolas Obouhow (1892–1954). Grimaud introduced Boulez to these interests of hers, and her enthusiasm for non-Western music proved especially stimulating for Boulez. Jean Boivin writes:

> It was in Messiaen's company, and led by him, that Boulez heard a recording of Balinese gamelan for the first time, around 1945. But another Messiaen disciple, Yvette Grimaud, showed interest in this area before Boulez, and it was she who introduced him to Madi Sauvageau [*recte*: Mady Sauvageot], who had just founded with Philippe Stern the record library at the Musée Guimet, the Paris centre for the study of Eastern civilisations.[33]

Both Grimaud and Boulez confirm that non-European music played an important role in their private class with Messiaen. Boulez wrote that

> European music was not at all the central focus of our studies: engaging with Asia and Africa taught us that musical tradition was not limited to

---

[32] Antoine Goléa, *Rencontres avec Olivier Messiaen* (Paris: Julliard, 1960), p. 147.

[33] Boivin, *La Classe de Messiaen*, p. 52: 'C'est bel et bien en compagnie de Messiaen, et conduit par lui, que Boulez entendit pour la première fois, vers 1945, un enregistrement de gamelan balinais, mais une autre disciple de Messiaen, Yvette Grimaud, précédait Boulez sur ce terrain, et c'est elle qui le présenta à Madi Sauvageau, qui venait de créer, avec Philippe Stern, la phonothèque du musée Guimet, à Paris, où était concentrée l'étude des civilisations orientales.'

our region, and it captivated us because these are places where music was, more than an art object, a real way of life: this was an indelible branding.[34]

Messiaen's class served as an introduction to musical traditions which have a different social function from the classical music that was more familiar to his students. But most of all, one is struck by Boulez's emotional language. Much like Messiaen's description of Boulez as a 'flayed lion', Boulez's 'indelible branding' is a strong, violent physical metaphor, displaying the power and intensity of his feelings. Another student in this group, Jean Prodromidès, gives more specific detail about the non-Western musics they were introduced to in Messiaen's class. Other than the gamelan, he recalls discovering 'the Balinese kecak, a bit of Tibetan music, and not forgetting Hindu music which nobody else knew [...]. I remember going to the Musée de l'Homme and seeing Gilbert Rouget who was then the curator and listening to 78s of Balinese gamelan music.'[35]

When a student, Boulez copied a number of scores by hand, including a *Chant funèbre* for voice and piano by Yvette Grimaud dating from 1943. Its bracketed subtitle reads 'Poème extrait des rites des tribus du Haut-Abanga' (Poem, extract of rites of the tribes of Haut-Abanga; the present-day location of this is north-west Gabon). A tantalising extract exhibited at the Bibliothèque Nationale de France in 2022 shows the opening page: the bass voice is marked 'd'une voix étouffée' (with a muffled voice). His performance mode changes from humming (*bouche fermée*) to rhythmicised speaking, and the piano part opens with irregular rhythmic clusters in the extreme bass register of the type that Boulez would soon use in *Notations* and elsewhere, illustrated in Ex. 2.1.

During these exceptionally creative years of the late 1940s, Boulez briefly considered a career as an ethnomusicologist and carried out research in the Musée Guimet record library at the suggestion of Grimaud. Here, he transcribed field recordings that had been made for the 1931 Exposition Coloniale. The museum planned a major field

[34] Originally written for a Domaine Musical programme of 15 April 1959 and published in Pierre Boulez, *Points de repère*, ed. Jean-Jacques Nattiez, 2nd edition (Paris: Christian Bourgois, 1985), p. 552: 'La seule Europe n'avait point le privilège de nos investigations; approcher l'Asie et l'Afrique nous apprit que les prérogatives de la tradition n'étaient pas circonscrites, nous ravit au stade où la musique était, plus qu'un objet d'art, un véritable mode d'être: brûlure indélébile.'

[35] Cited in Boivin, *La Classe de Messiaen*, p. 339: '[...] le kecak de Bali, un peu la musique tibétaine, sans oublier bien sur la musique hindoue, que personne ne connaissait [...]. Je me rappelle avoir été au Musée de l'Homme, avoir vu Gilbert Rouget qui en était conservateur à l'époque, et avoir entendu des disques soixante-dix-huit tours de gamelan balinais.'

Ex. 2.1 Yvette Grimaud, *Chant funèbre (poème extrait des rites des tribus du Haut-Abanga)*: opening bars.

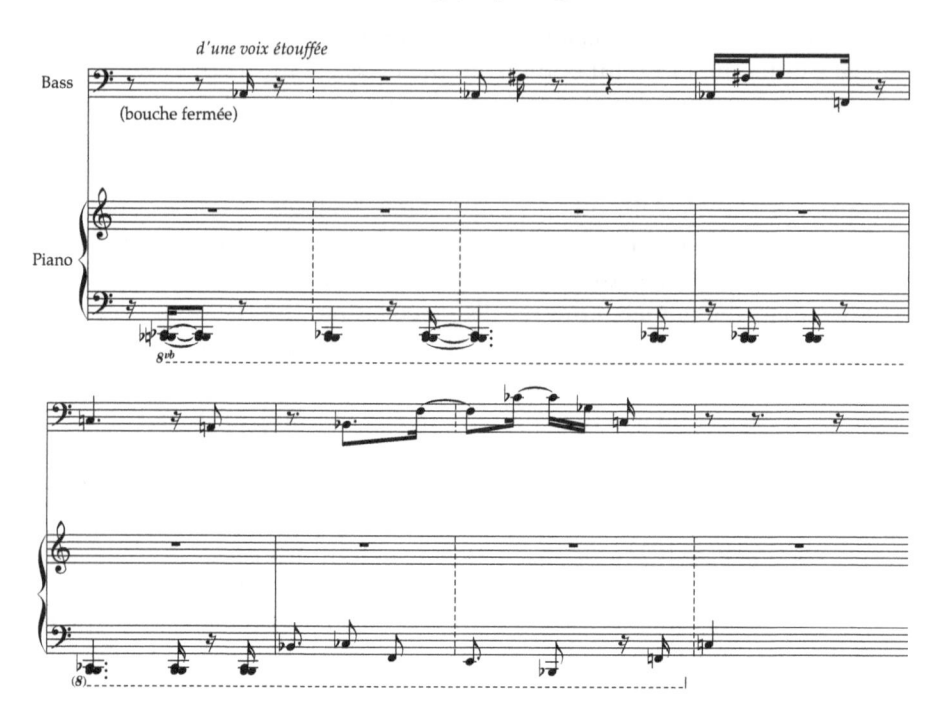

trip to French Indochina in 1947 involving Boulez, but the mission was cancelled following the outbreak of war in December 1946.[36]

The circle surrounding Messiaen also put Boulez in contact with others who gave him opportunities and connections in his formative years. Guy Bernard-Delapierre, for instance, also promoted concerts of contemporary music and was especially interested in composers who experimented with quartertones. One of the most prominent of these was Ivan Wyschnegradsky (1893–1979), of Russian origin and resident in Paris, who was recognised in the 1930s and 40s as a musical pioneer, though his work is rarely performed today. Bernard-Delapierre promoted a concert of his music at the Salle Chopin-Pleyel in Paris on 10

[36] See Luisa Bassetto, 'Ritratto del compositore come apprendista etnologo: Pierre Boulez prima dell'incontro con André Schaeffner', *Musicalia*, vol. 7 (2010), pp. 61–82, at p. 62: 'J'ai songé un moment faire de l'ethnologie musicale, et s'il n'y avait pas eu la guerre d'Indochine, je serais parti en mission au Cambodge, dans l'hiver 45–46'. For Grimaud's impact on Boulez, see also Tobias Bleek, 'Pierre Boulez: *Douze Notations*', *Explore the Score*, http://www.explorethescore. org/pierre-boulez-douze-notations-history-and-context-composing-within-narrow-confines.html [accessed June 2023].

November 1945, including his *Premier fragment symphonique*, op. 23b (1937), and *Cosmos* (1939–40) for four pianos, two tuned normally and two a quartertone distant, played by Grimaud, Loriod, Nigg and Boulez. The concert also featured *Linitte* (1937) for the same instruments plus two sopranos (Gisèle Peyron and Mady Sauvageot) and an alto (Lili Fabrègue).[37] This was certainly the 20-year-old Boulez's first public performance in a major concert hall. Looking back at this performance forty years later, Serge Nigg wrote:

> We had spent long days working under the direction of an author who looked like a prophet, visibly inspired by Heaven, and whose long arms, beating immutable quavers, pointed alternatively at each of us as if to denounce with a vengeful finger his melodic lines quartered between the four pianos. But what joy finding ourselves as if immersed in the magical world of micro-intervals, unreal harmonies, in a fantastical atmosphere, an Ali-Baba's cavern where diamonds, carbuncles and other precious sound gems glittered.
>
> The letdown was hard the day after the concert, when we returned to the ordinary sound world, a bit commonplace and prosaic, of our good old 12-note scale of which the chromatic intervals seemed to us to flirt with gaping holes in which all enchantment had vanished.[38]

While Boulez's musical interests changed dramatically and quickly during his formative years, his connection with Wyschnegradsky continued when in 1951 he participated in the world premiere of his *Deuxième fragment symphonique*, for the same four-piano formation as before and 'percussion ad libitum'. On this occasion, Boulez reunited with Grimaud, and the two were joined by Ina Marika and Claude Helffer.[39] In a long letter to Cage sent in December 1951, Boulez said Wyschnegradsky's piece was 'very bad, and the sounds themselves become heavy'.[40]

---

[37] See http://www.ivan-wyschnegradsky.fr/fr/catalogue/ [accessed June 2023]. André Souris programmed Wyschnegradsky's *Also sprach Zarathustra*, also for four pianos two of which are tuned a quartertone distant, in Brussels in 1947. Souris also conducted a concert at the École Normale de Musique including Wyschnegradsky's *Premier fragment symphonique* for the same instrumentation, performed by Grimaud, Loriod, Nigg and Boulez, which was broadcast on 30 January 1948; see O'Hagan, *Boulez and the Piano*, p. 112.

[38] Serge Nigg, programme note for Association Ivan Wyschnegradsky concert (January 1985), http://www.ivan-wyschnegradsky.fr/en/catalogue/ [accessed June 2023], translated by John Tyler Tuttle; original French not available here.

[39] http://www.ivan-wyschnegradsky.fr/fr/catalogue/ [accessed June 2023].

[40] Jean-Jacques Nattiez (ed.) and Robert Samuels (trans.), *The Boulez–Cage Correspondence* (Cambridge: Cambridge University Press, 1993), p. 118 (Jean-Jacques

Interlude: Boulez and the ondes Martenot

Messiaen was also important to Boulez because of his association with the early electronic instrument the ondes Martenot, an enthusiasm shared by several of his contemporaries who were especially attracted to its microtonal capability. The instrument has survived largely because Messiaen used it, most notably in the *Turangalîla-symphonie* (1948), and his future sister-in-law Jeanne Loriod became the leading exponent of the ondes in the twentieth century. Boulez discovered the ondes Martenot when he attended the rehearsals of Messiaen's *Trois petites liturgies de la Présence Divine*, which was composed between 1943 and 1944, though not premiered until April 1945. However, many of Boulez's closest classmates were familiar with the instrument well before this date. The intriguing role played by the ondes Martenot in Boulez's musical formation is worth exploring in some detail.

The ondes was introduced to the Parisian public by its inventor, Maurice Martenot, at the Paris Opéra on 20 April 1928, though it gained a much wider audience when it was featured at the Paris Exposition Internationale of 1937. During this exhibition, Martenot's sister Ginette directed an ensemble of eight female ondistes; they all wore flowing Grecian-style white gowns and gave at least one performance most days from mid-September to November 1937.[41] These were not live performances – the musicians mimed to recordings that were diffused through loudspeakers on the outdoor site – but the unique sound of the ondes ensemble and striking appearance of the performers made a big impact, and the instrument aptly combined the twin themes of the exhibition, art and technology. Both Maurice and Ginette Martenot were awarded a Grand Prix de l'Exposition for their participation in the festival, and eleven of the eighteen composers commissioned to write works for the exhibition wrote for the ondes.[42]

An advertisement published in the *Guide du concert* on 1 October 1937 shows that the ondes performance schedule included both Ginette Martenot's ensemble and other artists. One of these performers was

---

Nattiez (ed.), *Pierre Boulez/John Cage correspondance*, Paris: Christian Bourgois, 1991, p. 187: 'J'ai joué dans un concert à quatre pianos des œuvres avec quarts de ton de Wyschnegradsky. C'est très mauvais, et les sons eux-mêmes deviennent lourds').

[41] Peter Asimov, 'Une invention "essentiellement française": seeing and hearing the ondes Martenot in 1937', *Musique, images, instruments*, vol. 17 (2018): pp. 107–26, at p. 109. A promotional film of the ensemble can be viewed at https://www.youtube.com/watch?time_continue=1&v=vs75G_OaI5U&feature=emb_logo [accessed June 2023].

[42] Asimov, 'Une invention "essentiellement française"', p. 116.

the 13-year-old Serge Nigg, billed as 'Un jeune virtuose des Ondes' (Peter Asimov rightly points out that he is the only performer on the programme to be described explicitly as a virtuoso).[43] Boulez's future classmate was therefore an extremely early adopter of the ondes, and while Yvette Grimaud did not participate in the 1937 Exposition, she was another young pioneer of the instrument. As she was introduced to Messiaen in 1938 by Maurice and Ginette Martenot (when she was 18 years old), one assumes that like Nigg, she was learning the instrument from the Martenot family. Grimaud was also a child prodigy whose performances on the piano when she was just 11 years old attracted media attention in Algiers, her hometown; her other early public performances included accompanying the cellist Paul Tortelier in Rennes in 1942.[44]

Boulez, on the other hand, was no prodigy. Yvonne Loriod learned the standard repertoire of the piano, including all of Beethoven's piano sonatas and Mozart's piano concertos, as a child, but while Boulez learned to play the piano well, he had none of the intensive childhood immersion in music of his future classmates, and he heard his first live orchestral performances while studying in Lyon in his final two years of secondary school. However, although he discovered the ondes Martenot later than Nigg and Grimaud, he learned to play the instrument to professional standard in the mid-1940s when the only way to access lessons was through the Martenot family. Boulez also attended Martenot's lessons at the Conservatoire, recalling that 'They asked me to follow his class because it was then not well known, not many pupils had enrolled. I accepted, although I had already mastered the instrument. The arrival of the first pupils justified the existence of this class.'[45] Jeanne Loriod was also a pupil in this first ondes Martenot class, which started in 1947. In his memoirs, the Belgian composer Karel Goeyvaerts, who studied composition at the Paris Conservatoire under Messiaen in 1947, wrote that he took private ondes lessons with Martenot at his home. He recalled: 'Maurice Martenot's electronic instrument was the height of fashion at the time. Some of Messiaen's pupils had tried it out: Boulez and Grimaud were completely sold out on waves [ondes]; [Yvonne] Loriod left hers to her sister.'[46]

---

[43] See Asimov, 'Une invention "essentiellement française"', p. 111.

[44] Critique published in *L'Ouest-Eclair* (29 April 1942): p. 2.

[45] Meïmoun, interview with Boulez: 'On m'a demandé de suivre sa classe car elle était encore peu connue, assez peu d'élèves y étaient encore inscrits. J'ai accepté, alors que je maitrisais déjà parfaitement l'instrument. La venue des premiers élèves a permis d'entériner l'existence de cette classe.'

[46] Karel Goeyvaerts, 'Paris – Darmstadt 1947–1956: excerpt from the autobiographical portrait', in *The Artistic Legacy of Karel Goeyvaerts. A Collection of*

Perhaps surprisingly, there are multiple connections between the contemporary enthusiasms for the ondes Martenot and for non-Western musics. Previous large-scale exhibitions in Paris, such as the 1931 Exposition Coloniale, also had a strong international focus and featured performances by musical ensembles from the French colonial empire and beyond, and for 1937, many of the musical contributions to the exhibition reflected the absorption of non-Western musics or themes into French music. Maurice Martenot himself was inspired by musics from outside the Western tradition; indeed, as Asimov put it, he

> integrated his experience of Javanese and Indian musics into the construction of the instrument. [...] Martenot was seduced by a gamelan performance in Surabaya, Java, during a marathon world tour in 1930–31, and he decided in response to develop the *diffuseur métallique*, a speaker containing a metal gong in place of a membrane. In a separate anecdote, a fortuitous encounter between Ginette Martenot and Rabindranath Tagore laid the groundwork for Maurice Martenot to work, in collaboration with Indologist Alain Daniélou, on a model of the instrument with an adjustable keyboard, designed to adapt to various Indian modes.[47]

Two musical contributions to the 1937 exhibition show how different composers combined this new French instrument with non-European sources of inspiration. Pierre Vellones, one of the first composers to write for ondes Martenot, contributed *Fête fantastique*, which juxtaposed the ondes with instruments borrowed from the collection at the Musée de l'Homme,[48] and Mady Sauvageot's *Danse rituelle araucane* was written for ondes and piano and based on a Chilean tribal theme. Asimov states that Sauvageot's work

> manifests a sound of 'exotic' ritual with an insistent percussiveness and biting timbres in extreme registers; the thematic material is structured around, and doubled in, tritones. The programme annotation contending that no other instrument possesses such timbres has intriguing implications which further clarify the link between the ondes Martenot and musical 'otherness'.[49]

Essays, Revue belge de musicologie / Belgisch Tijdschrift voor Muziekwetenschap, vol. 48 (1994): pp. 35–54, at p. 36.

47   Asimov, 'Une invention "essentiellement française"', p. 118.

48   Asimov, 'Une invention "essentiellement française"', p. 122.

49   Asimov, 'Une invention "essentiellement française"', p. 120. Sauvageot's arrangement appeared on a 1958 recording *Musique rituelle à travers temps et pays* which featured transcriptions for percussion, voice and ondes Martenot of traditional and religious music from many different countries and periods, from the French and Spanish Middle Ages to traditional Scottish, Armenian and Brazilian music.

While today, the ondes Martenot is most often associated with otherworldly sci-fi effects, in France in the 1930s and 40s the instrument's connection with otherness was rather linked to non-Western musics. It is as if the ondes could act as a conduit between Western instruments (such as the piano) and other cultures, with percussion instruments frequently acting as an intermediary. The instrument also embodies the fascination with timbre that is a continuing thread in French music history.

The importance of Mady Sauvageot (1898–1987) to Boulez in his formative years has been underestimated. She was a pioneer in ethnomusicology in France who worked in the sound recording department of the Musée Guimet and also a singer who was involved in both the 1945 Wyschnegradsky concert promoted by Bernard-Delapierre, and the first (partial) performance of Boulez's initial version of *Le Visage nuptial* in 1947, a work that includes parts for two ondes Martenot. By introducing Boulez to the museum's recorded collections and by championing his early work, Mady Sauvageot was another woman who had a decisive impact on his musical evolution.

Yvette Grimaud's combined expertise as a pianist, composer, developing ethnomusicologist and ondes Martenot enthusiast encouraged and amplified many of Boulez's own concerns. As a composer, she was an early champion of the ondes; while little of her music is now available for study, a 2014 auction catalogue of her manuscripts notes that works she composed included *Mélopée* for two ondes Martenot and piano (1940) and a piece titled with the expression marking 'Très lent – expressif' (Very slow – expressive) for ondes or cello and piano (1943).[50] Most intriguingly where Boulez is concerned, her work was brought to wider attention when her *Trois pièces* for voice, ondes Martenot and piano were performed at the ISCM music festival in Palermo in 1948. Its instrumentation is strikingly similar to that of the first version of *Le Visage nuptial*.

This combination of ondes Martenot and piano is not one that is immediately obvious from a sonic perspective as there are few obvious points of contact between the sonorities of the two instruments, but perhaps the duo is intended to reflect more conventional duet partnerships such as the cello and piano, possibly with the piano in an accompanimental role. (One is reminded that Maurice Martenot was himself a cellist, and conceptually he viewed the ondes as a string instrument, not a member of the keyboard family.) Grimaud was far from the only French composer to treat the ondes as a pseudo-string instrument.

---

[50] See https://www.gazette-drouot.com/lots/4034774 [accessed June 2023].

Jacques Tchamkerten notes that the earliest composers for ondes, such as Jacques Chailley, Honegger and Canteloube, were attracted to 'the extremely expressive characteristic of the *jeu au ruban*', referring to one of the playing techniques where the finger slides up and down a metallic strip. But for Tchamkerten, Jolivet's *Trois poèmes pour ondes Martenot et piano* (1935) 'opened up the instrument to a new world of expression. Contrary to his predecessors, he demanded sounds from the instrument which were increasingly husky, piercing and heart-rending, representing the glorious violence and the unashamedly primitive character of the music.'[51] The second of Jolivet's pieces for ondes and piano is an adaptation of the third piece of his piano suite *Mana*, 'La Princesse de Bali', a movement that had a strong impact on Boulez.

This connection between non-Western musics and the ondes Martenot therefore represents a confluence that reflects the contemporary cultural environment of young French composers of the 1930s and 1940s. Boulez's own introduction to the ondes came through Messiaen's *Trois petites liturgies*, where the ondes is paired with gamelan-like metallophones, piano, celesta and a female chorus. Messiaen later used the instrument in his *Turangalîla-symphonie*, where it often doubles or otherwise enhances the string sound, but this is its last appearance in his output until the opera *Saint François d'Assise* (1975–83), written over thirty years later.

Although none of Boulez's published works employ the ondes Martenot, several of his early pieces feature the instrument. While he was initially interested in its sonority (as the first version of *Le Visage nuptial* makes clear) and its microtonal capability, it appears that the challenges of accurate performance led him to abandon precise microtonal notation. For instance, material from his *Quatuor pour ondes Martenot* of 1945–6 was recycled in other works, omitting the microtones. The ondes is used in his first, unpublished orchestration of *Notations* (1945–6) and incidental music for the Henri Michaux play *Chaînes* (1946), which is also an unpublished curiosity, as well as the first version of *Le Visage nuptial*. For *Chaînes* and *Le Visage nuptial*, the ondes and vocal parts both feature microtonal notation.

Beyond his invention, Maurice Martenot was well connected in the French musical scene, having in 1942 been co-founder with Pierre Schaeffer of the experimental 'Studio d'essai' at Radio France. And his impact on Boulez's musical development stretched beyond his role as

51 Jacques Tchamkerten, 'From *Fête des belles eaux* to *Saint François d'Assise*: the evolution of the writing for ondes Martenot in the music of Olivier Messiaen', in Christopher Dingle and Nigel Simeone (eds.), *Olivier Messiaen: Music, Art and Literature* (Aldershot: Ashgate, 2007), pp. 63–78, at pp. 63–4.

ondes tutor. He organised a musical evening in winter 1946 'at which Boulez himself gave the first performance of his First Piano Sonata';[52] the only information about this private concert appears in secondary sources, such as Joan Peyser's account which mentions that the conductor Roger Désormière and the composers Nicolas Nabokov (another Russian émigré) and Virgil Thomson were present.[53] (Yvette Grimaud gave the public premiere of the sonata later that year.)

Supporting himself in Paris, the young Boulez was a freelance ondiste and he made important connections through this side job. Dominique Jameux specifically notes that he 'was an ondiste at the Folies-Bergère from 1945'.[54] Pierre Larrieu, the musical director at the Folies-Bergère, was himself a prominent player of the ondes, which was then a popular source of sound effects that contemporary audiences would have considered cutting-edge. Larrieu released an LP of incidental music with himself as ondes soloist in the late 1950s to early 1960s.[55]

Most significantly for Boulez, he met Jean-Louis Barrault and Madeleine Renaud when their theatre company, then based at the Théâtre Marigny, required an ondes player. When Boulez joined the Renaud–Barrault company, it was originally as one of two musical directors, the other being Maurice Jarre. Not at that time known as a composer, Jarre had trained as a timpanist, and his work as percussionist complemented Boulez's role with the company as pianist and ondiste. Boulez soon became sole musical director of the Renaud–Barrault company, and Jarre acted as the musical director of the Théâtre National Populaire from 1951 to 1963. Boulez's work for the Renaud–Barrault company involved performing and directing a wide variety of work, first of all in 1946 incidental music by Honegger for Gide's translation of *Hamlet* for which he played ondes Martenot and Jarre was the percussionist.[56]

The premiere of Messiaen's *Trois petites liturgies de la Présence Divine* was a notorious musical event in the Paris calendar, and while Boulez

---

[52] See Dominique Jameux, *Boulez* (Paris: Fayard, 1984), p. 36: 'une soirée au cours de laquelle l'auteur lui-même crée sa *Première Sonate*'; this book, translated into English by Susan Bradshaw, was published by Faber in 1991.

[53] Joan Peyser, *Boulez: Composer, Conductor, Enigma* (London: Cassell, 1976), p. 53.

[54] Jameux, *Boulez*, p. 31: 'Boulez est *ondiste* au Folies-Bergère!'

[55] See https://www.youtube.com/watch?v=DJrnHXbtMWo [accessed June 2023].

[56] A short extract of this production was later recorded and is perhaps the only surviving example of Boulez playing the ondes Martenot; it can be accessed at https://soundcloud.com/daniel-plante-511223801/boulez-plays-the-ondes-martinot-1948-honegger-hamlet-excerpt [accessed June 2023].

and his classmates were not the object of the controversy, they were present. The first performance of Messiaen's piece was originally scheduled for June 1944, under the auspices of the Concerts de la Pléiade. This series of ten concerts with the aim of promoting contemporary French music began in February 1943 and was financed by the Nouvelle Revue Française, the publishers of the prestigious Pléiade literary series. As each concert was to feature two new works commissioned by the organisation, the series provided a rare opportunity for contemporary music to be heard during the war years.[57] The concerts were private, invitation-only events, and there is an interesting additional connection in that André Schaeffner, a close friend of Boulez from the late 1940s, organised them from 1943 to 1947.[58]

However, complications after the Liberation of Paris, including frequent power cuts, meant that the premiere of *Trois petites liturgies* was delayed until 21 April 1945, the first Pléiade concert since the Liberation. On this occasion, Yvonne Loriod was the piano soloist, Ginette Martenot played the ondes Martenot, Yvette Grimaud the celesta, and the orchestra and female chorus were conducted by Roger Désormière. Boulez had a small part to play in the premiere, as page turner for the vibraphone player (who may have been Félix Passeronne, a pioneering percussionist who introduced Messiaen to many tuned instruments including the vibraphone, marimba and xylorimba).[59]

The audience, according to Boulez, was 'very enthusiastic' but 'the scandal was in the press'.[60] Messiaen's premiere took place amid much contemporary debate about the value of his music, generally referred to in the press as 'le cas Messiaen' (the Messiaen case). Bernard Gavoty (who wrote for the newspaper *Le Figaro* under the pseudonym Clarendon) was one of his main detractors, being particularly exercised by Messiaen's written commentaries on his works. For his part, Claude Rostand's colourful account of *Trois petites liturgies* referred to 'this work of tinsel, false magnificence and pseudo-mysticism, this work with dirty nails and clammy hands, with bloated complexion and unhealthy flab, replete with noxious matter, looking about anxiously like an angel

[57] Dunbar and Aprahamian, 'The news from Paris', p. 15.
[58] Rosângela Pereira de Tugny (ed.), *Pierre Boulez, André Schaeffner: correspondance 1954–1970* (Paris: Fayard, 1998), p. 18. André Schaeffner had been prominent in Paris arts administration for a number of years; in 1929 he was 'secrétaire artistique de l'Orchestre symphonique de Paris'. See Myriam Chimènes (ed.), *Francis Poulenc: correspondance 1910–1963* (Paris: Fayard, 1994), p. 317.
[59] Boivin, *La classe de Messiaen*, p. 339.
[60] Roger Nichols, 'Interview – Pierre Boulez on Messiaen' (March 1986), published in *From Berlioz to Boulez* (London: Kahn & Averill, 2022), pp. 303–7, at p. 306.

wearing lipstick'.[61] While Messiaen was understandably hurt by this hostile reaction, 'For his students [...] the event was galvanizing: Nigg later described the *Trois petites liturgies* as "symbolizing the spiritual renewal of the country" after the terrible years of German occupation.'[62]

Messiaen explicitly termed the group of metal percussion instruments in *Trois petites liturgies* a 'gamelan', making a direct connection with the Balinese and Javanese musics he played to his private students. There are some notable differences between Messiaen's and Boulez's approaches to non-European musical sources. Messiaen was no ethnomusicologist: he might have incorporated Hindu (Sharngadeva) rhythms in significantly modified form in his works, though his source for the list of 127 rhythmic formulas was an encyclopaedia article. (There is a parallel here with the list of harmonic formulas he gave his Conservatoire harmony students.) Messiaen's use of Albert Lavignac's *Encyclopédie de la musique et dictionnaire du Conservatoire* as a source parallels Erik Satie's enthusiasm for discovering facts in the Larousse encyclopaedia which he later incorporated in his compositions.

What Boulez and Messiaen had in common was their emotional reaction to non-Western music; it is not at all true to say that they were attracted solely to exotic sonorities that could stimulate them in their own compositions. For instance, Messiaen saw Balinese gamelan and dancers at the Exposition Coloniale in 1931, and he describes his response to this performance in his posthumously published treatise:

> I saw and heard, for the first time, Anak Agung Gede Mandera, his Balinese gamelan orchestra, and the wonderful movements of the eyes, neck and hands. The sounding and visual rhythms impressed me so strongly that I have been marked, impregnated, transformed for my whole life. Here I'd like to acknowledge my sisters and brothers from Bali, who love rhythm just as I do.[63]

He was attracted by the visual spectacle and movement of the dancers at least as much as by the music; he also stresses the Debussy connection

---

[61] Cited in Hill and Simeone, *Messiaen*, p. 151.

[62] Sprout, 'The 1945 Stravinsky debates', pp. 114–15.

[63] Olivier Messiaen, *Traité de rythme, de couleur, et d'ornithologie (1949–2002)*, vol. 1 (Paris: Leduc, 2000), pp. 59–60; cited in Yves Balmer, Thomas Lacôte and Christopher Brent Murray. *Le Modèle et l'invention: Messiaen et la technique de l'emprunt* (Lyon: Symétrie, 2017), p. 385: 'j'ai vu et entendu, pour la première fois, Anak Agung Gede Mandera, son orchestra balinais, ou gamelang, et les merveilleuses danses des yeux, du cou, des mains, dont les rythmes sonores et visuels devaient m'impressionner de façon si durable que j'en suis resté marqué, imprégné, transformé pour toute ma vie. Je tiens à saluer ici mes sœurs et mes frères de Bali, qui aiment le rythme comme moi.'

when writing about his enthusiasm for gamelan. As far as his music is concerned, the multiple metallophones and gongs of *Trois petites liturgies* and *Turangalîla*, for instance, would never have been written if he had not encountered the metallic sonorities of the gamelan.

Messiaen was also inspired by sound recordings, specifically by recordings from the collection of the Musée de l'Homme which he borrowed and listened to in March 1944 at Guy Bernard-Delapierre's home.[64] While Boulez was also stimulated by recordings, his long acquaintance with Schaeffner and other ethnomusicologists including Simha Arom ultimately led to a deeper engagement with the context of the sounds he loved. He also acquired a collection of gongs and bells of all sorts, as photographs of his work room at his home in Baden-Baden demonstrate, and several of his published letters to Schaeffner deal with his attempts to buy specific instruments.[65]

Boulez's student compositions: *Trois Psalmodies, Notations*

Peter O'Hagan has detailed Boulez's compositional activity for 1944–5, when he was still studying counterpoint with Vaurabourg-Honegger and harmony at the Conservatoire with Messiaen. These earliest compositions predate his use of serial techniques. The principal fruits of this period were two piano works, each comprising three movements: *Prélude, Toccata et Scherzo* (winter 1944–5) and *Trois Psalmodies*, started in summer 1945. Neither is published, and the former was not performed in Boulez's lifetime, though since his death it has been championed by the Dutch pianist Ralph van Raat, who gave the public premiere at the Philharmonie in Paris in September 2018.[66] O'Hagan notes the influences of Messiaen, Jolivet and Honegger on the musical language of this work.

The same might be said of *Trois Psalmodies*, but this piece is more interesting in the context of this discussion because it also illustrates Boulez's developing literary and musical tastes. First, the title is striking. Moving away from the generic movement descriptors of the *Prélude, Toccata et Scherzo*, Boulez uses a title which immediately evokes a

---

[64] Balmer, Murray and Lacôte, *Le Modèle et l'invention*, p. 385; see also Hill and Simeone, *Messiaen*, p. 181.

[65] Photographs now housed in the Paul Sacher Stiftung, Boulez collection. See also Pereira de Tugny (ed.), *Pierre Boulez, André Schaeffner: correspondance*, pp. 35–6 for details about Boulez's attempts to acquire non-Western percussion instruments.

[66] Seth Colter Walls, 'A teenage Pierre Boulez, heard for the first time', *New York Times* (19 April 2019), https://www.nytimes.com/2019/04/19/arts/music/pierre-boulez-piano.html [accessed June 2023].

religious musical genre, specifically the singing or intonation of psalms. Boulez's upbringing was conventionally religious for a Frenchman of his background in that he was brought up nominally in the Catholic faith (he attended a Catholic primary school, Institut Victor Laprade),[67] and although as an adult he was not a church attender, he used titles with religious connotations throughout his life. It is possible that his use of the title 'Psalmodie' was prompted by Messiaen, specifically by the movement titles of his *Trois petites liturgies* ('Antienne', 'Séquence', 'Psalmodie'), which was composed just before Boulez's work, though there is an earlier piano piece of this title by Boulez whose date is uncertain.[68] O'Hagan contends that

> Messiaen's incorporation of the form of responsorial psalmody into this work suggested to Boulez the point of departure for his own pieces. The sectional form of the first two pieces particularly, with their juxtaposition of rhapsodic passages with passages in strict rhythm is reminiscent of the first of Messiaen's *Liturgies*, where the almost improvisatory style of the piano writing provides contrast with the chorale-like character of the vocal passages.[69]

O'Hagan also notes that the end of the manuscript of the first *Psalmodie* features the dedication 'En souvenir de Saint-Henri', referring to the saint whose feast day is 13 July, one day before the completion date indicated on this score.[70] (It is perhaps significant, given the religious connotations of the title of his work, that Boulez chose not to cite the obvious national celebration associated with 14 July, the date of completion.) If the psalmody reference does indeed refer to a structuring device, it is intriguing that Boulez returned to similar titles as late as his Third Piano Sonata, a preliminary version of which was performed by the composer in 1958: the first movement of this is titled 'Antiphonie', and the unpublished and incomplete fifth and final movement also shares its title with a movement of *Trois petites liturgies*: 'Séquence'.

But there are also unequivocally secular ideas behind *Trois Psalmodies*. The manuscripts of the first piece feature a quotation from André Gide's semi-autobiographical *Les Nourritures terrestres* (1895), a loosely linked narrative in both poetry and prose that expresses Gide's rejection of his conservative religious upbringing and his sensual awakening in North

[67] Christian Merlin, *Pierre Boulez* (Paris: Fayard, 2019), p. 21.
[68] The Paul Sacher Stiftung catalogues this as 'Psalmodie 0' and has dated it 1943 (Boulez collection). Its opening is cited as Ex. 13 in Gerald Bennett, 'The early works', in Glock (ed.), *Pierre Boulez*, pp. 41–84, at p. 52. Bennett believes 1944–5 is a plausible date for this piece.
[69] O'Hagan, *Boulez and the Piano*, p. 24.
[70] O'Hagan, *Boulez and the Piano*, p. 23.

Africa. Boulez quotes only five lines of a fourteen-line poem: the first and last, and three central lines.[71]

> Je sais la source où j'irai rafraîchir mes paupières [...]
> Source froide où toute la nuit va descendre.
> Eau de glace où le matin transparaîtra
> Grelottant de blancheur. Source de pureté. [...]
> Quand j'y viendrai laver mes paupières brûlées.

> [I know the source where I will refresh my eyelids [...]
> Cold source where night will fall.
> Icy water from whence morning will emerge
> Shivering with whiteness. Source of purity. [...]
> When I will come there to wash my burning eyelids.]

The lines omitted by Boulez focus on different aspects of nature (woods, leaves) and on night falling. He also leaves out a striking phrase which is more explicit about human feelings as evening draws in: 'déjà la caresse de l'air / Nous invitera plus au sommeil qu'à l'amour' (already the breeze's caress / Will invite us more to rest than to love). Gide's poem, written during a convalescent trip to Blida in Algeria in 1893, was composed during a period of self-discovery. In *Les Nourritures terrestres*, the poem is followed by a 'Lettre à Nathanaël' which continues the theme of sensual awakening in nature and ends 'I believe the path I follow is my path and that I follow it as I should. A vast confidence has become habitual to me which would be called faith, had I taken any vows.'[72] Nathanaël is a young boy who is the object of the author's interest; though Gide would marry his cousin Madeleine in 1895, this was to be a celibate marriage and his principal orientation was towards boys.

Gide was a major cultural figure in France during Boulez's formative years – he was awarded the Nobel Prize for Literature in 1947 – and, given Boulez's use of an epigraph from *Les Nourritures terrestres*, it might be assumed that the author was important to the composer. Also, it cannot have escaped Boulez's attention that his classmate Serge Nigg's first composition was a setting of Gide's *Perséphone* which drew on the same source as Stravinsky's large-scale work of 1934.[73] But Boulez soon distanced himself from Gide and crossed out the epigraph in red pencil.

---

[71] On sketch material for the first *Psalmodie*, housed in the Paul Sacher Stiftung, Basel (Boulez collection, 577-0563).
[72] Original French: 'Je crois que la route que je suis est *ma* route, et que je la suis comme il faut. Je garde l'habitude d'une vaste confiance qu'on appellerait de la foi, si elle était plus assermentée.'
[73] Dunbar and Aprahamian, 'The news from Paris', p. 15.

When asked directly by O'Hagan in 2013 whether Gide had influenced him, Boulez responded:

> No, Gide was no influence on me. I knew his books, and this kind of literature was rather 'flappy' in 1947. No, I saw him as a translator: he was very pompous – he was the great old man, and had the reputation of being very frank about sexual affairs: there was something very precious about him which didn't attract me at all.[74]

(The first Renaud–Barrault theatre project with which Boulez was involved was a production of *Hamlet* in a translation by Gide.) This is not the only example of Boulez rewriting history from a later vantage point to reflect the evolution of his tastes, and perhaps also the composer is alluding to the widespread condemnation of Gide's sexual preferences.

Why might the Gide quotation have appealed to Boulez? The lines he chose are emotionally intense, focusing on opposites: heat/ice, fire/water, night/morning, burning/shivering. While Gide was no surrealist, his reference to 'burning eyelids' irresistibly evokes the gaze, or indeed the closed eye, that recurs many times in surrealist art and literature; witness Man Ray's photography, Dalí's closed eye in *The Great Masturbator* and many other paintings and films, Magritte's staring *False Mirror*. More obviously where Boulez is concerned, the juxtaposition of religious references and a quotation from Gide that focuses on the sensual world (and, as Boulez would have been aware, marks the author's rejection of his religious upbringing) must have been significant to a young man of 19 or 20 in the process of self-discovery. Years later, Boulez's conversation with O'Hagan shows that he grew to find Gide's 'pompous' and 'precious' attitude, and his sexual frankness, distasteful, but these remarks were made with the benefit of hindsight.

As for the musical content of *Trois Psalmodies*, this unsurprisingly reflects the young Boulez's extensive musical explorations of the period. Some of these influences would prove more durable than others. Sketches for the opening of the first *Psalmodie* place the work in a Debussy-style impressionist universe, with sustained chords overlaid by a melody marked 'comme une improvisation' which might be considered evocative of flute music heard at Blida. (The same town inspired Jolivet's *Cinq incantations* for solo flute, composed in 1936.) Even at this stage, Boulez's musical language goes considerably beyond Debussy, avoiding octaves and preferring the more astringent seventh and ninth, though unsurprisingly the young composer lacks Debussy's subtle variation and sense of timing. Also, following Messiaen's practice, the *Psalmodies* have no time signature.

---

[74] O'Hagan, *Boulez and the Piano*, p. 328.

The second *Psalmodie* opens with an F sharp in the treble register which is repeated in irregular rhythm and underpinned by chords. This repetition creates an incantatory effect, and the chords have a purely sensual value as sonority, being harmonically non-functional; one is reminded of Debussy as a student telling his teacher Ernest Guiraud 'Pleasure is the law'. O'Hagan notes that the fair copy of the second *Psalmodie* 'contains the additional subscription below the opening bars, *comme une gamelang* [sic] [...] at this stage [Boulez] is likely to have been equally influenced by such gamelan-influenced exemplars as the movement "La Princesse de Bali" from Jolivet's *Mana*'.[75]

While Jolivet is an obvious ancestor of this piece, the third *Psalmodie* features both ostinato drum-like figures reminiscent of Jolivet's incantatory style, and explicit references to both Honegger and Hindemith: the head of the manuscript score features the annotation 'Hindemith – étude p[our]/piano' and 'phrase mélodique longue accompagnée – Honegger'. Perhaps the Hindemith reference is to his recently published *Ludus tonalis*, and O'Hagan points out that the Honegger 'long accompanied melodic phrase' cites the 'Lamento' from his *Danse des morts* (1938)[76] – the orchestral work that so impressed the young Boulez when he heard it in Lyon in the early 1940s. The Honegger fragment is developed and accompanied by low bass clusters of the type that appear in 'La Princesse de Bali'. This is the first appearance of what would become a common trope in Boulez's early work. Some of the textures of the third *Psalmodie* strongly resemble the *Notations*, though a pianistic idea that is the sole focus of an individual *Notation* is in the third *Psalmodie* a fragment that is juxtaposed with other distinctive ideas.

Boulez's *Trois Psalmodies* was the first work of his to be performed in public, together with the twelve *Notations* which were on the same programme. Yvette Grimaud, dedicatee of the *Psalmodies*, was the soloist for the world premiere on 12 February 1946 at the concert society Le Triptyque; four years later, she would give the first public performance of Boulez's Second Piano Sonata for the same organisation. The aim of Le Triptyque, according to its founder Pierre d'Arquennes, was 'to promote French music played by young performers'; founded in 1934 under the auspices of Paul Dukas, Ravel and Albert Roussel, it soon branched out to include music by non-French composers.[77]

---

75   O'Hagan, *Boulez and the Piano*, p. 25.

76   O'Hagan, *Boulez and the Piano*, p. 26.

77   See Sarah Barbedette, *Poétique du concert* (Paris: Fayard, 2014), p. 113: 'promouvoir la musique française par des interprètes jeunes'. See also http://le.triptyque.free.fr/ [accessed June 2023].

Almost two months after this concert, one of very few contemporary reviews of early Boulez performances was published in *Les Étoiles* on 9 April 1946. It is signed by 'Serge Niff', which it must be assumed is an ill-disguised pseudonym of Boulez and Grimaud's friend and classmate Serge Nigg, who was already a published author; certainly, it is impossible that the critique was written by someone without inside knowledge of Boulez's musical trajectory. This author writes of *Trois Psalmodies*:

> If the overall form of the work is slightly imperfect in the balance of its sections, some of which seemed a bit long, it shows genuine qualities in its rhythmic invention and harmonic combinations. Although it is not a dodecaphonic work, it makes us aware of the ever-growing impact of the 'serial system' on the young school of composers.[78]

Bearing in mind that modern discussion of Boulez's music is dominated by technical matters, specifically about serialism, it is extraordinary that this very early review already places Boulez within this frame, even though serial technique is not employed in the work under discussion. By early 1946, Boulez, Niff/Nigg and their comrades had already made contact with Leibowitz, and this review reflects their contemporary musical exploration rather than the Boulez who composed *Trois Psalmodies*. Boulez himself spoke of *Trois Psalmodies* many years later in these terms:

> I knew very little of Schoenberg's music at that time, precisely two pieces, both from his atonal but not serial period: *Pierrot lunaire* [1912] and the Three Piano Pieces, op. 11 [1909–10]. When I composed the *Trois Psalmodies*, I knew nothing about serialism, not even that it existed, but I felt strongly the necessity of an atonal musical language.[79]

Writing about his Three Piano Pieces, Schoenberg himself said to Ferruccio Busoni that he strove 'for: complete liberation from all forms, from all symbols of cohesion and logic. Thus: away with "motivic

---

[78] Serge Niff, 'La Musique', *Les Étoiles* (9 April 1946), p. 5: 'Si cette œuvre recèle quelques imperfections dans la forme générale, dans le balancement des périodes dont certains nous ont paru un peu longues, elle révèle de sérieuses qualités dans l'invention rythmique et dans les combinaisons harmoniques. Quoique n'étant pas dodécaphonique, elle nous fait sentir l'emprise de plus en plus grandissantes qu'exerce sur la jeune école le "système sériel".'

[79] Goléa, *Rencontres avec Pierre Boulez*, p. 20: 'De Schoenberg, à 1'époque je connaissais très peu de choses, exactement deux œuvres, toutes deux de la période atonale, mais non encore sérielle: *Pierrot Lunaire* et les *Trois Pièces* Opus 11. Lorsque je composai les *Trois Psalmodies*, j'ignorais jusqu'à l'existence de la musique sérielle, mais j'avais le sentiment très net de la nécessité de l'atonalité.' Boulez also knew Schoenberg's *Herzgewächse* well by late 1945, because he participated in a performance on 5 December that year directed by Leibowitz.

working out." Away with harmony as cement or building bricks. Harmony is *expression* and nothing else. Then: Away with pathos!'[80] It was this expressionist Schoenberg that Boulez knew at the time of composing *Trois Psalmodies*.

In summer 1945, Boulez both completed a set of twelve *Notations* and composed the first two of three movements of a quartet for ondes Martenot. Peter O'Hagan and Susanne Gärtner both note the strong resemblance between the ondes quartet and the second *Psalmodie*; O'Hagan describes it as a 'transitional work' particularly because its second and third movements were soon recast as a sonata for two pianos.[81] But it is also a work where Boulez seems to be working out his dual passions for the new instrument and non-Western musics. The obsessive, incantatory first movement contrasts the 'clavier' (keyboard) and 'percussion' performing techniques of the instrument, the lower voice being given a low repeated C that is almost entirely in rhythmic unison with the more arabesque-like upper voice. The final movement of the quartet was completed in March 1946, predating his First Piano Sonata.

Boulez's *Notations*, twelve pieces for piano each with twelve (unmeasured) bars, were premiered by Yvette Grimaud on 12 February 1946 on the same programme as the *Trois Psalmodies*, though the work was not published until 1985. The fetish focus on the number twelve is, of course, no accident in the context of Boulez's discovery of the dodecaphonic language. All twelve pieces are based on a twelve-note row (in its primary form: A flat, B flat, E flat, D, A, E, C, F, C sharp, G, F sharp, B natural), and Boulez's dedication of his work to Nigg further underscores the location of these piano pieces in the nascent serial school of Paris.

Boulez orchestrated eleven of the *Notations* in December 1945–January 1946, omitting the sixth piece because of its pianistic texture of extremely rapid staccato semiquavers,[82] but this exercise was unpublished and is not related to the later larger-scale orchestral reworking of some of the pieces. This manuscript is still titled 'Douze Notations' as Boulez intended the sixth, in its original piano scoring, to be part of the performed sequence, following no. 11.[83] While Boulez does not use time

[80] Letter of c. 18 August 1909, cited in Mark Berry, *Schoenberg* (London: Reaktion, 2018), p. 64. Emphasis in original.

[81] O'Hagan, *Boulez and the Piano*, pp. 34–5.

[82] Bleek, 'Pierre Boulez: *Douze Notations*'. June 2023 The manuscript is now housed in the Paul Sacher Stiftung, Boulez collection.

[83] Manuscript housed in the Paul Sacher Stiftung, Boulez collection, starting at 577-0601. The order of the pieces in this orchestrated version is: 10, 1, 2, 4, 8, 9, 5, 7, 3, 11, 6 [for solo piano], 12.

signatures, he does indicate how the pieces should be conducted, using shapes in each bar to represent two beats (down–up) or three beats (a triangle). The larger-scale orchestral expansion of *Notations* 1–4 was completed in 1980, *Notation* 7 was published in 1997, and Boulez also worked on orchestrations of the fifth, sixth and eighth pieces.

There is a good deal more to the *Notations* than their dodecaphonic aspects. Boulez's musical language shows that, even at this early stage, serialism coexisted with other influences, especially with the incantatory world of Jolivet's music of the 1930s. Jolivet, who had first heard Schoenberg's music in Paris in 1927, noted about the musical language of his piano suite *Mana*: 'I was led to abandon both the strict Schoenbergian system and Varèse's theories in favour of a return to the actual sources of music. In a word, to magic.'[84] Boulez, however, found a way of synthesising, if not the 'strict Schoenbergian system' then certainly his expressionist tendencies, with magic, and specifically with Jolivet's *Mana*. This connection is most evident if we examine the opening of 'La Princesse de Bali', the third piece of *Mana*, with its pulsating low bass clusters which have a value purely as rhythm, not precise pitch. This sonority is a world away from traditional classical musical language, instead making a connection with musics driven by a percussive beat whose purpose is ritualistic.

These percussive bass clusters we hear in *Mana* are appropriated by Messiaen in two of his *Quatre études de rythme* (1949–50), the two works entitled *Île de feu*, which are both dedicated 'à la Papouasie' (to Papua New Guinea). However, exactly the same clusters were used extensively by Boulez in his piano music before Messiaen composed his studies. A cluster of the type in 'La Princesse de Bali' appears in three of Boulez's *Notations* (numbers 2, 9 and 12; see Exx. 2.2a–c for the Jolivet and two Boulez examples), and sketch evidence shows that Boulez intended an unpitched sonority, as these notes are given a cross head used for untuned percussion notation.[85] This cluster stands apart from the rest of the musical material of the *Notations* as it has no connection with the underlying twelve-note row. It is as if the cluster is a 'found object' (a surrealist *objet trouvé*) employed by Boulez in different contexts: the second *Notation* is very loud and largely consists of extensive glissandi, while the ninth is a very slow and quiet piece which juxtaposes

---

[84] Cited in Lucie Kayas, *André Jolivet* (Paris: Fayard, 2005), p. 132: 'j'ai été amené à abandonner aussi bien le strict système de Schoenberg que les théories de Varèse au profit d'un retour aux sources mêmes de la musique. En un mot, à la magie.'

[85] Paul Sacher Stiftung, Boulez collection, 577-0596. For Yvette Grimaud's use of the same gesture in *Chant funèbre* (1943), see p. 70.

Ex. 2.2a André Jolivet, 'La Princesse de Bali' (*Mana*, 3): opening bars

Ex. 2.2b Boulez, *Notations*, 9: bars 5–8

Ex. 2.2c Boulez, *Notations*, 12: final bars

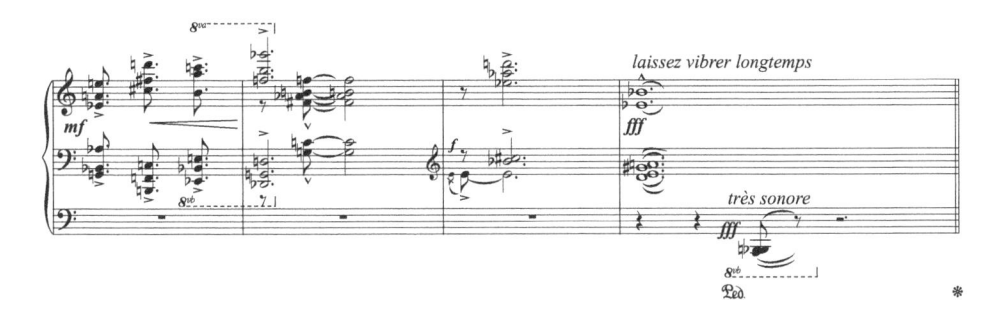

contrasting musical material. In *Notation* 9, bars 5, 8, 10 and 12 each feature three percussive unpedalled bass clusters, like a low thud. The cluster reappears in the trenchant chord-based final *Notation*, whose tempo marking is 'Lent. Puissant et âpre' (Slow. Powerful and bitter); a very loud cluster, marked 'fff très sonore', concludes both the first phrase at bar 8 and the piece as a whole. The ringing bass cluster, left to vibrate, is therefore the final statement of the set of *Notations*.

The orchestrations of the second, fifth, seventh and ninth *Notations* feature significant roles for the ondes Martenot. The second piece features huge glissandi which work perfectly on the instrument (the end of the glissando is underlined by a cluster chord played on the piano); in the fifth, the instrument points up the unearthly extreme high register of the melody, and in the seventh and ninth, the top melodic line is given to the ondes. The chordal accompaniment in the ninth *Notation* is given to the harp and piano, and the reiterated clusters are played by a solo bass drum, giving them the untuned percussive character that was impossible in the piano original. This identification of the thudding cluster with untuned percussion is also seen in the final bar of the orchestrated twelfth *Notation*, where the extremely loud and resonant concluding gesture is allocated to the tam-tam, and the opening of the second *Notation* again replaces the piano cluster with a bass drum.

Other *Notations* show the impact of non-Western musics on Boulez at this very early stage of his compositional career. Boulez himself acknowledged the influence of Asian musics on the musical language of the seventh *Notation*, while the manuscript in the Paul Sacher Stiftung shows that the eighth was originally titled 'Afrique', a title Boulez deleted before the work was published. The right-hand part of the eighth *Notation* focuses on only two pitches, E flat and B flat, marked 'Donner à cette figure tout son caractère de percussion' (Give this gesture a percussive character), iterated rapidly above chordal interjections in the left hand. The acciaccaturas before each chord should be played, according to Boulez's note on the manuscript, 'on the beat and strongly accented.'[86] Luisa Bassetto specifies that the title 'Afrique' 'relates to the rhythmic ostinato over a pedal of a fourth which is intended to evoke the African sanza.'[87] A sanza is a hand-held lamellophone with beads, metal discs or bottle tops attached to the body of the instrument which create buzzing sounds when the metal bars are pinged (it is also known as a kalimba or mbira), and the acciaccaturas are the pianistic equivalent of this ping.

The seventh *Notation* proved to be an exceptionally fertile source for Boulez. Its heading, 'Hiératique', is curious, and translating it into English as 'Hieratic' does not dispel the mystery. Unlike those of the other pieces in the collection, its heading is not, strictly speaking, a tempo marking; Boulez would not have liked the comparison, but this indication would not be out of place in Satie's Rosicrucian piano pieces of the late 1880s and early 1890s. While the piece sounds nothing like Satie, its block construction, based on three different types of musical material which are alternated, is not unlike Satie's much longer *Le Fils des étoiles* (1892). Boulez's seventh *Notation* is a solemn processional – surely what was meant by 'Hiératique' – and as in the *Trois Psalmodies*, Boulez uses a title with religious connotations. When Claude Helffer questioned him about the unusual heading, Boulez defined the term as something '... connected with sacred things belonging to priests ...'[88]

In a video interview filmed when he was 87, Boulez identifies a specific starting point for the seventh *Notation*:

> This piece recalls Asian music. I was listening to a lot of non-European music at the time. Once I heard a dirge sung to save the soul of a man who had drowned. [...] I'd say the piece doesn't undergo true development,

[86] Paul Sacher Stiftung, Boulez collection, 577-0591: 'La petite note sur le temps et très accentuée.'

[87] Luisa Bassetto, 'Études d'ethnomusicologie. Projets et découvertes', in Sarah Barbedette (ed.), *Pierre Boulez* [exhibition catalogue] (Paris: Actes Sud, 2015) pp. 77–9, at p. 79: 'renvoyait à l'ostinato rythmique sur une pédale de quarte destiné à évoquer la *sanza* africaine.'

[88] Cited in Peter O'Hagan, *Pierre Boulez: sur Incises* (Geneva: Contrechamps, 2021), p. 227: '... qui concerne les choses sacrées qui appartiennent aux prêtres ...' (punctuation as in original).

only variation – those breathing motifs now with more notes, now with fewer, but always similar in outline.[89]

Here, Boulez does not explicitly state how the 'Asian music' or 'dirge' elements were transferred to his piece, but his reference to the piece lacking development should be understood to mean that he is locating the structure outside the Western classical music tradition.

Boulez's interest in non-Western musics also became a means of escaping from the rigidity of serial processes. In what must be interpreted as a critique of Leibowitz, Boulez said:

> This interest was also a reaction against what represented European twelve-tone music in this period. Of course I was interested in questions about musical language, but the sort of dodecaphonic tradition which risked to become academicism irked me deeply. And I must say that non-European musics represented, compared to that, a breath of fresh air.[90]

In his preface to the published correspondence between himself and André Schaeffner, Boulez also specifically refers to non-Western music as an opening to 'a different type of rhythm, form or sonority'.[91]

The seven-note cell at the core of the seventh *Notation* – which is not heard in totality until the final bars of the work – also suggests that there is more than one fetish number at the heart of *Notations*, and in fact there was also more than one *objet trouvé*. Julian Anderson notes strong links between Jolivet and this piece: 'Compare, for example, the opening bar of *Mana* with the obsessive recurring gesture featured throughout Boulez's *Notations* No. 7: both melodic and harmonic content, as well as rhythmic profile are clearly very similar.'[92] The tempo of the two pieces might be very different, but there are striking parallels in the musical language of both (Exx. 2.3a and b).

---

[89] http://www.explorethescore.org/pierre-boulez-douze-notations-boulez-video-interview.html [accessed June 2023]; English subtitles by Tobias Bleek.

[90] Cited in Bassetto, 'Ritratto del compositore come apprendista etnologo', p. 62: 'Cet intérêt était aussi une réaction contre ce que représentait le dodécaphon-isme européen à l'époque. J'étais bien sûr intéressé par les questions de langage, mais l'espèce de tradition dodécaphonique qui risquait de devenir académique m'agaçait profondément. Et je dois dire que les musiques extra-européennes représentaient, face à cela, un grand bol d'air frais.'

[91] Pierre Boulez, 'Avant-propos' to Pereira de Tugny (ed.), *Pierre Boulez, André Schaeffner: correspondance*, pp. 9–10: 'l'ouverture bienvenue sur des univers non européens, tant comme témoins d'une civilisation, d'une fonction, que de la pensée rythmique, formelle ou sonore'.

[92] Julian Anderson, 'Jolivet and the *style incantatoire*', in Caroline Rae (ed.), *André Jolivet: Music, Art and Literature* (Abingdon: Routledge, 2019), pp. 15–40, at p. 32.

Ex. 2.3a André Jolivet, 'Beaujolais' (*Mana*, 1): opening bars

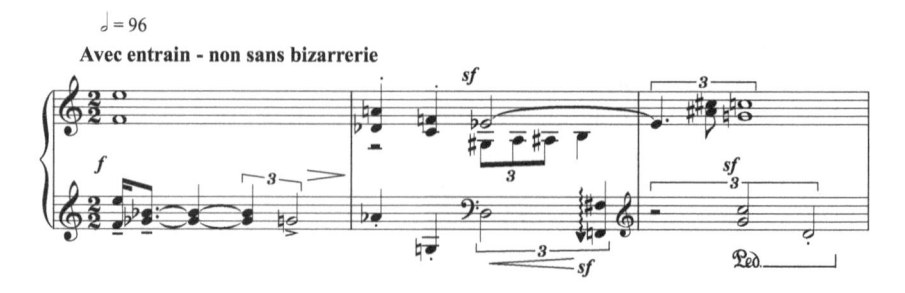

Ex. 2.3b Boulez, *Notations*, 7: opening bars

The seventh *Notation* proved an extraordinarily fertile source for Boulez: based on *objets trouvés* from Jolivet and an Asian traditional source he did not specifically name, in later years it became in its own right an *objet trouvé* that he used in many works.

Conclusion

Boulez's casual references to the musics of very different cultures, generically termed 'Asian' or 'African', might lead him to be accused of appropriation and a fundamentally colonial mentality, whatever his ethnomusicological interests. One of his reasons for dipping into other musics was typically provocative, as he stated that for him as a creative artist, a shallow acquaintance of another culture is more stimulating than a profound knowledge. He claimed that

> the more the windows on other [cultures] were small, the more my imagination was powerful. Too much knowledge of things inspires us to respect it and forbids spontaneous usage. In contrast, a sporadic knowledge shakes up the imagination: beginning with a small kernel, the grain of sand in the oyster becoming a pearl, that your idea is given

flesh, without being preoccupied by a deeper preliminary study of civilisations.[93]

These non-Western sonorities are transformed in the prism of Boulez's own thought and combined with diverse other influences.

There are also other ways of exploring Boulez's encounter with non-Western musics, bearing in mind that he appreciated the seriousness of purpose of cultures that treat music as part of everyday spiritual life; he always had a horror of music being considered solely as entertainment. The comparative literature scholar Xiaofan Amy Li's penetrating analysis of two authors who interested Boulez greatly, Artaud and Michaux, allows us to view Boulez under a different angle. Li references Debussy's friend Victor Segalen, who 'revolutionised the "exotic" into an ethical instead of colonial (i.e. unethical) position' in his *Essai sur l'exotisme* (1911). She continues: 'one can love the difference of the Other without appropriating it, and understand difference aesthetically and philosophically, leaving behind the political struggle between cultures for power domination. [...] I believe that Artaud and Michaux are "exoticists" in this Segalenian sense rather than naïve Orientalists.'[94] Boulez's stress on the ethical function of music in the cultures he studied allows us to place him alongside these authors.

Boulez was genuinely interested in the social and cultural dimension of non-Western musics. I remember him being interviewed by Edwin Roxburgh at the Royal College of Music on 27 March 2000, when he displayed real passion about a gamelan ensemble for people local to the newly opened Cité de la Musique in the nineteenth arrondissement of Paris. His animation when talking about how collective musical performance can bring people together contrasted strongly with his urbane, professional responses to questions about his own musical career. Of course, his approach to non-Western instruments was that of a Western composer interested in timbre, but he also recognised and appreciated their cultural context and significance. He told Martine Cadieu:

> But if I have been influenced by knowledge and study of these [non-Western] civilisations, it's not only on a spiritual level. More than

---

[93] Pierre Boulez, 'Existe-t-il un conflit entre la pensée européenne et non-européenne?', in Hans Oesch, Wulf Arlf and Max Haas (eds.), *Europäische Musik zwischen Nationsmus and Exotik* (Winterthur: Amadeus, 1984), pp. 131–45, at p. 139, cited in David Walters, 'The aesthetics of Pierre Boulez', PhD thesis, Durham University, 2003 (available at Durham E-Theses Online: http://etheses.dur.ac.uk/3093/), p. 248 in his translation.

[94] Xiaofan Amy Li, *Comparative Encounters between Artaud, Michaux and the Zhuangzi. Rationality, Cosmology and Ethics* (London: MHRA/Legenda, 2015), pp. 10–11.

an aesthetic based on pleasure, I found an ethical approach to existence. The influence is in my mind, not in my work. Here are the three key points of this influence: temporal structure (the conception of time is different); the concept of the anonymous author; the concept of a work which is not admired as a masterpiece but as part of spiritual life.[95]

Boulez thus identified with the seriousness of purpose of music created for spiritual reasons. He also suggests in this statement a distaste for the Western cult of the author, which must be connected to his consistent refusal to give people outside his close personal circle access to his private life.

In his formative years, spent in Paris during and after World War II, Boulez encountered people and ideas who would strongly mark his music and ideas. His teachers were certainly important to him for the musical techniques and ideas they imparted, but above and beyond this, his exchange of ideas with fellow students was fundamental to his development. With other adventurous young musicians such as Yvette Grimaud, Yvonne Loriod and Serge Nigg, Boulez explored and performed music which was at the cutting edge; music which moved beyond the chromatic scale, beyond the European mainstream and beyond standard acoustic instrumentation. These young people were fortunate to be supported by well-connected patrons, such as Guy Bernard-Delapierre, who provided sympathetic venues and audiences for their explorations, and the role played by private supporters continued to be vital for Boulez beyond his formative years as he moved towards the foundation of his Domaine Musical concert series in the 1950s. While Boulez's music appeared rarely on public concert programmes in Paris in the second half of the 1940s, his supporters ensured that his music was at least heard by influencers including the critics Pierre Souvtchinsky and Boris de Schloezer, representatives of the international avant-garde including John Cage and Virgil Thomson, and future patrons including Suzanne Tézenas. And professional artistic contacts made by Boulez in this period, most notably Jean-Louis Barrault and Madeleine Renaud,

---

[95] Martine Cadieu, *A l'écoute des compositeurs* (Paris: Minerve, 1992), pp. 150–4, at p. 151 (interview originally published as 'Musique traditionnelle, un paradis perdu?' in *Le monde de la musique Unesco*, vol. 9 no. 2, 1967): 'Mais si la connaissance, l'étude de ces civilisations m'a influencée, ce n'est que sur le plan spirituel. J'ai trouvé davantage une éthique de l'existence qu'une esthétique de la jouissance. L'influence est dans mon esprit, non dans mes œuvres. En voici les trois points principaux: – la structure temporelle: la conception du temps est différente. – le concept d'anonymat – le concept de l'œuvre non admirée comme chef d'œuvre mais comme élément de vie spirituelle.'

ensured that he could both make a living from music and broaden his artistic horizons.

For Boulez, the music of Messiaen and Jolivet provided him with models that engaged with intellectual and musical currents that would prove crucial to the development of his own musical language. One of the most important of these aspects was his discovery of non-Western musics, a discovery that naturally reflected the environment in which he lived and worked. Above all, it is remarkable that the different spheres of Boulez's interests overlapped to such a strong degree. We see André Schaeffner organising the Pléiade concert series that was the location for many important Messiaen premieres including *Trois petites liturgies*; Mady Sauvageot, a curator at the Musée Guimet, singing in the first partial performance of Boulez's *Le Visage nuptial*; André Souris programming Boulez's Sonatine and providing the composer with a direct link with the Belgian surrealist movement. The shared interests of Boulez and many of his student contemporaries – the ondes Martenot, non-Western music, quartertones – appear diverse on the surface, but they were all part of the small world that was the avant-garde musical scene of mid-1940s Paris.

Above all, the speed of Boulez's development in his formative years was astonishing. As he told Roger Nichols, 'in late 1945, I reacted very quickly. I think that teaching is a very quick process. That's a kind of shock in your life, and if you don't have this shock, years of studying will not really make up for it.'[96]

---

[96] Undated conversation between Boulez and Nichols in English cited in Nichols, *From Berlioz to Boulez*, p. 324.

3

SERIALISM AND SURREALISM: BOULEZ'S INSTRUMENTAL MUSIC 1946–8

Boulez, Leibowitz and aesthetic protests

The final key influence on the young Boulez was the Second Viennese School. Schoenberg, Berg and Webern were very little known in France in the mid-1940s, and René Leibowitz (1913–72) can be credited with introducing Boulez to these composers, whatever their subsequent disagreements. Most publications on Boulez highlight the importance of Webern's serial language to the young composer, but Schoenberg was arguably a stronger influence on his earliest works. Michel Leiris's article on Schoenberg, first published in a programme book for one of Leibowitz's concerts, ends with words that could equally apply to Boulez:

> Going far beyond the solutions proposed by his contemporaries, who were infatuated with Reason, Humour or Brutality, Arnold Schoenberg genially takes part in this process, because – abandoning himself entirely to this 'inner constraint' whose slave he declares himself to have been – he is not afraid to place music on a point that is steeper and more vulnerable than any other: vertigo's very crest, bristling with saw teeth.[1]

---

[1] Michel Leiris, 'Quant à Arnold Schoenberg', in *Brisées* (Paris: Mercure de France, 1966), pp. 20–4, at p. 24: 'Dépassant de beaucoup les solutions proposées par ses semblables qu'envoûtait la Raison, l'Humour ou la Brutalité, Arnold Schoenberg participe génialement à ce procès, parce que – s'abandonnant tout entier à cette 'contrainte intérieure' dont il déclare lui-même avoir été l'esclave – il n'a pas craint de situer la musique sur un point plus que tout autre abrupt et menacé: la crête même du vertige, hérissé de dents de scie.' I have modified Lydia Davis's English translation published as *Brisées: Broken Branches* (San Francisco: North Point Press, 1989), pp. 13–17, at p. 17.

It was the hyper-emotional, expressionist Schoenberg that Boulez knew before February 1945, when he attended a concert at the home of Claude Halphen, a young supporter of contemporary music. Boulez told Antoine Goléa that this was

> my first encounter with serial music. Songs by Max Deutsch and a piece by André Casanova, a young student of Leibowitz, were performed, and Leibowitz directed Schoenberg's Wind Quintet. It was like an illumination for me. I had a passionate desire to get to know this music, most of all, in the first instance, to learn how it was constructed.[2]

This prompted Boulez to attend Leibowitz's private classes from spring 1945 to autumn 1946, again as part of a group of fellow private students of Messiaen including Nigg, Grimaud and Loriod. Nigg told Jean Boivin that he instigated the 'defection' of Messiaen's students to study with Leibowitz, whom he had met through his first French pupil, André Casanova (1919–2009).[3]

February 1945 also witnessed one of the most notorious events involving the group of students. Stravinsky's *Danses concertantes* (1941–2) was given a Paris premiere on 27 February 1945 by the Société Privée de Musique de Chambre, and a small group of Messiaen's students, led by Boulez, protested against what they perceived as the old-fashioned neoclassical style of this work, shouting and blowing police whistles. Nigg's Concertino for piano, percussion and wind instruments (1944) was premiered on the same programme, and he took the leading role in bringing the students' opinions to public attention. On 14 April 1945, Nigg published an article 'La Querelle Strawinsky [sic]' in *Combat*, a newspaper that described itself as an 'organe du Mouvement de libération française' (organ of the French liberation movement). Responding to criticism of the students' attitude, Nigg aimed to set the record straight:

> For these 'young idiots' whom critics have been attacking on all sides, every artistic enterprise ought to be, if not an undisputed success, at least the sign of a deeply felt anxiety. As far as I know, this is simply their

[2] Antoine Goléa, *Rencontres avec Pierre Boulez* (Paris: Julliard, 1958), p. 27: 'C'est dans son salon que se place ma première rencontre avec la musique sérielle. On y donnait des mélodies de Max Deutsch, une œuvre d'André Casanova, un jeune élève de Leibowitz et, sous la direction de celui-ci, le Quintette pour instruments à vent de Schönberg. Ce fut, pour moi, comme une illumination. J'eus le désir passionné de me familiariser avec cette musique et surtout, pour commencer, d'apprendre comment c'était fait.'

[3] Leslie A. Sprout, 'The 1945 Stravinsky debates: Nigg, Messiaen, and the early Cold War in France', *Journal of Musicology*, vol. 26 no. 1 (2009): pp. 85–131, at p. 116 footnote 74.

formulation of the fundamental laws of the ethics of artistic creation. But this is taken the wrong way, because they are then immediately treated as 'conformists of non-conformism', of 'neo-academicism', or of being 'adepts of modernity at all cost'.[4]

The students, in Nigg's argument, considered that neoclassicism was decadent and mediocre, an inadequate response to contemporary concerns. Even if Messiaen did not participate in the protest, he shared their distaste for neoclassical composers, writing in October 1945 that these composers were 'placing around their works a modern sauce that fools the ears of the public, who imagine they have heard "modern" music'.[5] Nigg's article continues:

> People accuse a certain type of music (whether atonal or not) of appearing to be too heavily reliant on research, of being 'cerebral' and therefore fundamentally excluding spontaneity. I don't see how [Beethoven's] *Grosse Fuge*, [Bach's] *Art of Fugue*, [Bartók's] *Music for Strings, Percussion and Celesta* or [Schoenberg's] *Erwartung* can be anti-musical and devoid of emotion.[6]

This critique seems highly prescient regarding the future reception of Boulez's music – the opinion that music which is highly constructed cannot also be emotionally impactful is a critical commonplace that this book aims to dispel – but it is important to note that the Stravinsky *Danses concertantes* protest predated Boulez's and his comrades' study with Leibowitz and had nothing to do with atonality or serialism. Leslie Sprout correctly underlines that 'The 1945 protests against Stravinsky were not about the decisive embrace of a single musical style; rather, they were about the desire of young French composers to play an active role in shaping the postwar future of music in France, even as they

---

4   Serge Nigg, 'La Querelle Strawinsky', *Combat* (14 April 1945), n.p.: 'Pour ces "jeunes imbéciles" sur lesquels la critique fait feu de toutes pièces, toute entreprise artistique semble se devoir d'être, sinon le gage d'une réussite certaine, du moins le signe d'une inquiétude profondément ressentie. A ma connaissance, ils ne font que formuler là, très simplement, les lois élémentaires d'une éthique de la création artistique. Mais mal leur en prend, car les voilà traités aussitôt du "conformistes du non-conformisme", de "néo-académistes", ou "d'adeptes de la modernité à tout prix".'

5   Cited in Leslie A. Sprout, *The Musical Legacy of Wartime France* (Berkeley and Los Angeles: University of California Press, 2013), p. 177.

6   Nigg, 'La Querelle Strawinsky': 'On accuse certaine musique (atonale ou autre) paraît-il trop recherchée dans ses diverses combinaisons, d'être "cérébrale", ce qui exclurait, à priori, toute spontanéité; je ne vois pas en quoi le "16e quatuor" (grande fugue), "l'Art de la fugue", "la musique pour cordes, célesta et percussion" ou "Erwartung" seraient des œuvres antimusicales et dépourvues d'émotion?'

were still uncertain as to what stylistic shape that future would take.'[7] Perhaps the most important message to be drawn from Nigg's article is his stress on the ethical dimension of music, his profound belief that music should respond to the troubling times that marked the end of World War II. Boulez shared Nigg's belief in the seriousness of purpose of music, but their practical engagement with this belief sharply diverged. Unlike Boulez, Nigg was a politically active member of the Parti Communiste de France, and his stylistic evolution in the late 1940s reflected his growing belief that music should be easily understood by people. And just as Nigg's role as a young and controversial Parisian music polemicist was soon to be usurped by Boulez, he was also shortly to be replaced by Boulez as the most prominent young composer in France.

Born in Poland of Russian Jewish heritage, René Leibowitz moved with his family first to Berlin, and then around 1926 to Paris. Leibowitz began his musical education in Berlin as a violinist; some sources state that he studied at a later date with Schoenberg or Webern, though firm evidence of this is lacking. It appears that he was introduced to twelve-tone music by the German pianist and composer Erich Itor Kahn in the early 1930s, and he adopted this style as a composer. In Paris, he moved in artistic and intellectual circles as the friend of writers including Theodor Adorno, Georges Bataille and Claude Lévi-Strauss and artists including Pablo Picasso and André Masson; he also wrote for *Les Temps modernes*, the prominent literary journal edited by Jean-Paul Sartre and Simone de Beauvoir.

While Leibowitz identified primarily as a composer, he is now best remembered as a conductor and teacher. His name appears alongside some of his private students in a concert given on 5 December 1945 (Fig. 3.1), where Leibowitz conducted musicians from the Orchestre National de France in a programme of his own Chamber Concerto, op. 18, Schoenberg's Chamber Symphony, op. 9, and the French premieres of *Herzgewächse* (Foliage of the heart), op. 20, and Webern's Symphony, op. 21. Boulez played the harmonium in *Herzgewächse* (1911), a setting of Maeterlinck for coloratura soprano, harp, celesta and harmonium, and Grimaud reprised the role of celesta player she had assumed in the premiere of Messiaen's *Trois petites liturgies*. The 30 November 1945 issue of *Combat* included a preview of the concert in which Leibowitz was described as 'the principal representative in Paris of Schoenberg's school'. In the same preview, Webern's death on 15 September, 'assassinated by a Nazi', was recalled.

---

[7]   Sprout, *Musical Legacy*, p. 154.

Fig. 3.1 Leaflet promoting Paris concert of 5 December 1945

Leibowitz published several books on the Second Viennese School, most notably *Schoenberg et son école* (1947) and *Introduction à la musique de douze sons* (1949), and his ideas had a strong impact on Boulez in both positive and negative senses. During their classes with Leibowitz, the group studied works including Webern's Symphony, op. 21; Concerto for nine instruments, op. 24; Piano Variations, op. 27, String Quartet, op. 28, Cantata no. 1, op. 29, and Variations for orchestra, op. 30. These were very recent pieces indeed, the Variations being composed in 1940. Boulez's hand copies of all these scores, some of which feature annotations explicating the serial workings, are now part of the Boulez collection in the Paul Sacher Stiftung. David Walters notes Leibowitz's friend Adorno's influence on him as a writer and points out that Boulez's 'dialectical approach is strikingly similar to that of Leibowitz'.[8] It is true that 'Boulez's first four published articles, dating between 1948 and 1951, all discuss Leibowitz's ideas in some manner',[9] though this is generally by attacking his former teacher.

---

[8] David Walters, 'The aesthetics of Pierre Boulez', PhD thesis, Durham University, 2003, p. 27, available at Durham E-Theses Online: http://etheses.dur.ac.uk/3093/.

[9] Walters, 'The aesthetics of Pierre Boulez', p. 27.

Indeed, while Boulez's discovery of twelve-tone composition had a lasting impact on his music, his opinion of Leibowitz as a teacher deteriorated rapidly and never recovered. He railed against Leibowitz's view of the historical inevitability of Schoenberg, and considered Leibowitz's teaching style to be 'the worst academicism'[10] and his analyses of Schoenberg 'an arithmetical countdown'[11] These views had antecedents in the Paris musical world: as early as 1939, André Schaeffner publicly criticised Leibowitz's Germanocentric view of music history and his lack of understanding of Stravinsky,[12] and one of Boulez's first published articles, in which he strongly criticised Leibowitz, prompted his meeting with Schaeffner, who was to become a close friend.[13]

Boulez explained his reservations about Leibowitz in some detail to André Souris in a letter of 17 December 1947:

> If I attack [Leibowitz] insistently and quite forcefully, it's not for personal reasons. [...] I think he has a kind of monopoly on analytic explanation which raises him – in his view, at least – to the status of a Mohammed. *Insh-Arnold*. He considers himself the apostle of a new religion. [...] Added to his cumbersome terminology, his total absence of irony or a sense of humour ought to warn people against those who are most eager to follow the current trends in music. That's why he isn't a good propagandist: his clumsy and stupid proselytising leads to catastrophic results (not violent reactions, but BOREDOM). [...] Without boasting, I am one of the only ones who can, in the technical sense, clearly show that some of his viewpoints are complete nonsense.[14]

---

[10]   Sprout, 'The 1945 Stravinsky debates', p. 119.

[11]   Joan Peyser, *Boulez: Composer, Conductor, Enigma* (London: Cassell, 1977), p. 75.

[12]   Maxime Joos, 'Variations esthétiques (Schloezer, Boulez, Schaeffner)', *Revue de musicologie*, vol. 91 no. 2 (2005): pp. 401–424, at pp. 416–7.

[13]   Pierre Boulez, 'Trajectoires: Ravel, Stravinsky, Schoenberg', *Contrepoints*, 6 (1949): pp. 122–42; English translation by Stephen Walsh, 'Trajectories', in Boulez, *Stocktakings from an Apprenticeship*, pp. 188–204.

[14]   Cited in Susanne Gärtner, *Werkstatt-Spuren: Die Sonatine von Pierre Boulez* (Bern: Peter Lang, 2008), pp. 133–4 footnote 4, letter dated by Souris: 'Si je l'attaque [Leibowitz] avec insistance et assez brutalement, ce n'est pas une question personnelle. [...] Je pense en effet qu'il détient une sorte de monopole de l'exégèse qui le maintien – à ses propres yeux du moins – à la hauteur d'un Mahomet. *Inch'Arnold*. Il se voit l'apôtre d'une nouvelle religion [...]. De plus sa terminologie lourde, son absence complète d'un sens quelconque de l'ironie ou de l'humour préviennent contre lui-même les gens les plus *disposés* à suivre les démarches actuelles de la musique. C'est en ce sens qu'il ne fait pas de la bonne propagande: son prosélytisme maladroit et stupide entraîne au contraire des résultats catastrophiques (pas de réactions violentes, mais L'ENNUI). [...] Sans me vanter, je suis un des seuls – techniquement parlant – à pouvoir démontrer efficacement le non-sens total de certaines de ses vues.'

Boulez paid a price for his criticisms of Leibowitz. As a conductor, one of few people organising contemporary music concerts in the post-war years, and specifically as a proponent of serial music, Leibowitz was an influential figure in the small Paris contemporary music scene, and it is noteworthy that he did not include Boulez's music in his concerts. Leibowitz's festival of dodecaphonic music held in Paris on 25 and 29 January 1947 included works by his French students André Casanova, Antoine Duhamel and Serge Nigg, the British composers Elisabeth Lutyens and Humphrey Searle, and the Belgian André Souris, but not Boulez. The festival programme displays direct connections with the Paris surrealist circle; a portrait by André Masson illustrated the programme, and the text by Michel Leiris on Schoenberg, cited at the start of this chapter, was published here for the first time.[15] Boulez hoped to meet Souris at this concert but, as François Meïmoun indicates, Souris was unable to travel to Paris and 'Boulez sent him an acid critique of the event.'[16] In this letter to Souris, Boulez derided Duhamel and Casanova's works as 'pure academic cliché', Nigg as 'Wagnerising' and Leibowitz's own Overture based on the tone row of Schoenberg's *Ode to Napoleon* as 'truly a cream tart for the Master's birthday'[17] (it is clear this was not intended as a compliment). If Boulez was critical of his peers in private, he was even more scathing about them in a published article, 'Incidences actuelles de Berg', which appeared in *Polyphonie* early in 1948. Arguing that Berg's music is 'the starting point of an alarming return to Wagner', Boulez wrote, 'If Berg drags in his wake people as uninteresting as Duhamel and Casanova, that is truly irrelevant and means nothing whatsoever to us. Worms have always flourished on corpses.'[18]

---

[15] Leiris's article was originally written in 1929 for *Documents*, though not then published. It became more widely available in his collection *Brisées*: see note 1 above.

[16] François Meïmoun, *La Construction du langage musical de Pierre Boulez: la Première Sonate pour piano* (Paris: Aedam Musicae, 2019), p. 149 note 108: 'Souris n'ayant pas fait le déplacement à Paris, Boulez lui adresse un compte-rendu acide sur les événements.'

[17] Meïmoun, *Construction du langage musical* (citing correspondence housed in the Belgian National Library), pp. 148–9: 'du pur poncif académique [...] wagnérisant [...] une véritable tarte à la crème pour l'anniversaire du Maître.'

[18] Pierre Boulez, 'Incidences actuelles de Berg', *Polyphonie*, no. 2 (1948): pp. 104–8, at p. 107: '[...] le point de départ d'un retour à Wagner assez ahurissant. Que Berg entraîne dans son sillage des gens aussi peu intéressant que Duhamel et Casanova, ceci, à vrai dire, ne nous importe guère et ne nous émeut pas le moins du monde. De tout temps, les vers ont proliféré sur les cadavres.'

Serialism was a central aspect of Boulez's musical language, but far from the only one, and its predominance in discussions of his musical style has overshadowed other, equally vital aspects. Here, I will focus on Boulez's Sonatine for flute and piano (1946) and first two piano sonatas, but rather than exploring their serial workings, I will situate these pieces in their broader musical and cultural context. The intensity and visceral power of Artaud and the surreal conflation of explosion and stasis, pithily expressed in Breton's fragment 'explosante-fixe', are at the heart of the instrumental works of Boulez's formative period, though he conceals their emotional world beneath the neutral titles 'Sonata' and 'Sonatine'.

Why did Boulez choose these traditional titles for works which have nothing whatsoever to do with the classical form's tonal conflicts? In an interview, he said, 'I choose as titles forms which have lost any real connotation',[19] and while this might suggest that the titles were used almost in opposition of their traditional significance as classical forms, other associations with the term 'Sonata' may have been more relevant. A 'sonata' does not, by the first half of the twentieth century, need to be a form founded on tonal argument; the name can also denote a large-scale, serious instrumental work and, since at least Beethoven, its number and type of movements has been flexible. In fact, Beethoven's two-movement Piano Sonata in F sharp, op. 78, was Boulez's model for his First Piano Sonata: according to the pianist Jean-Efflam Bavouzet, who rehearsed the sonata with the composer in 1989, Boulez wanted to emulate Beethoven's 'dialectic between long phrases and short phrases, and between dry and resonant musical elements'.[20] The contrast between the long-breathed phrases of the slow introduction of Beethoven's op. 78 and the staccato, short, choppy phrases of the second movement typifies this oppositional relationship of the two movements.

Contemporary sonata models for Boulez include Berg's single movement Piano Sonata, op. 1 (1907–9), and still closer to him, Jolivet's First Sonata (1945) and Nigg's First Sonata (1943), both of which were premiered by Grimaud, who was also the dedicatee of Nigg's work. And indeed Leibowitz wrote in his *Introduction à la musique de douze sons* that 'It is impossible to invent two things at

[19] Pierre Boulez, 'Prenons garde à la démagogie', interview with Richard Millet, *Revue des deux mondes* (2001), no. 1, pp. 28–34, at p. 31: 'Je choisis pour titre des formes qui ont perdu toute connotation réelle.'

[20] Conversation between the author and Jean-Efflam Bavouzet, 12 April 2022: 'la dialectique entre phrases courtes et phrases longues, et entre les éléments secs/résonnants.'

the same time, and serial technique, which is already an astounding invention, needed to be experienced first with traditional compositional means.'[21] In this, he was following the practice of all three members of the Second Viennese School, who all used titles such as 'Sonata', 'Symphony' and 'Concerto'. At the same time, we must remember Boulez and his comrades' disdain for neoclassicism, expressed most forcefully during their protest against Stravinsky's *Danses concertantes*; new music, for Boulez, could never be a matter of putting new wine into old bottles.

Boulez's First Piano Sonata was composed between March and June 1946 during the time of his studies with Leibowitz and was dedicated to him, though it later underwent considerable modification.[22] Yvette Grimaud performed a revised version of the first movement which was broadcast on 10 June 1947 (the composer was not present at this performance),[23] and Boulez made a final revision of the work in 1949 that was published two years later by Amphion.[24] Of the three early works under discussion here, it is the least assimilable to traditional sonata models. Rather, the musical style of this work is indebted to Schoenberg's piano music, as Boulez told Joan Peyser:

> As for the First Sonata, that was influenced by the first pieces in Schoenberg's Opus 23 as well as the Opus 11 which I had on my piano for a long time. The third piece of Opus 11 introduced me to a style of piano writing that was different from anything I had known. There is a great density of texture and a violence of expression that conveys a kind of delirium.[25]

So what drew Boulez to these pieces was their Artaud-esque emotional world, their violence. Certainly, the last of Schoenberg's op. 11 piano pieces is often dense in texture, more so than anything in Boulez's First Sonata. Schoenberg's sudden shifts in dynamic level, frequently from

[21] René Leibowitz, *Introduction à la musique de douze sons* (Paris: L'Arche, 1949), p. 267: 'Il est impossible d'inventer deux choses à la fois et la technique de douze sons qui constitue déjà par elle-même une innovation foudroyante avait besoin d'être éprouvée d'abord avec des moyens de composition traditionnels.'

[22] Peter O'Hagan, *Pierre Boulez and the Piano* (Abingdon: Routledge, 2017) goes into detail about the different versions (pp. 49–68).

[23] François Meïmoun, interview with Pierre Boulez, https://www.musicologie.org/publirem/entretien_avec_pierre_boulez.html [accessed June 2023]. (Meïmoun: 'Étiez-vous présent à cette nouvelle création?' Boulez: 'Non et je dois dire que, hormis quelques exceptions dont celle-ci, la radio passait alors complètement à côté de nos préoccupations.')

[24] See O'Hagan, *Boulez and the Piano*, p. 66.

[25] Peyser, *Boulez: Composer, Conductor, Enigma*, p. 39.

one extreme of the spectrum to the other, and its great rhythmic mobility are more akin to this Boulez work.

Other musical influences on the First Piano Sonata that Boulez did not publicly acknowledge were cut from the first version. The low bass cluster which is used extensively in *Notations* is a feature of the first movement of this sonata, usually in a form that accumulates the notes one by one – in fact, it is the opening gesture of the first version of the piece – and as we have seen, this feature can be traced back to Jolivet's *Mana*. Again, the cluster appears in a fixed register, always in the extreme bass of the piano where it has a percussive sonic identity, not something that is easily perceivable as particular pitches. These clusters were largely excised from later iterations of the First Piano Sonata, in what looks like a prime example of Boulez editing a score to get away from an early influence that he considered all too obvious.[26]

This critical editing can be seen when comparing the first bars of the original with the final published version (Exx. 3.1a and b). The tempo (slow), the idea of opening with a collection of short, sparse gestures that strongly contrast in register, which starts quietly but has a sharp crescendo at the end of the final gesture, is common to both versions. But Boulez excises the growing cluster gesture from bar 1 of the original version and also cuts the melodically static high repeated Es, preferring to move the musical argument forward more dynamically in his published version. He also cuts an irregularly repeated B flat from bars 11–16, probably both because it was overtly reminiscent of Jolivet's incantatory style, and because its tritone relationship with the repeated E in bars 2–3 was too obvious a riposte to the classical sonata opposition between tonic and dominant. Very few of the numerous bass cluster and incantatory passages survive in the published version of the first movement, and a similar slow incantatory section which couples the extreme bass with extreme treble registers was removed from the final page of the score.[27]

---

[26] Julian Anderson, 'Jolivet and the *style incantatoire*: aspects of a hybrid tradition', in Caroline Rae (ed.), *André Jolivet: Music, Art and Literature* (Abingdon, Routledge, 2019), pp. 15–40, at p. 32. Anderson particularly draws attention to the similarity between Jolivet's 'La Princesse de Bali' and Boulez's sonata: 'Compare, for example, bars 9–13 and bars 19 to the end of Jolivet's third movement with the very similar sounding deleted segments in the first movement of the Boulez Sonata'. A copy of Boulez's first version is housed in the Paul Sacher Stiftung, Boulez collection, 0577-0807 to 0577-0828.

[27] This excised section was placed between the 'Très ralenti' and 'Rapide' indications on the last page of the published score (p. 19, between eleven and ten bars from the end).

Ex. 3.1a Boulez, First Piano Sonata, original version: bars 1–3

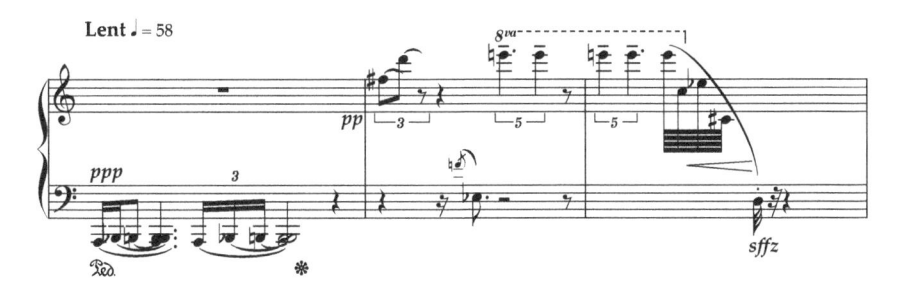

Ex. 3.1b Boulez, First Piano Sonata, published version: bars 1–2

Ex. 3.2 Boulez, First Piano Sonata, first version: bars 25–9

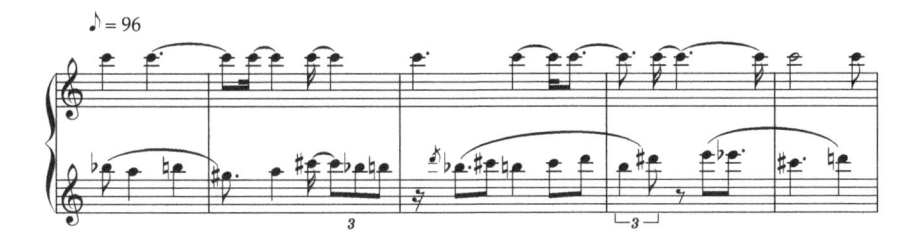

Ex. 3.2 illustrates bars 25–9 of the original version and typifies material that Boulez deleted. Several influences are clear in these bars: first, the irregularly reiterated high Cs in the top line show Boulez emulating Jolivet's incantatory style overlaid with Messiaen-like irrational rhythms. As in Messiaen's piano music, no time signatures are provided. Jean-Efflam Bavouzet, who inserted time signatures on his own copy when learning the piece, proposed to Boulez that he, Bavouzet, could make an edition of the sonata with these indications, but Boulez

responded: 'You do what you want, but I fear that pianists would place accents on the downbeat [if such an edition were created].'[28]

Another ancestor of this passage is Bartók: the reiterated melodic line which winds around conjunct intervals is highly reminiscent of the Hungarian composer's style. We know that Boulez studied selected Bartók works during Messiaen's private lessons, and another manuscript housed in the Paul Sacher Stiftung, composed around a year before the First Piano Sonata, illustrates the young Boulez's exploration of Bartók's style. This manuscript, dating from around 1945, is a setting of Psalm 97 'dans le style de Béla Bartók', composed for the four standard choral voice types and notated in a manner characteristic of French contrapuntal teaching, using the soprano, alto, tenor and bass clefs. Psalm 97 as set by Boulez features the same narrowly winding highly chromatic lines as the excised section of the First Piano Sonata, and its 5/8 time signature further aligns the setting with Bartók's musical language. A transcription of this piece for string quartet, for which individual parts survive, suggests both that it might have been performed for this instrumental formation and that Boulez might have been proud of this student work.[29]

The published score of the First Piano Sonata is in two movements, both of which feature abrupt contrasts of texture and dynamics, disjunct lines and extreme registral contrasts, and lasts around ten minutes in performance. In the first movement, the opposites of fast/ slow, silence/sound and loud/soft are juxtaposed in a musical argument which is extremely volatile, and bass clusters act as punctuation points (including at the end of the movement). The second movement consists of material in moderate tempo which is often lyrical in character and on one occasion is labelled 'excessivement souple' (excessively supple), and contrasting, much faster material which is typically in two polyphonic, rapidly moving voices. These voices are frequently highly disjunct and in contrary motion and together form dissonant intervals of sevenths, seconds or ninths. But it would be incorrect to suggest that this movement explores a straightforward dialectic of opposites, as there is a good deal of flux between the two extremes of tempo. Most of all, it is impossible for the listener to anticipate what might come next. Boulez's expression markings reveal this restlessness and instability: 'nettement

[28] Conversation between the author and Jean-Efflam Bavouzet: 'Vous faites comme vous voulez, mais j'ai trop peur que les pianistes mettent les accents sur les temps.'

[29] Both Psalm 97 and its transcription for string quartet are housed in the Paul Sacher Stiftung, Boulez collection, from 577-0348.

plus vif et plus violent' (notably livelier and more violent), 'plus animé et plus nerveux' (faster and more nervous); and Bavouzet confirms that speed was far more important to Boulez than accuracy; he even told the pianist, '60% of the notes is fine – it's the speed that counts.'[30] The final chord is marked 'arpéger très brutal et très sec' (very brutally and very drily arpeggiated). This second movement thus combines violence and extreme mobility with a rigorous contrapuntal language, with two voices often mirroring each other.

In his article 'Propositions', published in 1948, Boulez asks a rhetorical question: why seek so much complexity in a musical work? He replies: 'To match methods of composing with the variety of the dodecaphonic language with a rhythmic language that is also perfectly "atonal".' Therefore, both rhythmic and harmonic/contrapuntal language are equal in complexity, volatility and unpredictability, and again to cite 'Propositions', 'the principle of variation and of constant renewal will implacably guide us.'[31] And as we have already seen, 'Propositions' ends with Boulez's statement that music should be 'collective hysteria and magic, violently modern – along the lines of Antonin Artaud [...].'[32] The ultimate goal of this constant mobility and transformation, this uncompromising modernity of both contrapuntal and rhythmic language, is thus an Artaud-esque 'organised delirium' – and, as Boulez's remarks about Schoenberg's piano style reveal, this 'delirium' was also something he was drawn to not only in Artaud, but also in Schoenberg. Clearly, Boulez was not only attracted to the serial language of Schoenberg, but also to the emotional impact of his music; the two aspects are inseparable.

Shortly before his death, Leibowitz said of Boulez's piece:

> I thought he wrote too fast, too carelessly, that he threw in too many notes. When he started his First Sonata, I told him he knows my address. He should send me the work bit by bit. Then I could help him as he went along. But he brought in the completed manuscript. I didn't like it at all.

---

30 Conversation between the author and Jean-Efflam Bavouzet: 'Il a dit que 60% des notes, c'était bien – c'est la vitesse qui compte.'

31 Pierre Boulez, 'Propositions', *Polyphonie*, no. 2 (1948), pp. 65–72, at p. 72: 'Pourquoi rechercher une telle complexité? Pour faire correspondre à des moyens d'écriture aussi variés que ceux de la dodécaphonie un élément rythmique d'une parfaite 'atonalité' lui aussi. [...] le principe de la variation et du renouvellement constant nous guidera impitoyablement.'

32 Boulez, 'Propositions', p. 72: '[...] envoûtement et hystérie collectifs, violemment actuels – suivant la direction d'Antonin Artaud [...].'

Joan Peyser reports that Leibowitz corrected the score in red pen, Boulez shouted at him 'Vous êtes merde!' ('You are shit!'), and before the work was published, he angrily crossed out the dedication to Leibowitz.[33] His former teacher's critique of this piece precipitated a breach in their relationship that proved permanent.

Peter O'Hagan wondered why Leibowitz might have reacted against the work, pointing out that Leibowitz's conservative rhythmic language is a world away from Boulez's, and he may also have disliked the 'extremes of register, with three contrasting ideas juxtaposed within the space of a few bars'[34] at the start of the first version of the sonata. Moreover, the serial workings of Boulez's piece are not easily discernible as he tends to combine strict and freer approaches, in contrast with Leibowitz, whose music of the 1940s features highly legible serial workings. Boulez's series

> incorporates all the possible intervals from semitone to perfect fifth, making it particularly rich in melodic possibilities, and [...] it resists obvious segmentation into Webernian three-or four-note cells. Since such a model of regular cells was favoured by Leibowitz in his own compositions and was doubtless one which he would have encouraged his students to adopt, Boulez's basic series would not have commended itself to a teacher seeking evidence of the pupil's absorption of his teaching.[35]

At the same time, one wonders whether at least some aspects of Leibowitz's criticisms hit home, as the published version of the First Piano Sonata is considerably more concise than the first version Boulez showed to Leibowitz.

The only published critical response to the June 1947 broadcast of the First Piano Sonata, by Roland-Manuel, describes the composer as 'a new atonalist of strict observance';[36] the composer was then so little known that his surname is spelt 'Boulèze' throughout the review. Roland-Manuel, a composer closely associated with Satie in the 1910s and early 1920s, conveys little sympathy with the musical language of 'M. Boulèze, [who] in his piano sonata, engages seriously with the formalities of "serial" musical language where he finds, not charm which is not his aim, but a sort of icy discourse which contrasts with the

---

[33] Peyser, *Boulez: Composer, Conductor, Enigma*, p. 39. Peyser also cites the Leibowitz statement, though it is not clear whether she was the interviewer.

[34] O'Hagan, *Boulez and the Piano*, p. 52.

[35] O'Hagan, *Boulez and the Piano*, pp. 52–3.

[36] [Alexis] Roland-Manuel, 'Musiciens inédits: Wladimir Golschmann à l'Orchestre National', *Combat* (15–16 June 1947), p. 2: 'un nouvel atonaliste de la stricte observance.'

effusions of M. Roger Depraz's quartet [...].'[37] Certainly there is nothing conventionally 'charming' in Boulez's First Sonata, but it is notable that even at this very early stage in Boulez's musical development, a critic's view of the rigours of serialist language completely outweighs any other possible reaction to his music.

✦

Boulez's Sonatine for flute and piano was composed in February 1946 and is similar in duration to his First Piano Sonata, but the diminutive title 'Sonatine' immediately suggests the work might fit into the established French tradition of pieces for woodwind instruments. For instance, the identically titled contemporaneous works by Dutilleux (1943) and Pierre Sancan (1946) were both written as test pieces for the final-year flute competition at the Paris Conservatoire. But rather than his Sonatine being a continuation of this tradition, Boulez's work seems to be undermining the style from within. There are features of Boulez's piece that align with the Conservatoire test piece format, such as the overall duration of around eleven minutes with contrasting sections that vary in tempo and show off different playing techniques of the flute. Two specific sections are close to the French tradition of flute pieces. Firstly, the 'Très modéré presque lent' passage which first appears from bar 97 is based on tremolo material alternating with rapid ascending and descending eruptions on both instruments (Ex. 3.3). Together with several of the *Notations*, this writing typifies Boulez's fusion of serialism with florid, ornamental writing characteristic of his French forebears. This quasi-arabesque gesture is commonplace in French music and ideally suited to the flexible flute, and the underpinning tremolandi create the combination of mobile rhythm and static harmony which is typical of Ravel's musical textures. Second, the central scherzando section beginning at bar 151 marked 'avec humeur', with characteristic staccato repeated notes, is closest to the witty French tradition of flute music, but Boulez's repeated notes appear in a context of starkly contrasting dynamic levels and disjunct melodic phrases. These angular lines, combined with extreme dynamic and rhythmic fluctuation, move Boulez's Sonatine far from the insinuating, pleasing style of traditional Conservatoire test pieces for the flute.

---

[37] Roland-Manuel, 'Musiciens inédits', p. 2: 'M. Boulèze, dans sa sonate pour piano, se plie avec sérieux aux formalités de la musique 'sérielle'. Il y trouve, à défaut d'un agrément qui n'entre pas dans son propos, une espèce de tenue glacée qui contraste avec les effusions du quatuor où M. Roger Depraz s'abandonne au hasard des rencontres.'

Ex. 3.3 Boulez, Sonatine: bars 97–102

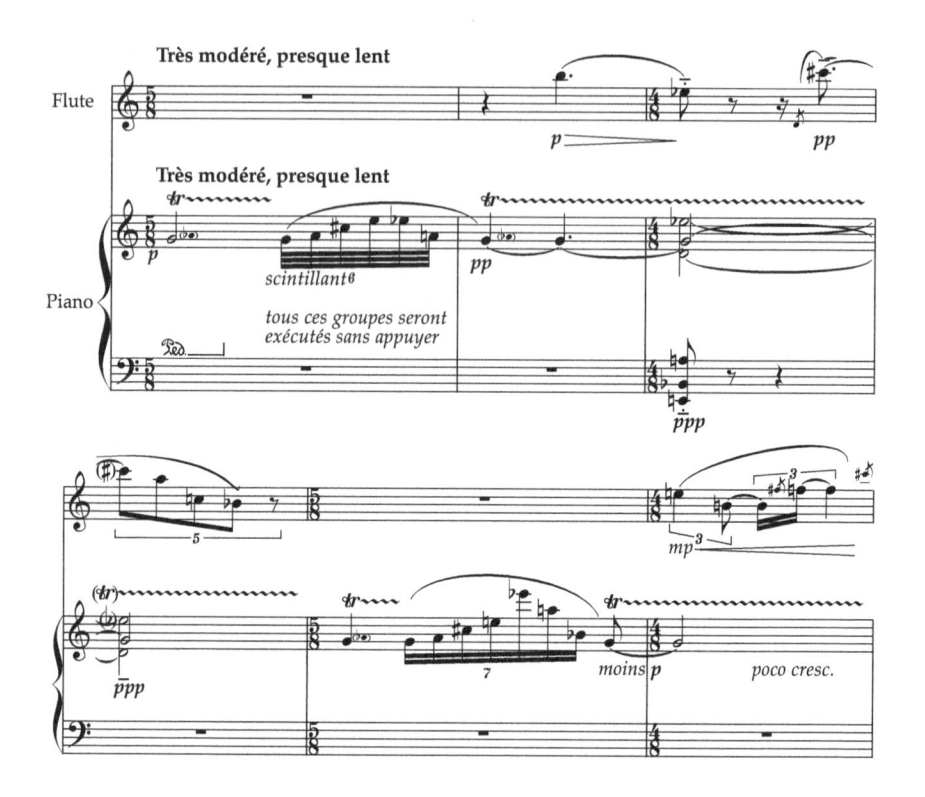

Moreover, this is not a piece in which the flute is the soloist and the piano has a purely accompanimental role. The piano has an important solo section (from the 'Tempo rapide' indication at bar 343), and when the flute rejoins the discourse, it reduces the tempo and temperature of the argument. The two instruments are unequivocally equal partners in the extremely mobile climax of the work, a climax that immediately reduces in tempo to a restatement of the tremolo 'Très modéré, presque lent' material. And the flute has a final surprise in store in the last bar when it ascends to a top F (equating to the highest F on the piano keyboard), which is a fourth above the official highest note of the instrument.

Boulez himself stated that the structural model for his Sonatine was Schoenberg's Chamber Symphony, op. 9; he 'emulated its synthesis of four movement-types'.[38] This single-movement multi-sectional work was, as Susanne Gärtner has pointed out, also the model for Leibowitz's own Chamber Concerto, op. 10 (1944). Boulez's correspondence with

---

[38] Paul Griffiths, *Boulez* (Oxford: Oxford University Press, 1978), p. 11.

Souris indicates that he also studied Leibowitz's Chamber Concerto while composing his Sonatine.[39]

The premiere of Boulez's Sonatine was intended for Jean-Pierre Rampal (1922–2000), who met Boulez when they were both students at the Conservatoire and became the pre-eminent French flautist of his generation. Like Boulez, Rampal was a brilliant student, winning first prize in flute in 1944 after only four months at the institution (Jolivet's *Chant de Linos* for flute and piano was the newly commissioned test piece for the 1944 competition). Rampal recalls that Boulez was 'intransigent, passionate and highly intellectual' and that he was 'honoured' when he asked him to play the work.[40] Leibowitz had dedicated his op. 12 sonata for flute and piano (1944) to Rampal, and the flautist was one of the performers involved in the recording of Schoenberg's Wind Quintet, op. 26, made under Leibowitz's direction that was a revelation for Boulez.[41]

The manuscript of the flute part housed in the Paul Sacher Stiftung shows that Rampal was originally the dedicatee, though his name was later deleted and despite the connections and affinities between flautist and composer, it was not Rampal who ultimately gave the first performance of Boulez's work. Boulez did not want Rampal's regular partner, Robert Veyron-Lacroix, to be the pianist, and Rampal was put off by its difficulty and the lack of barlines. For these reasons, Rampal could not commit to learning the work, even though he 'felt that the piece had a strong emotional impact'.[42] (Manuscript evidence shows that Boulez added barlines and time signatures in pencil at a later stage, and these are included in the published version of the Sonatine.)

The piece was premiered not in Paris, but in Brussels, at the instigation of André Souris, who had invited Boulez to submit a piece to the concert series 'Aspects de la musique d'aujourd'hui' run by the Séminaire des Arts, a concert organisation that Souris had run since 1944 with the aim of bringing together early and contemporary music. In a letter to Souris, dated 9 December 1946, Boulez offered him four possible works for this programme: in descending order of preference, they were *Le Visage nuptial* (which he titled 'Cinq mélodies sur le Visage nuptial de René Char');

39 Susanne Gärtner, 'Pierre Boulez's Sonatine (1946/1949)', in Edward Campbell and Peter O'Hagan (eds.), *Pierre Boulez Studies* (Cambridge: Cambridge University Press, 2016), pp. 25–55, at p. 34; Leibowitz's concerto is scored for wind quintet, violin, viola, cello and double bass.

40 Jean-Pierre Rampal, *Musique, ma vie. Mémoires* (Paris: Calmann-Lévy, 1991), p. 168: 'Il était intransigeant, ardent et très intellectuel.'

41 Gärtner, 'Pierre Boulez's Sonatine', p. 27.

42 Rampal, *Musique, ma vie*, pp. 168–9: 'Je sentais bien que l'œuvre avait une forte charge émotionnelle.'

the Sonatine for flute; First Piano Sonata, and his quartet for four ondes Martenot.[43] Perhaps bearing in mind the difficulty of employing two ondes Martenot players for *Le Visage nuptial*, Souris selected the Sonatine and engaged Herlin Van Boterdael (flute) and Marcelle Mercenier (piano) to perform it. Mercenier later gave the Belgian premiere of several significant contemporary piano works, including Boulez's Third Piano Sonata and Stockhausen's *Klavierstücke* 1–4. Souris greatly admired both performers, describing Mercenier as 'already the most brilliant collaborator in my concert series' and Boterdael as 'a very able flautist, then soloist at the Théâtre de la Monnaie, [whose] stunning technique allowed him to overcome difficulties which were then unprecedented.'[44]

Boulez told Souris:

> if you work on my Sonatine with the two performers, may it be above all alive, may it produce an impression of shock, of violence. It seems to me that's the main thing that is missing from all the works of the atonal 'school.' The word 'school' is horrid, don't you think? It will always be indigestible. That's exactly the impression I had at those concerts [Leibowitz's festival]. Anything other than that boring mish-mash that might be produced by any member of that 'school' whose *academic* paternity is all too obvious.[45]

Souris was particularly close to Boulez at this time, being also the editor of the journal *Polyphonie* that published Boulez's first significant article, 'Propositions'. In a draft of this article written at the same time as the Sonatine, Boulez drew an even closer parallel between Artaud and his own rejection of anything smacking of a 'school':

---

[43] Letter cited in Meïmoun, *La Construction du langage musical*, p. 87. (This extract is not present in the published version of the thesis.)

[44] André Souris, *La lyre à double tranchant: écrits sur la musique et le surréalisme*, ed. Robert Wangermée (Liège: Mardaga, 2000), pp. 181–2: '[...] par Marcelle Mercenier, qui était déjà la plus brillante collaboratrice de mes concerts, et par un très habile flûtiste, Herlin Van Boterdael, alors soliste au Théâtre de la Monnaie, et sa technique étourdissante lui permit de vaincre des difficultés qui étaient cependant inédites.'

[45] Gärtner, *Die Sonatine von Pierre Boulez*, p. 143; Boulez did not date the letter but Souris noted he received it on 31 January 1947: '[...] si vous faites travailler ma Sonatine aux deux interprètes – que ce soit avant tout vivant et qu'elle produise une impression de *choc*, de *violence*. C'est ce qui manque le plus, me semble-t-il, à toutes les œuvres de l'"'école" atonale. Quel vilain mot que celui d'école, vous ne trouvez pas? Il restera éternellement indigeste. C'est exactement l'impression que j'ai eue à ces concerts. Tout plutôt que ce méli-mélo ronronnant dont on pourrait aisément attribuer à n'importe qui de "l'école" – encore une fois – la paternité *académique*.'

So, following on from Artaud's expression 'today's theatre must be a theatre of hysteria', music should become a phenomenon of collective hysteria; those who do not participate in it will feel violently excluded. Now, as part of this sonic sorcery, rhythm must be linked to sound and have an equally important role. Above all, let's make music that is alive – in the sense that it obliges listeners to be involved – and not a sub-growth of Wagner, Berg or Schoenberg.[46]

There could be no closer connection between this statement and the sentiments Boulez expressed in his letter to Souris. For Boulez, this 'phenomenon of collective hysteria', of 'violence, shock, life', was very clearly an emotional prerequisite for music. The above passage, which was excised from the final version of 'Propositions', might also suggest a critique of traditional audience behaviour in a classical concert hall; listening in silence and applauding politely is precisely the opposite of what Boulez sought for his own music. And this was not just something he was impelled to create as a composer: his notorious behaviour in the concert hall, arriving equipped with whistles to protest against Stravinsky's neoclassical language, comes from the same source. It cannot be stressed enough that Boulez cared passionately about music, and an overwhelming Artaud-esque emotional response is something he wanted to provoke in his audience.

Boulez's Sonatine was premiered on 28 February 1947, a week after Leibowitz had conducted a programme in Brussels that he had given in Paris in January as part of his festival of twelve-tone music. Souris's introduction to Leibowitz's 'Hommage à Schoenberg' programmes includes the striking proto-Boulezian statement 'I salute Schoenberg as detonator of a supreme explosive power.'[47] Boulez was also unable to attend the Brussels performance, but 'subsequently he learned with pleasure from Souris that the Sonatine had provoked vociferous

[46] Cited in Werner Strinz, "'Il y a un couteau que je n'oublie pas": Antonin Artaud et Pierre Boulez', in Florence Fix, Pascal Lécroart and Frédérique Toudoire-Sur-lapierre (eds.), *Musique de scène, musique en scène* (Paris: L'Harmattan/Orizons, 2012), pp. 21–33, at p. 23: 'Enfin, suivant le mot d'Artaud "le théâtre d'aujourd'hui doit être un théâtre d'hystérie", la musique devrait devenir un phénomène d'hystérie collective, ceux qui n'y participent pas se sentiront violemment exclus. Or, dans l'envoûtement par le son, le rythme doit être lié au son et avoir une part également importante. Faisons avant tout de la musique vivante – dans le sens où elle oblige les auditeurs à participer – et non une sous-mouture de Wagner, Berg ou Schoenberg.' The complete text can be found in the Paul Sacher Stiftung Boulez collection, microfilm 025.1.854.

[47] Robert Wangermée, *André Souris et le complexe d'Orphée: entre surréalisme et musique sérielle* (Liège: Mardaga, 1995), p. 249: 'Je salue en Schoenberg le détenteur d'une souveraine puissance d'éclatement.'

protests'.[48] The impression of 'shock' and 'violence' that Boulez hoped his work would produce came to pass.

This Brussels performance also had an impact on the piece itself. As Souris explained,

> The work was naturally played from the manuscript and after working in great detail, Marcelle Mercenier proposed to me that cuts should be made, which she justified not because of the work's excessive difficulty, but for reasons of formal balance. It's noteworthy and to Mercenier's credit that these cuts, which I adopted myself, were also adopted by Boulez, who recognised their validity and took account of them in the published edition of the Sonatine.[49]

There seems to be no surviving correspondence between Souris and Boulez (or indeed between Mercenier and Boulez) about this fascinating detail, which is all the more regrettable because Boulez's apparent acceptance of the proposed cut is in extreme contrast to his negative reaction to Leibowitz's suggestions for revision of his First Piano Sonata. Boulez and Souris would finally meet in Brussels in April 1947, when Boulez was in the Belgian capital with the Renaud–Barrault company playing ondes Martenot for a Jacques Prévert pantomime drawn from the film *Les Enfants du Paradis*.[50] The music for this production was by Joseph Kosma; as so often, Boulez's employment as musical director with the company meant he had to engage with music that was, to say the least, far distant from his own creative preoccupations.

Boulez's revision of his Sonatine was made in April 1949; Gärtner believes that this was prompted by the possibility of publication, following Cage's introduction to the publishers Heugel and Amphion. But while Boulez's first two piano sonatas were published soon after this introduction (the second by Heugel in 1950 and the first a year later by Amphion), the Sonatine was not published until 1954, and its revised version was premiered in 1956 at Darmstadt by Severino Gazzelloni (flute) and David Tudor (piano).[51] It is also true that the revisions 'elimi-

---

[48] Undated letter from Boulez to Souris, cited in Gärtner, 'Pierre Boulez's Sonatine', p. 30.

[49] Souris, *La Lyre à double tranchant*, pp. 181–2: 'L'œuvre fut naturellement exécutée sur le manuscrit et après un travail très approfondi, Marcelle Mercenier me proposa d'y pratiquer des coupures, ce qu'elle justifiait non par des raisons de trop grande difficulté, mais pour des questions d'équilibre formel. Chose piquante et qui est tout à l'honneur de Mercenier, ces coupures, que j'avais moi-même adoptées, furent aussi adoptées par Boulez, qui en reconnut le bien-fondé et qui en tint compte lors de l'édition de sa *Sonatine*.'

[50] See Wangermée, *André Souris*, p. 273.

[51] Gärtner, 'Pierre Boulez's Sonatine', pp. 30–1.

nate the features whose Balinese or magic connotations are particularly salient: clusters in the extreme bass register [...] and everything that recalls the incantatory style of Jolivet'.[52] As with the First Piano Sonata, here we see Boulez using a revision to strip his music of footprints which are too obviously derivative of other composers.

Boulez's Second Piano Sonata is on a quite different scale from both the Sonatine and the First Sonata. Lasting about half an hour in performance, it is in four movements, 'Extrêmement rapide' (extremely fast), 'Lent' (slow), 'Modéré, presque vif' (moderate, almost fast) and 'Vif' (lively), which one could map on to the traditional large-scale Romantic sonata structure of fast first movement – slow movement – scherzo – fast finale. It was completed in 1948, though not premiered until 29 April 1950, once more by Yvette Grimaud. Listeners are immediately struck by the stupendous level of technical challenge for the performer in this sonata, which allegedly prompted the formidable pianist Yvonne Loriod to burst into tears when she first encountered the score.[53] The 'violence, shock, life' that Boulez sought in music is allied to rigorous contrapuntal workings, often with highly disjunct individual voices, as in the First Piano Sonata but on a much larger scale. And Susan Bradshaw correctly points out that 'It was typical of Boulez that he should arrive at the annihilation of sonata form not by an intellectual decision, but by an emotional exploration of its extreme limits as a perceptible (and workable) frame'.[54]

Peter O'Hagan notes that the work

started life as an independent *Variations-Rondeau* completed as early as May 1946 and dedicated to Andrée Vaurabourg-Honegger. It was eventually to become, in revised form, the third movement of the Second Sonata. Its overall shape is essentially fixed at this stage, with three modified returns of the brief opening Scherzo section, marked Modéré, presque vif in the published version, separated by somewhat more extended episodes. The first draft of *Variations-Rondeau* provides labels for this sectional structure: the three episodes were conceived as 'Variations' but interestingly, the first return of the opening section is marked 'Deuxième Répons Rondeau Rétrograde contraire' [Second Response Rondo Retrograde

52 Strinz, 'Artaud et Boulez', p. 26: 'élimine les éléments dont les connotations balinaises ou magiques sont les plus flagrantes: les clusters dans l'extrême grave [...] et tout ce qui rappelle le style incantatoire de Jolivet'. See also Gärtner's detailed analysis of the revisions to the Sonatine.
53 David Fanning, sleeve note for Maurizio Pollini's recording of Boulez's Second Sonata and other works, Deutsche Grammophon 447 431–2 (1995).
54 Susan Bradshaw, 'The instrumental and vocal music', in William Glock (ed.), *Pierre Boulez: A Symposium* (London: Eulenburg, 1986), pp. 127–229, at p. 158.

inversion]. This confirms the conscious nature of Boulez's serial thinking with regard to structure as early as 1946.[55]

While the titles of the four movements might suggest a large-scale classical sonata structure, Boulez's aim was not continuity with this tradition – quite the opposite. As he later wrote, 'My experiment was to destroy what was first-movement sonata form, to dissolve slow-movement form by means of the trope, to dissolve repetitive scherzo-form by means of variation form, and finally, in the fourth movement, to destroy fugal and canonic form.'[56] Specifically, Beethoven's op. 106 sonata (the 'Hammerklavier') was Boulez's explicit model, and using Beethoven's largest and most technically challenging piano sonata as a prototype immediately shows the scale and ambition of Boulez's work. More precisely, John Keillor notes that the fugal subject of the Beethoven is quoted on the first page of Boulez's work, and he sees Boulez's use of imitative counterpoint as another overt homage to Beethoven's op. 106.[57] Fugal textures come to the fore in the finale, with a fugue subject that starts in the very lowest register of the piano. In this sonata, Boulez is using op. 106 as a found object, but not as something to be quoted or even revered: it was a formal model to be obliterated. Indeed, the instrument itself comes close to obliteration in the last movement, such is the violence of the pianist's gestures.

Boulez's preface stresses that 'All contrapuntal voices are equally important: there are no principal nor secondary voices.' Concepts of foreground and background, or more precisely of Schoenberg's *Hauptstimme* and *Nebenstimme*, are therefore absent. He also notes that 'Articulating the musical structure is left to the interpreter's judgement, both where the varied relationships of the sonorities are concerned, and regarding a degree of freedom in tempo fluctuation. Especially in slow tempi, what tend to be referred to as "expressive nuances" should absolutely be avoided.'[58] The composer uses scare quotes to demonstrate his horror of anything that might suggest a Romantic, sentimental

---

[55] Peter O'Hagan, 'Boulez and the Foundation of IRCAM', in Richard Langham Smith and Caroline Potter (eds.), *French Music since Berlioz* (Aldershot: Ashgate, 2006), pp. 303–30, at p. 308.

[56] Cited in Paul Griffiths, sleeve note for Maurizio Pollini Edition, vol. 9: Debussy Etudes, Boulez Second Sonata, Deutsche Grammophon 471 359-2 (2001).

[57] John Keillor, 'Pierre Boulez: Second Sonata.' https://www.allmusic.com/composition/piano-sonata-no-2-mc0002365595 [accessed June 2023].

[58] Pierre Boulez, preface to published score of *2ème Sonate pour piano* (Paris: Heugel, 1950): 'Tous les contrepoints sont également importants; il n'y a ni parties principales, ni parties secondaires. Le soin d'articuler l'architecture musicale est laissé à l'intelligence de l'interprète, tant par les rapports variés de la dynamique sonore, que par une certaine liberté de fluctuation dans le tempo.

approach to his score. Boulez's insistence that all voices should be equal further ensures that it is extremely difficult to pick out individual lines to follow. Rather, textures and (ever-mobile) rhythms are the most easily perceptible elements of the work. Individual lines are extremely disjunct, obliterating any notion of melody: notes that are beamed and grouped together on the score are frequently widely spaced and often overlap in register with other groups. At the same time, sketch material for the sonata housed in the Paul Sacher Stiftung includes several pages of lists of different transpositions and inversions of its tone row, indicating the rigorous serial thought behind the chaotic surface. This is an intentionally disorientating, uncompromising, radical work.

One starting point for an exploration of the emotional world of the sonata is Boulez's performance indications, especially in the febrile first and fourth movements. The first movement has a narrow range of related indications: 'très marqué et très sec' (very marked and very dry); 'sec' (dry); 'percuté' (percussive); 'très sec et très arraché' (very dry and snatched); 'très sec'. Towards the end of the movement, the nuances become more extreme: 'de plus en plus martelé' (more and more hammered; p. 12); 'rapide et violent' (p. 13); 'très violent, percuté' (p. 15, on the penultimate system). This dry, highly percussive incisiveness is pushed to a still more extreme state in the finale. The word 'percuté' abounds in this movement, and these are the most noteworthy performance markings (Table 3.1).

This is a piece where the piano is fundamentally treated as a percussion instrument to be attacked by the performer. The striking performance instruction 'pulvériser le son' is the term which most pithily encapsulates the overwhelming violent passion of the work; what Boulez means is that there is no perceivable metre, so complex and fast-moving is the texture, and no sense of linear continuity as the piano writing is exceptionally disjunct, as seen in Ex. 3.4. While Boulez tends to be pigeonholed as a cerebral composer, this work above all others shows that this intellectual side coexists with extreme visceral energy. But where does the crushingly intense emotional mood of Boulez's sonata come from? René Char's contemporary collection Le Poème pulvérisé, written in 1945 and published two years later, immediately springs to mind as a possible source for this expression marking, and in August 1948 Boulez asked Char's permission to set a fragment of this collection, A la santé du serpent; Char approved of his proposed outline, though the project did not ultimately materialise.[59] More generally, the Second

Éviter absolument, surtout dans les tempos lents, ce que l'on convient d'appeler les "nuances expressives".

[59] Correspondence housed in the Paul Sacher Stiftung, Boulez collection.

Table 3.1 Boulez, Second Piano Sonata: fourth
movement, significant performance markings

Page of published score/French	English translation
p. 38: Brusquement vif et très heurté – sans presser et avec une grande rigueur dans le tempo – dans une nuance forte, exaspérée	Brusquely lively and very abrupt – without pushing forward, with great temporal rigour – loud, exasperated
p. 45, second system: Les attaques nettement plus dures – de plus en plus haché et brutal	Attacks notably harsher – more and more choppy and brutal
p. 46, third–fourth systems: Plus vif. Encore plus violent (au début surtout dans la qualité du son)	Livelier. Still more violent (initially especially in the sound quality)
p. 47 (penultimate page), first system: Extrêmement vif pulvériser le son; attaque brève, sèche, comme de bas en haut. [Left hand, same bar] rester *sans nuances* dans la très grande force	Extremely lively, pulverise the sound; short, dry attack, as if from below to above. Remain *expressionless* while hugely forceful

Ex. 3.4 Boulez, Second Piano Sonata, fourth movement:
'pulvériser le son', p. 47 of published score

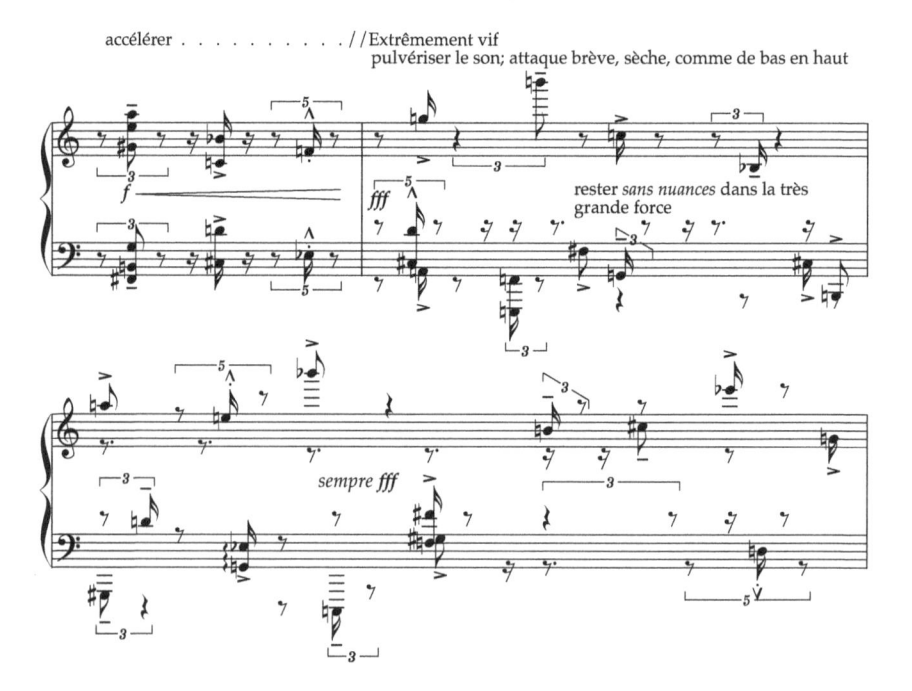

Piano Sonata is the work that can be most closely and convincingly linked to Artaud's performance style and Theatre of Cruelty aesthetic.

Let us first return to one of the most important early statements by Boulez, in his article 'Propositions' which was written at the same time as the Second Piano Sonata. The principal topic of this article is rhythm in music, and it ends: 'I have a personal reason for giving such an important place to the phenomenon of rhythm. I think that music should be a collective hysteria and magic, violently modern – along the lines of Antonin Artaud and not in the sense of a simple ethnographic reconstruction in the image of civilisations more or less remote from us.'[60] Rhythm, therefore, has magical properties; it is a binding force between people that can lead to rapture, to out-of-body experiences. Boulez's own music, composed to be performed in concert halls and other spaces associated with Western classical music, is far from the communal, binding experiences of the traditional musics with which he was familiar, but this article strongly suggests that he wanted the emotional impact of his music to be as powerful as those communal rituals that culminate in trance states. Surely Boulez's 'collective hysteria and magic' specifically references Artaud's involvement in collective rituals; by extension, music should be seen as a performative experience that binds performer and public together in the moment, with rhythm as the fundamental unifying element.

How did Boulez achieve this sonic and rhythmic sorcery? We could interpret the angular lines, constant dynamic fluctuation, extreme technical demands and abrupt changes in tempo as an Artaud-style intense expression of emotion. A concrete illustration of this in Artaud's work is *Pour en finir avec le jugement de Dieu* (1947–8), the first part of which is the final recorded verbal performance by Artaud. It must be recalled that Boulez was composing his Second Piano Sonata shortly after he attended a live performance by Artaud at Galerie Loeb in July 1947, an event that had an enormous impact on him. One notorious section of *Pour en finir*, performed by Artaud in the Radio France recording, speaks of collecting the sperm of American boys for ultimate use in artificial insemination (from 'Il paraît que, parmi les examens' to 'prêt à toutes les tentatives de fécondation artificielle qui pourraient ensuite avoir lieu', at 1′20″ to 1′49″ of the Radio France recording). The spectrogram of this extract of the recording (Fig. 3.2) shows the abrupt marked

---

[60] Boulez, 'Propositions', p. 72: 'J'ai enfin une raison personnelle pour donner une place si importante au phénomène rythmique. Je pense que la musique doit être envoûtement et hystérie collectifs, violemment actuels – suivant la direction d'Antonin Artaud, et non pas une simple reconstitution ethnographique à l'image de civilisations plus ou moins éloignées de nous.'

Fig. 3.2 Antonin Artaud, *Pour en finir avec le jugement de Dieu*:
spectrogram of recording from 1'20" to 1'49"

contrasts in register and dynamics of Artaud's performance, pushing
the voice to extremes. This strongly parallels Boulez's very wide leaps
and sudden moves from one end of the dynamic spectrum to another in
his Second Piano Sonata. Edmund Mendelssohn is right to suggest that
'Perhaps we can hear something of Artaud's "shouts, noises, and rhythmic effects" in the musical language that Boulez forged in his Piano
Sonata no. 2 (1948), written after Boulez heard the raving dramatist
in person.'[61] Indeed, for Boulez, Artaud was primarily a live performer
rather than a theoretician.

This disjunction of line is also a feature of the works by Schoenberg
that most interested Boulez in this period. Boulez performed the harmonium part in one of these pieces, *Herzgewächse*, under Leibowitz
in 1945, and in the next chapter we will see that there are strong parallels between this piece and the first version of *Le Visage nuptial*.
Schoenberg's Suite, op. 25, often features the same widely ranging lines
as Boulez's Second Piano Sonata, though while Boulez aimed to destroy
the classical sonata, Schoenberg's work retains some of the rhythmic lilt
of the Baroque dance suite. Schoenberg's second movement, Gavotte,
is far more mobile and disjunct than Baroque music, though the 'not
hasty' tempo ensures the underlying pulse of the gavotte is still present.

In his Second Piano Sonata, Boulez pushes this type of musical
expression to far more extreme places. As he wrote in 'Propositions',
Boulez wanted to give rhythm the same 'atonal', unpredictable character
as the pitch content of his pieces, and he goes far beyond Schoenberg
in the rhythmic flux and extreme discontinuity of his material. This

---

[61] Edmund Mendelssohn, 'Ontological appropriation: Boulez and Artaud', *Twentieth-Century Music*, vol. 18 no. 2 (2021): pp. 281–310, at p. 286.

produces something that is overwhelming, which is too complex to perceive in its individual elements, but which hits the listener with force as a sonic and emotional experience.

Boulez gave a private performance of extracts of his Second Piano Sonata to Pierre Souvtchinsky early in November 1947, soon after he had drafted the slow movement. Their correspondence reveals that Souvtchinsky

> must have raised some reservations about the music he heard, since Boulez wrote to him excusing his own playing (although without explaining the circumstances that this formidably complex movement had only been completed a few days previously), and requesting that he have the opportunity to perform it again after Souvtchinsky had time to study the score.[62]

While O'Hagan notes that the slow movement was not altered after this initial performance, it is striking that Boulez was willing to engage with Souvtchinsky's views about the piece in a way he was not able to do with Leibowitz.

A review of the premiere of the completed work is of interest as one of very few published accounts of early Boulez performances. Written by a performer from another age – Hélène Jourdan-Morhange, the violinist and close friend of Ravel – the review was published in a newspaper founded by the Communist Party, *Ce soir*, on 11 May 1950 with the striking headline 'Schoenberg surpassed: Two new works by [Jean-Louis] Martinet and Boulez'. Jourdan-Morhange wrote:

> According to his admirers, Pierre Boulez is a musical Rimbaud, a dazzling character whose writings for the review *Contrepoints* inform us of his intransigence. It's not even a matter of destroying Ravel and Debussy – indeed, they are dead! – but of disavowing Schoenberg, who is accused of not going to the furthest extreme of his dodecaphonic revolution. It's difficult for me to follow Pierre Boulez, because I admit I was so bored by his 30-to-35-minute-long sonata that I forbid myself from talking about it … I don't understand. I am one of those listeners who demand from music what the Greek philosophers called a 'moral force'. It was Aristotle who saw people's faces relax and their expressions lighten when a performance was beautiful … Well, the audience the other evening didn't radiate goodness; rather, it was boiling. Anger and laughter were about to spill over, but the listeners were extremely polite, because after this half-hour of boredom or of insurrection, they didn't even whistle – they were thus far more polite than the young Boulez supporters who noisily

---

[62] O'Hagan, *Boulez and the Piano*, p. 75.

left the room when music returned in the guise of Schumann played by the two charming pianists Jacqueline Bonneau and Geneviève Joy.[63]

It would appear, then, that Jourdan-Morhange's previous knowledge of Boulez was based more on his writings than on his music; Boulez's reputation as a polemicist was already overshadowing his compositions, not least because his music was even less widely disseminated than his articles written for specialist publications. Karel Goeyvaerts, a friend of both Boulez and Grimaud, also attended the premiere performance on 28 April 1950. He recalled:

> Yvette was slight in stature, not built to make a big sound. Although she mastered the complex rhythms of the piece, her fingers were not quite up to doing justice to the sharp contrasts in dynamics which characterised the work. There were a few wolf-whistles and Yvette, wearing a sort of negligee she had made herself, acknowledged our applause with a sort of 'Thanks all the same!'[64]

Boulez was not present at this public premiere as he left Paris on the date of the performance for a two-month tour of South America with the Renaud–Barrault company. However, his recollection of Grimaud's performance of the work suggests he agreed in broad terms with Goeyvaerts's account; 'It was a shame; she didn't have the necessary energy to play my works. Her playing was refined in the second

---

[63] Hélène Jourdan-Morhange, 'Schoenberg dépassé: Deux œuvres nouvelles de Martinet et Boulez', *Ce soir* (11 May 1950): p. 2: 'Pierre Boulez est, au dire de ses admirateurs, un Rimbaud de la musique. Nature fulgurante dont les écrits dans la revue *Contrepoints* nous ont instruits sur son intransigeance. Il n'est même plus question de détruire Ravel et Debussy – ils sont bien morts! – mais de désavouer Schoenberg, accusé de ne pas aller jusqu'au bout de la révolution dodécaphonique. Il m'est difficile de suivre Pierre Boulez, car j'avoue m'être tant ennuyée en écoutant sa sonate qui dure 30 ou 35 minutes que je m'interdis d'en parler ... Je ne comprends pas. Je fais partie des auditeurs qui réclament encore ce que les philosophes grecs appelaient les "forces morales de la musique". C'est Aristote qui voyait les visages se détendre et l'expression devenir meilleure quand l'œuvre exécutée était belle ... Eh bien, le public de l'autre soir n'irradiait pas la bonté: il était en ébullition. La colère et les rires était au bord de la cuve, mais la politesse des auditeurs fut extrême, puisqu'après cette demi-heure d'ennui ou de révolte, ils n'ont même pas sifflé – en cela beaucoup plus polis que les jeunes adeptes de Boulez qui quittèrent la salle avec fracas cependant que Schumann et la musique réapparaissaient par l'entremise des deux charmantes pianistes Jacqueline Bonneau et Geneviève Joy.'

[64] Karel Goeyvaerts, 'Paris – Darmstadt 1947–1956: Excerpt from the autobiographical portrait', in *The Artistic Legacy of Karel Goeyvaerts. A Collection of Essays*, *Revue belge de Musicologie / Belgisch Tijdschrift voor Muziekwetenschap*, vol. 48 (1994): pp. 35–54, at p. 40.

movement, but the first and fourth movements lacked energy.'[65] He was a good deal more forthright and sexist on the matter in a letter to John Cage dated 13 June 1950: 'As for the concert in which my sonata was performed, I don't give a damn about it. I don't believe Yvette Grimaud played it well, she must have played it in too feminine a manner.'[66] Did the Boulez–Grimaud friendship founder because of his views of her piano performance? This was the last of his works that she premiered, and one wonders whether Grimaud became aware of Boulez's condescending, gendered view of her performance and distanced herself from his music as a result.

Cage was important to Boulez in the late 1940s, not least because he introduced Boulez to two Parisian publishers in late summer 1949, when he visited Paris. O'Hagan studied manuscripts of the second and third movements of Second Sonata which are now housed in Northwestern University, bearing a dedication 'For John Cage, in memory of your visit to Paris which was very enriching for both of us.'[67] Cage also had a central role in the promotion of the Second Piano Sonata as he introduced the work to the pianist David Tudor, who gave the American premiere on 18 December 1950.

Tudor was not only new to Boulez's music, but through Boulez's article 'Propositions' he also encountered Artaud's name for the first time, and Artaud's 'revolutionary ideas about theatre would permanently alter his conception of the performance of modern music.'[68] Prompted by Boulez's article, Tudor read Artaud's *Le Théâtre et son double* and was particularly struck by a phrase in 'Le Théâtre alchimique' (1932): 'It seems to me that where simplicity and order rule, no theatre or drama can exist, and true theatre, like poetry too but in different ways, emerges from anarchy which is organised after philosophical battles which are

---

[65] François Meïmoun, *Entrietien avec Pierre Boulez: la naissance d'un compositeur* (Paris: Aedam Musicae, 2010), p. 40: 'C'était dommage, elle n'avait pas l'énergie pour jouer mes œuvres. C'était raffiné dans le second mouvement, mais les premier et quatrième mouvements manquaient d'énergie.'

[66] English translation by Robert Samuels in Jean-Jacques Nattiez (ed.), *The Boulez–Cage Correspondence* (Cambridge: Cambridge University Press, 1993), p. 63 (Jean-Jacques Nattiez (ed.), *Pierre Boulez/John Cage correspondance*, Paris: Christian Bourgois, 1991, p. 101: 'Quant au concert où on a donné ma Sonate, je m'en fous complètement. Je ne crois pas qu'Yvette Grimaud l'ait bien jouée, elle a dû le jouer d'un façon trop féminine').

[67] See O'Hagan, *Boulez and the Piano*, p. 76.

[68] Eric Smigel, 'Recital hall of cruelty: Antonin Artaud, David Tudor, and the 1950s avant-garde', *Perspectives of New Music*, vol. 45 no. 2 (2007): pp. 171–202, at p. 172.

the impassioned side of these primitive fusions.'[69]It is impossible to read this extract without thinking of Boulez's famous expression that, following the example of Artaud, he wanted to take delirium and organise it. Eric Smigel comments,

> Recognizing the pertinence of 'chaotic violence' to Boulez's sonata, Tudor began to interpret its disjunctive pitches as physical objects being projected into the performance space. The music was to be experienced not in terms of a developmental narrative requiring the application of memory, but rather as a visceral engagement with the present [...].[70]

Following Artaud's imprecations, however, involves not only emulating the 'chaotic violence' mentioned in his text, but also recognising that his theatrical alchemy involves organisation and thought as its other ingredient. This essential duality (Artaud often refers to 'le double' in his article), a duality which for Artaud is collapsed in the alchemy of the ideal theatrical performance, is once again the quintessential characteristic of surrealism, when apparent opposites are united in a culminating point.

This both/and unification in the Second Piano Sonata of serial workings and a delirious surface both represents a culmination of Boulez's formative period and looks forward to his 'total serial' phase of the early 1950s. Boulez said:

> in my Second Sonata, which I still like very much as a kind of organised counterpoint, the registers were not only a little bit, they were [totally] anarchic. There was some direction but not enough control for me. Then when I began to work with total serialism and all the parameters, it was no longer possible to control anything.[71]

More than anything, this encapsulates the paradoxical meaning of the term 'chance' as applied to Boulez's music.

A similar paradox was articulated by Breton when he referred to 'convulsive beauty', first in *Nadja* and later, in more developed form, in *L'Amour fou*. In the latter story, he explains the meaning of this term:

[69] Antonin Artaud, *Le Théâtre et son double* (1938; reprinted Paris: Gallimard, Folio edition, 1964), pp. 77–8: 'Il me semble bien que là où règnent la simplicité et l'ordre, il ne puisse y avoir de théâtre ni de drame, et le vrai théâtre naît, comme la poésie d'ailleurs, mais par d'autres voies, d'une anarchie qui s'organise, après des luttes philosophiques qui sont le côté passionnant de ces primitives unifications.'

[70] Smigel, 'Recital hall of cruelty', pp. 172–3.

[71] David Gable, 'Ramifying connections: an interview with Pierre Boulez', *Journal of Musicology*, vol. 4, no. 1 (Winter 1985–6): pp. 105–113, at p. 111.

The word 'convulsive', which I've used to describe the only type of beauty that, according to me, must be used, would be meaningless in my eyes if it were conceived in movement and not at the precise arresting of this movement. For me, convulsive beauty can exist only if one acknowledges the reciprocal relationship that links the object in movement and at rest.[72]

Elsewhere in *L'Amour fou*, Breton expresses this relationship in paradoxical formulations including 'explosante-fixe' – and this expression was used by Boulez as the title of several interrelated works from the 1970s to 1990s.

The coexistence of what is static (the original form of a tone row) and what is in motion (the row's realisation in a musical work) is fundamental to serial musical workings and therefore to Boulez's compositional language. The series, or fragments thereof, can appear in vertical form (chords), or horizontally as a solo line or in counterpoint, but the unchanging identity of the series is what guarantees the consistency of the musical language. From the initial version of the First Piano Sonata, we might see Boulez stress the immutability of the tone row by associating each pitch with a specific register – an idea he may well have acquired from Webern's Symphony, op. 21, which he studied with Leibowitz.[73] Beyond this, the typical Boulezian musical gesture of a sustained note followed by elaborate arabesque unfurling is another manifestation of explosion arising from stasis. As music is an art form that can only exist in time, it is peculiarly apt to realise the both/and paradoxes of 'convulsive beauty', and Boulez's Second Piano Sonata also demonstrates that the piano, with its quickly decaying sonority, is the ideal instrument to express Artaud-esque delirium. Capable of a much wider dynamic and registral range than most other instruments, piano music also needs to constantly move on to the next gesture before the sound has completely died away if it is to exist at all.

Much of the Second Piano Sonata was composed at speed from 12 September 1947 to the first weeks of 1948, a period that immediately followed several key encounters in Boulez's life, one being his attendance

---

[72] André Breton, *L'Amour fou* (Paris: Gallimard, 1937), p. 15: 'Le mot "convulsive", que j'ai employé pour qualifier la beauté qui seule, selon moi, doive être servie, perdrait à mes yeux tout sens s'il était conçu dans le mouvement et non à l'expiration exacte de ce mouvement même. Il ne peut, selon moi, y avoir beauté – beauté convulsive – qu'au prix de l'affirmation du rapport réciproque qui lie l'objet considéré dans son mouvement et dans son repos.'

[73] This is illustrated in Boulez, 'Propositions' as Ex. 2 (p. 68) which demonstrates both the fixed registers of the tone row and its realisation in the First Piano Sonata, though this passage was deleted from the final version of the piece.

at the reading by Artaud in July 1947. He looked back on the other meeting, or meetings, in 1954 in a letter to Karlheinz Stockhausen: '1947, the year when I made the acquaintance of Char, and when I became aware of myself. Now all that has gone and I can't think of it without sadness.'[74] All what has gone? The context of the letter suggests this might be a reference to a *Symphonie-concertante* that he was working on in the first half of 1947, a work he subsequently lost, but is more plausible that the expression 'tout cela est disparu' (all that has gone) has a more profound significance. By 1954, Boulez was in the middle of composing *Le Marteau sans maître*, based on Char's poetry, so Char was unequivocally still present in his life, at least in the form of his work. But Boulez never recaptured the speed of composition, and perhaps not the white heat of inspiration, that so marks his music up to 1948. Were there other, more personal encounters that had a strong impact on him at the end of his formative period, other losses that meant more to him? Was he lamenting the passing of his heady coming-of-age period when, as he put it, 'I became aware of myself'?

The abiding impression of the Second Piano Sonata is of uncompromising violence and destruction, and Paul Griffiths is right to state that this emotional mood is not superficial in character:

> it is expressive of a whole aesthetic of annihilation, and in particular of a need to obliterate what had gone before. Boulez's techniques of rhythmic manipulation rapidly destroy the profiles of his cells, and his proliferating serial method threatens the unifying power of the series. One need look no further than [...] *Le Visage nuptial* [...] for confirmation that this last destruction proceeded through love.[75]

This extraordinary vocal work is one of two settings Boulez made in the late 1940s of René Char; both will be discussed in the next chapter.

---

[74] Letter of 1954, housed in the Stockhausen Foundation and cited by O'Hagan, *Boulez and the Piano*, p. 74: '1947, l'année où j'ai fait connaissance de Char, et où j'ai pris conscience de moi-même. Enfin, tout cela est disparu; ce n'est pas sans mélancolie que j'y songe.'

[75] Griffiths, *Boulez*, p. 16.

4

FUREUR ET MYSTÈRE: THE FIRST VERSIONS OF BOULEZ'S RENÉ CHAR SETTINGS

> Sometimes, discoveries which prove essential to your life take you una-
> wares and take your breath away; they cause a definitive rupture, both
> required and desired at the very same time as they stab you. [...] You
> might be staring inattentively at a newspaper and suddenly you recog-
> nise yourself; this blazing paragraph in front of you seems both to take
> you outside of yourself and to expand your capabilities, your grasp and
> your power beyond what you had previously imagined.[1]

BOULEZ'S STRIKING STATEMENT, PUBLISHED in the newspaper
Libération in 1983, captures the extraordinary impact of René Char
on his musical evolution. Elsewhere in this short article, written to cele-
brate the publication of Char's complete works, he uses metaphors of a
bomb going off, of having one's very being shaken to the foundations, of
a shock that 'liberates an energy that is wild, joyful, drunk with its new
existence. Of course, it's a young person's thing, it has to be!'[2] But while
this youthful flash of discovery cannot last, its ramifications, writes
Boulez, are profound:

> Its presence can be felt everywhere and nowhere. The relationship
> is unwittingly transformed; there is this force at the centre of your
> own proliferation. No, it wasn't two narratives which were for a while

[1]   Pierre Boulez, 'Si je pense à René Char', *Libération* (24 June 1983): 'Il arrive
      que les découvertes essentielles à votre définition vous prennent au dépourvu,
      agressent votre souffle; elles causent un ravage irrémédiable, requis et désiré
      dans l'instant même où elles vous cinglent. [...] Vous fixez sans grande attention
      les yeux sur des poèmes dans une page de journal et voilà, vous vous êtes recon-
      nu: ce paragraphe fulgurant subitement là, devant vous, il semble tout à la fois
      vous déposséder de vous-même et agrandir votre capacité, votre prise et votre
      pouvoir au-delà de ce à quoi vous avez jusqu'à présent songé.'
[2]   Boulez, 'Si je pense à René Char': 'libère une énergie sauvage, joyeuse, enivrée de
      sa neuve existence. Pour sûr, cela est juvénile, cela doit l'être!'

superposed; no, it's not a transplant, not osmosis; no, it's not a carrier wave. Rather, it is a permanent transgression of limits and of substance.[3]

However eloquently Boulez expresses himself, and however deeply felt this statement might be, its style is almost as remarkable as its substance. Writing about an artistic encounter which changed him profoundly and permanently, Boulez almost always narrates using the second rather than first person ('beyond what you previously imagined') and never once mentions Char by name. This combination of intensity of feeling and distancing is characteristic of Boulez's writing style when looking back on his heady formative years. And Gavin Thomas is surely right when he suggests that 'one could almost believe that this is not Boulez speaking of Char, but Boulez speaking of Boulez.'[4]

René Char's verse made a central and vital contribution to Boulez's artistic development. The early works explored so far are all for instrumental forces; Boulez had attempted to set poetry as a young composer, but these juvenilia remain unpublished and uncharacteristic of the musical style he would develop only a short time later. And whatever impact writers such as Artaud might have had on his developing artistic personality, only Char's words are set to music by Boulez and thus are explicitly at the core of his early work. Boulez employed Char's texts in three works, in order of composition *Le Visage nuptial* (1946), *Le Soleil des eaux* (1948) and *Le Marteau sans maître* (1953–5); the first two of these were revised several times, and the first versions that will be investigated in this chapter remain unpublished.

In another homage to Char, this time written for the newspaper *Le Monde* in 1990, Boulez asks a rhetorical question: why does a composer choose a particular poet? 'The response, which is as simple as it is mysterious, could be summarised in words from the Gospels: You would not seek me if you had not already found me ... The meeting, the coincidence come from a demand which is so deep, so urgent that it might be considered futile to ask questions about the why and how of the circumstances.' This quasi-religious trope continues: 'Three times, the work of René Char reprimanded me severely; three times, I responded to this threatening incitement [...].' But while *Le Visage nuptial* 'makes

3   Boulez, 'Si je pense à René Char': 'la présence se détecte partout et nulle part. La relation s'est insensiblement transfigurée: il y a cette impulsion au centre de votre propre prolifération. Non, ce n'était pas deux narrations pour un temps superposées; non, ce n'était pas une greffe, ou une osmose; non, ce n'était pas une onde porteuse. Il s'agit bien d'une permanente transgression de la limite et de la substance.'
4   Gavin Thomas, 'Work not in progress', *Musical Times*, vol. 136 no. 1827 (May 1995): pp. 225–9, at p. 229.

explicit the narration of the poem, is modelled entirely on its form, is literally articulated according to it', *Le Soleil des eaux* 'is more a linking text which reassembles musical ideas which are pre-existing but fragmentary and gives them a necessary cohesion'. On the other hand, *Le Marteau sans maître* 'has a more complex relationship where the presence of the poetry is not the only connecting factor. The poetry irrigates the totality of the musical invention, even when it has ceased to be present.'[5] Readers will be struck by the emotional violence of the encounter between text and composer: the text is not something that seduced, but a threat that demanded a response. And it is the passionate, intense and often violent emotion of *Le Visage nuptial* that Boulez captured, especially in the first version which he composed within five weeks.

The initial encounter between Boulez and Char happened via published poetry, as they did not meet in person until August 1947. Char's five poems titled *Le Visage nuptial* first appeared in the review *Cahiers d'art* in 1944 and were reprinted by the publisher Gallimard the following year in the collection *Seuls demeurent* (They alone remain). Finally, these poems were published as part of a larger collection, *Fureur et mystère* (Fury and mystery; 1948). As Boulez's first version of *Le Visage nuptial* was composed in October–November 1946, he must have known at least one of the early editions of Char's verse.

This first version of *Le Visage nuptial* has the unusual scoring of voice, two ondes Martenot, piano and percussion, and the title page of the manuscript, written entirely in lower case, shows that it was originally dedicated 'à olivier messiaen'. However, this dedication is vigorously crossed out in the manuscript housed in the Bibliothèque Nationale de France and replaced by an enigmatic 'A Pierre Souvtchinsky. Le <u>vrai</u> visage. P.B.' ('vrai' is underlined twice). The 'real' or 'true' face? Does

---

[5] Pierre Boulez, 'Un allié substantiel', *Le Monde* (1990); reprinted in *Regards sur autrui*, pp. 711–12: 'La réponse simple autant qu'énigmatique pourrait se résumer en la parole évangélique: Tu ne me chercherais pas si tu ne m'avais déjà trouvé... La rencontre, la coïncidence viennent d'une réclamation si profonde, si urgente qu'il peut paraître vain de se poser les questions circonstancielles du pourquoi et du comment. [...] Par trois fois, l'œuvre de René Char m'a lancé une objurgation; par trois fois j'ai répondu à cette incitation comminatoire [...]. *Le Visage nuptial* explicite la narration du poème, se modèle entièrement sur la forme, s'articule littéralement selon lui. [...] *Le Soleil des eaux* est bien davantage un texte de liaison qui va rassembler des idées musicales déjà constituées, mais éparses, et leur donner l'indispensable cohésion. *Le Marteau sans maître* s'attache à une relation plus complexe où la présence du poème n'est pas le seul facteur d'alliance. Il irrigue toute l'invention musicale, même lorsqu'il a cessé d'être là.'

Boulez mean that Souvtchinsky is the 'true' face of this work (which is implausible, as the first version of *Le Visage nuptial* certainly predates their meeting), or – more likely – is Boulez suggesting that the work is *his* true face? Souvtchinsky (1892–1985) was one of many Russian émigrés to whom Boulez was close; he settled in Paris in 1922 and became known as a writer on music (he and the composer Roland-Manuel were the ghost authors of *Poetics of Music*, published under Stravinsky's name in 1939). As he was from a wealthy background, he was also in a position to be a patron of young musicians, and he was one of the supporters that enabled Boulez's Domaine Musical concert series to get underway in 1954. Another dedicated copy of *Le Visage nuptial*, now in the Paul Sacher Stiftung, is also addressed to Souvtchinsky and is much less enigmatic: 'To my dear friend / Pierre Souvtchinsky /this Visage Nuptial which will / finally see the day / thanks to him.'[6]

Joan Peyser's startling remarks about the background to the composition of *Le Visage nuptial* suggest an autobiographical element to the work:

> In 1946 Boulez engaged in a brief, passionate sexual affair, the only one of his life so far as I know. It was a love-hate relationship so intense and tormented that he has said it could not possibly have gone on. The two joined in a double-suicide pact; Boulez will say nothing more about the affair, not even whether the other person went through with the fatal act. The need for suicide and the release from it proved to be a stimulus of enormous vitality for Boulez. Within the next few years he created a series of wild, courageous works each of which maintained that delicate balance between emotion and intellect. The escape from death – or from the love affair – apparently precipitated a burst of prodigious talent. [...] Unable to find words to express his deepest feelings, Boulez, throughout his career, has set poems that do exactly that for him. The first poem he chose after the end of this affair was *Le Visage Nuptial*, by René Char.[7]

Boulez never spoke in public about this alleged affair, nor, it should be noted, does Peyser present the story as a citation of Boulez's own words. She does, however, quote him as saying of *Le Visage nuptial* 'It was a strong love poem. It was a good poem for me. It was a meeting

---

6   Paul Sacher Stiftung, Boulez collection, 577-0881: 'A mon cher ami / Pierre Souvtchinsky / ce Visage Nuptial qui va / enfin voir le jour / grâce à lui.' The work, in a revised orchestral version, was not premiered until 4 December 1957 in Cologne, conducted by the composer. Boulez and Souvtchinsky's extensive surviving correspondence shows that they must have met by 1947 at the latest.

7   Joan Peyser, *Boulez: Composer, Conductor, Enigma* (London: Cassell, 1977), pp. 33–4.

with the fancies I was having at that time.'[8] More recent research carried out by Boulez's biographer Christian Merlin gives his 'fancies' a possible identity. Writing after Boulez's death, Merlin refers to a conversation he had with Boulez's sister Jeanne Chevalier (1922–2018), to whom the composer was very close; she confirmed that 'Pierre Boulez had a passionate affair with the actress Maria Casarès. The date she gave was 1945 or 46.'[9] Chevalier added that 'the actress was then the mistress of Albert Camus, she had no intention of leaving him, believing that it would be feasible for her to divide herself between both men. Pierre [Boulez] preferred to split from her rather than be involved in a *ménage à trois*.'[10]

Casarès (1922–96) was one of the great tragic actors of her day. She was born in Spain; her father was a minister in the Republican government and the family was forced to flee in 1936 at the outbreak of the Civil War, when Casarès and her mother moved to Paris. She first gained a reputation as a stage actor, making a big impression in November 1942 with her first major role in *Deirdre des douleurs* (a translation of J. M. Synge's *Deirdre of the Sorrows*), and her appearance in Marcel Carné's classic film *Les Enfants du paradis* (1945) brought her to a wider audience. An exceptionally versatile performer, Casarès participated in the recording of Artaud's *Pour en finir avec le jugement de Dieu* made in 1947, which also featured Boulez's close friend Paule Thévenin.

Did her and Boulez's paths cross when he started working for Jean-Louis Barrault and Madeleine Renaud in October 1946 (the month he also began *Le Visage nuptial*)? While Casarès and Boulez had a number of common acquaintances, there is frustratingly little documentary evidence of their connection. The surviving correspondence from Casarès to Boulez, three letters now housed in the Paul Sacher Stiftung and dating between 1949 and 1951, are at most friendly rather than passionate in tone, addressing the composer as 'Cher Boulez', 'Cher Pierre Boulez' or the only slightly more intimate 'Cher ami'. Christian Merlin wonders whether 1948 is a more convincing date for the affair, as Casarès performed for the first time with the Renaud–Barrault company at this time;[11] however, this postdates the first version of *Le Visage nuptial* and would therefore rule out her being the passionate personal

---

[8] Peyser, *Boulez: Composer, Conductor, Enigma*, p. 37.

[9] Christian Merlin, *Pierre Boulez* (Paris: Fayard, 2019), p. 42: 'Pierre Boulez avait eu une histoire d'amour ardente avec l'actrice Maria Casarès. Elle la date de 1945 ou 46.'

[10] Merlin, *Pierre Boulez*, p. 42: 'la comédienne était alors la maitresse d'Albert Camus, qu'elle n'avait aucune intention de quitter, estimant en revanche envisageable de se partager entre les deux hommes. Refusant l'idée d'un ménage à trois, Pierre préféra rompre.'

[11] Merlin, *Pierre Boulez*, pp. 42–3.

impetus behind its composition. To further complicate this story, the 1948 Renaud–Barrault production featuring Casarès was *L'État de siège*, a play by Camus. Merlin's suggestion that the Boulez–Casarès relationship might have been 'if not one-way, then at least extremely unbalanced'[12] seems plausible, if indeed there were a relationship.

A more aesthetically driven interpretation of what Peyser called a 'double-suicide pact' is more convincing. The opinion that 'The need for suicide and the release from it proved to be a stimulus of enormous vitality for Boulez' should be contextualised within the post-war period, expressing an extreme desire to rid oneself of a hated past in order to move forward. Rather than being a literal suicide pact, this might have been a metaphor standing for extreme feelings that could never have been acted out. The secret Acéphale group of the 1930s, led by Georges Bataille, considered suicide to be the ultimate (and unrealised) destination, and Artaud's writings on suicide might also place intense feelings akin to Boulez's on a literary plane – though for Artaud at least, there is never a strong dividing line between metaphor and life. As early as 1925, Artaud wrote:

> If I commit suicide, it will not be to destroy myself, but to put myself back together again. Suicide will be for me only one means of violently reconquering myself, of brutally invading my being, of anticipating the unpredictable approaches of God. Through suicide, I reintroduce my design in nature, for the first time I give things the shape of my will.[13]

Boulez's statements about destruction regarding the Second Piano Sonata also spring to mind: the violence and intensity parallel Artaud's, with both artists glimpsing the abyss and translating it creatively. In conversation with Roger Nichols, he drew a telling parallel with Japanese Kabuki theatre: 'There is a symbol of people, when they are dying, going through a transparent paper screen, and when they have gone through the screen they have gone beyond death. That's exactly what happens

---

12 Merlin, *Pierre Boulez*, p. 44: 'un sentiment sinon à sens unique, du moins fortement déséquilibré'.

13 Antonin Artaud, 'Sur le suicide' (published in the Brussels review *Le Disque vert*, 4th series, no. 1, 1925, co-edited by Franz Hellens and Henri Michaux): 'Si je me tue ce ne sera pas pour me détruire, mais pour me reconstituer, le suicide ne sera pour moi qu'un moyen de me reconquérir violemment, de faire brutalement irruption dans mon être, de devancer l'avance incertaine de Dieu. Par le suicide, je réintroduis mon dessin dans la nature, je donne pour la première fois aux choses la forme de ma volonté.'

to a young composer. He has to go through, otherwise he will never acquire his own personality.'[14]

Moving more into the realms of speculation, there is an unnerving parallel between Peyser's account and Schoenberg, one that is explicitly autobiographical and which really did culminate in a suicide. Schoenberg's first wife Mathilde left him briefly in 1908 for the young painter Richard Gerstl; the Schoenberg couple reconciled, but Gerstl took his own life in November that year at the age of 25. Schoenberg responded to this personal turmoil with an extraordinary series of works composed at white heat in 1908–9: *Erwartung, Das Buch der hängenden Garten*, Five Orchestral Pieces. Shortly afterwards he composed an opera to his own libretto, *Die glückliche Hand* (1910–13), which was explicitly based on the love triangle. Given Boulez's great enthusiasm for Schoenberg's work in the immediate post-war years, and in particular its evident influence on *Le Visage nuptial*, one wonders whether he was aware of the older composer's personal story, whether he somehow identified with him (or with Gerstl?) as well as with Schoenberg's intense creative journey.

What is certain is that Boulez's first meeting with René Char happened several months after the composition of the first version of *Le Visage nuptial*. Boulez recalled:

> In June 1947 I was part of a group of young people who wanted to start a literary review in the margins. We wanted to publish some texts by René Char and we went to see him, not without difficulty as he was known in l'Isle-sur-Sorgue as the son of the mayor and not as a poet, which shows the gap between the cultural importance of a man and his social importance.[15]

This 'literary review in the margins' was a project hatched by Boulez with Édouard Helman, Albert Diato and Armand Gatti, who had secured the support of the publishing house Éditions du Rocher and aimed to co-opt both Char and André Souris. Sadly, this project had no concrete outcome, though Char's presence in the pages of Christian

[14] Roger Nichols, 'Interview – Pierre Boulez on Messiaen' (March 1986), published in Nichols, *From Berlioz to Boulez* (London: Kahn & Averill, 2022), pp. 302–7, at pp. 302–3 (interview conducted in English).

[15] Cited in Merlin, *Pierre Boulez*, p. 58: 'Je faisais partie en juin 1947, d'un groupe de jeunes gens qui voulaient faire une revue littéraire, marginale. Nous voulions publier des textes de René Char et nous sommes allés le voir, non sans peine d'ailleurs, car il était connu à l'Isle-sur-Sorgues [sic] comme fils du maire et non comme poète, ce qui indique la marge entre l'importance culturelle d'un homme et son importance sociale.' Also see Peter O'Hagan, *Boulez and the Piano* (Abingdon: Routledge, 2017), p. 74.

Dotremont's review *Les deux sœurs* (1946–7) shows his willingness to collaborate with young artists in their circle.[16]

Boulez's continuing interest in Char's work is evidenced through his use of the poet's work during the following decade in *Le Marteau sans maître*, and he also told Char in a letter of 31 August 1948 that he planned to set his collection of aphorisms *À la santé du serpent* that year, but the project never came to fruition.[17] Merlin claims that Char had little sympathy with music, though his continuing admiration for Boulez is clear from an extract of a letter he wrote on 7 July 1953, after Boulez had rewritten *Le Visage nuptial* and was awaiting its performance: 'For me, you are the only composer whose work truly matters to me and has for a long time. That's all I can say, I don't admire many people ... I hope that *Le Visage nuptial* will finally be played. Please keep me updated.'[18]

Under the influence of Mallarmé's *Un coup de dés jamais n'abolira le hasard*, Boulez developed in the 1950s his 'work in progress' concept – the notion that a work never has a single, definitive form. While this concept as applied to his oeuvre postdates his formative years, we can see aspects of the essential modus operandi of the work in progress from his earliest works. Pieces might be composed, withdrawn, partially or totally reworked, or a single work might exist in a number of different iterations. Boulez's two Char cantatas each took some years to reach their final version, though one might argue that only now that the composer has died can we surmise that there exist 'final versions'. I will explore the first versions of these cantatas, focusing on their musical language and Boulez's approach to the texts.

Le Visage nuptial

The first version of *Le Visage nuptial* was composed for voice (Boulez specifies a soprano on the title page and uses the generic term 'chant' on the score), two ondes Martenot, piano and percussion.[19] In a letter to Souris dated 9 December 1946 in which Boulez proposes works for performance in Brussels, he refers to the piece as 'Cinq mélodies sur le

---

16   François Meïmoun, *La Construction du langage musical de Pierre Boulez: la Première Sonate pour piano*, thesis submitted to EHESS, Paris, 2018, p. 176.

17   Correspondence in Paul Sacher Stiftung, Boulez collection.

18   Letter in Paul Sacher Stiftung, Boulez collection: '[...] vous êtes pour moi le seul musicien dont l'œuvre m'importe au fond ici et pour longtemps. Voilà qui est dit, je n'ai pas l'admiration nombreux ... J'espère qui "Le Visage Nuptial" sera enfin joué. Merci de me tenir au courant.'

19   Many authors, including Goléa, Griffiths and Meïmoun, state that this version is for two voices (soprano and contralto), but this is inaccurate; the change to two soloists happens in the orchestral version.

Visage nuptial de René Char',[20] though this rather old-fashioned title is not present on the score. Each of the five movements is precisely dated at the end,[21] and these dates range from 26 October to 30 November 1946. The percussion ensemble is extensive, comprising two piccolo and one ordinary timpani, bass drum, side drum, military drum, Provençal drum, suspended cymbal, gong, tam-tam, two pairs of crotales (one high-pitched, the other low-pitched), triangle and, 'if possible', a balafon or xylophone ('if possible' no doubt because the balafon – an African xylophone – appears only once, at the very end of the second movement, where it plays a single chord).

This ensemble shows the debts Boulez owed to several composers and to non-Western music in general. The example of Messiaen's *Trois petites liturgies*, with its solo roles for ondes Martenot and piano and its very contemporary blend of electronic, European and pseudo-Asian sonorities with female voices, was surely important to Boulez. The inclusion of a balafon in a mixed ensemble also points the way towards Boulez's setting of *Le Marteau sans maître*, for which the composer explicitly used instruments that suggest sonorities beyond the Western classical tradition. However, André Jolivet and, further back in time, Schoenberg are both more pertinent sources of influence. Specifically, Jolivet composed *Trois poèmes* for ondes Martenot and piano in 1935, adapting material from his seminal piano suite *Mana*, whose impact on Boulez has already been highlighted in detail and continues in *Le Visage nuptial*. But Boulez also knew Jolivet's earliest orchestral work, *Danse incantatoire* for large orchestra and two ondes Martenot (1935), and he copied the orchestral version of *Cinq danses rituelles* (1939), which he analysed in Messiaen's class when the work was still unpublished. Boulez's handwritten copy of this score was still in his possession in 2005.[22]

Two pieces by Schoenberg are even closer to the structural, instrumental and vocal characteristics of *Le Visage nuptial*. First, *Herzgewächse*, op. 20 (1911), a setting in German translation of Maurice Maeterlinck's poem 'Feuillage du cœur' (Foliage of the heart; 1889) for coloratura soprano, harmonium, celesta and harp. While this is one of Schoenberg's least known works – a piece lasting three and a half minutes for a highly unusual ensemble is not likely to receive many

[20] See Meïmoun, *Construction du langage musical* (thesis), p. 87 note 466.
[21] There are copies housed in the Bibliothèque Nationale de France, BNF Ms 21613, and the Paul Sacher Stiftung (microfilm 577 of the Boulez collection features several copies).
[22] Julian Anderson, 'Jolivet and the *style incantatoire*: aspects of a hybrid tradition', in Caroline Rae (ed.), *André Jolivet: Music, Art and Literature* (Abingdon: Routledge, 2019), pp. 15–40, at p. 32.

performances – Boulez was very familiar with *Herzgewächse* as he had participated in a performance on 5 December 1945 as the harmonium player, under Leibowitz's direction.[23] Before then, he discovered the name of Schoenberg for the first time when reading Paul Landormy's book *La Musique française après Debussy* (1943), which cites the first phrase of *Herzgewächse*; a few years before he died, Boulez told François Meïmoun, 'I still remember this extract by heart.'[24] Surely Boulez had the *Herzgewächse* ensemble in mind when composing *Le Visage nuptial*: his piece also couples different keyboard instruments with a vocal part requiring an enormous range.

Schoenberg's pioneering vocal work *Pierrot lunaire*, op. 21 (1912), had a strong impact on the first version of *Le Visage nuptial*, first because the vocal part in *Le Visage nuptial* includes Sprechstimme (speech-song), and second, because each of the five movements features a different configuration of the small instrumental ensemble, just as Schoenberg used a variety of formations in each of the twenty-one movements of *Pierrot lunaire*. Boulez's instrumental layout for each of his movements is listed below:

1. Conduite: voice, 1 ondes, piano, percussion (suspended cymbal, side drum, gong, tam-tam)
2. Gravité: voice, 2 ondes, percussion (2 pairs of crotales, high and low; 'balafon si possible' in final bar)
3. Le Visage nuptial: voice, 2 ondes, piano, percussion (2 small timpani, one ordinary timpanum, bass drum, side drum without timbre, Provençal drum, military drum, suspended cymbal, tam-tam)
4. Évadné: voice, piano
5. Post-scriptum: voice, 2 ondes, percussion (2 small timpani, suspended cymbal, tam-tam)

(*Le Marteau sans maître* features a similarly varied selection of instruments from the core ensemble in each movement.) Beyond this instrumental diversity, Boulez uses contrasting registers or textures for the ondes Martenot parts in different movements, and his vocal writing ranges from speech to singing to Schoenbergian in-between Sprechstimme. And unlike Schoenberg's, his musical language includes quartertones, though only in 'Gravité' and 'Post-scriptum', the movements that do not include the piano.

---

[23] A beautifully calligraphed copy of *Herzgewächse* in Boulez's hand is now housed in the Paul Sacher Stiftung (Boulez collection, 577-4000).

[24] François Meïmoun, *Entretien avec Pierre Boulez: la naissance d'un compositeur* (Paris: Aedam Musicae, 2010), p. 17: 'je me souviens encore par cœur de cet extrait.'

Boulez's rapid composition of the first version of *Le Visage nuptial* might be understood in the light of Schoenberg's 1912 essay 'The relationship to the text', published in the review *Der blaue Reiter* alongside a facsimile of *Herzgewächse*. Here, Schoenberg described the spontaneous compositional outpouring he experienced when setting words to music. He wrote that

> inspired by the sound of the first words of the text, I had composed many of my songs straight through to the end without troubling myself in the slightest about the continuation of the poetic events, without even grasping them in the ecstasy of composing, and that only days later I thought of looking back to see just what was the real poetic content of my song. It then turned out, to my greatest astonishment, that I had never done greater justice to the poet than when, guided by my first direct contact with the sound of the beginning, I divined everything that obviously had to follow this first sound with inevitability.[25]

Schoenberg's publication of *Herzgewächse* alongside this text suggests that we should consider this work as a practical example of Schoenberg's theory of the relationship between text and music. The links between Schoenberg's words and Boulez's conception of a vocal work that is 'literally organised' according to a text are striking. Even more, the first version of *Le Visage nuptial*, composed extremely rapidly, has something of the spontaneous 'ecstasy of composing' mentioned by Schoenberg.

Boulez's vocal line is exceptionally challenging; it would be very interesting to learn what Mady Sauvageot, its first performer, made of his writing for the voice. The vocal line includes some pitches with crosses placed over the note stems, a notation first used by Schoenberg for the Sprechstimme he requires for *Pierrot lunaire*. As this was not standard notation in 1946, Boulez adds a note to his score, 'ce signe veut dire mi-parlé, mi-chanté' (this sign indicates half-spoken, half-sung), following in Schoenberg's footsteps. But unlike in *Pierrot lunaire*, whose vocal part was composed for an actress and mostly remains in the speech register, Boulez writes for an extremely wide vocal range, from F sharp below middle C to the B natural over two octaves above this pitch, and he adds even more challenge with frequent abrupt changes of register. This is further enhanced in the orchestral versions, in which Boulez changes the octave of some pitches to make the solo vocal lines even wider-ranging and more disjunct. In this sense, his

---

[25] Arnold Schoenberg, 'The relationship to the text', originally published in *Der blaue Reiter* in 1912 and reprinted in *Style and Idea*, ed. Leonard Stein, trans. Leo Black (London: Faber, 1975), pp. 141–5, at p. 144.

vocal line has greater affinities with *Herzgewächse*, whose concluding bars demonstrate the stupendous demands Schoenberg makes on the soprano. The climax, *pppp* on a high F, exceeds even Boulez's challenge to the vocalist in *Le Visage nuptial*, and Boulez, as if surprised by this pitch, writes in the name of the note on his hand copy (Fig. 4.1). Schoenberg's harmonium is opposed in sonority by the metallic, percussive celesta and harp, and in Boulez's piece this incisive sonic role is played by both the piano and percussion.

How can music be 'literally organised' according to a text? Susan Bradshaw rightly states that 'since poetry can be made to reflect something of its own form when placed in a musical setting, words themselves can be used as an alternative formal framework', and she notes this is the case for Boulez's two early Char settings, although her chapter shows that she was not able to consult the 1946 version of *Le Visage nuptial*.[26] The central, name poem of Boulez's *Le Visage nuptial* is unmeasured and therefore unequivocally a prose poem, though the other four are shorter and (for the most part) measured.

In the first movement, 'Conduite', the performers tend to be divided into two groups: the voice generally works with the ondes Martenot (only one is used in this movement), and the piano with the percussion ensemble. The work starts with Boulez's favourite clusters, already familiar from early works including *Notations*, here forcefully reiterated in the treble register accompanied by a cymbal roll (Ex. 4.1). As in the First Piano Sonata, this very Jolivet-like rhythmic incantation is removed from revised versions of the score. Another important feature of Boulez's musical language is apparent in the relationship between the voice and ondes. While the ondes sometimes anticipates the vocal line, as it were providing a cue for the singer, it more often provides what Boulez later termed a 'contradictory note', where a second line creates a strong dissonance with the first. He theorised this technique in *Penser la musique aujourd'hui*, published in 1963: 'take care to introduce, in the centre of the register bounded by octave relationships, one or more contradictory intervals whose tension will weaken or annul the effect of octave relationships and will thus divert the ear from its tendency to simplify'.[27]

[26] Susan Bradshaw, 'The instrumental and vocal music', in William Glock (ed.), *Pierre Boulez: A Symposium* (London: Eulenburg, 1986), pp. 127–229, at p. 147.

[27] Pierre Boulez, *Penser la musique aujourd'hui* (Paris: Denoël/Gonthier, 1963), p. 50: 'prendre soin d'introduire, à l'intérieur du registre délimité par les rapports d'octaves, un intervalle ou des intervalles contraires, de plus grande tension, qui en affaibliront ou en annuleront l'effet, et détourneront ainsi l'attention auditive de sa tendance simplificatrice'.

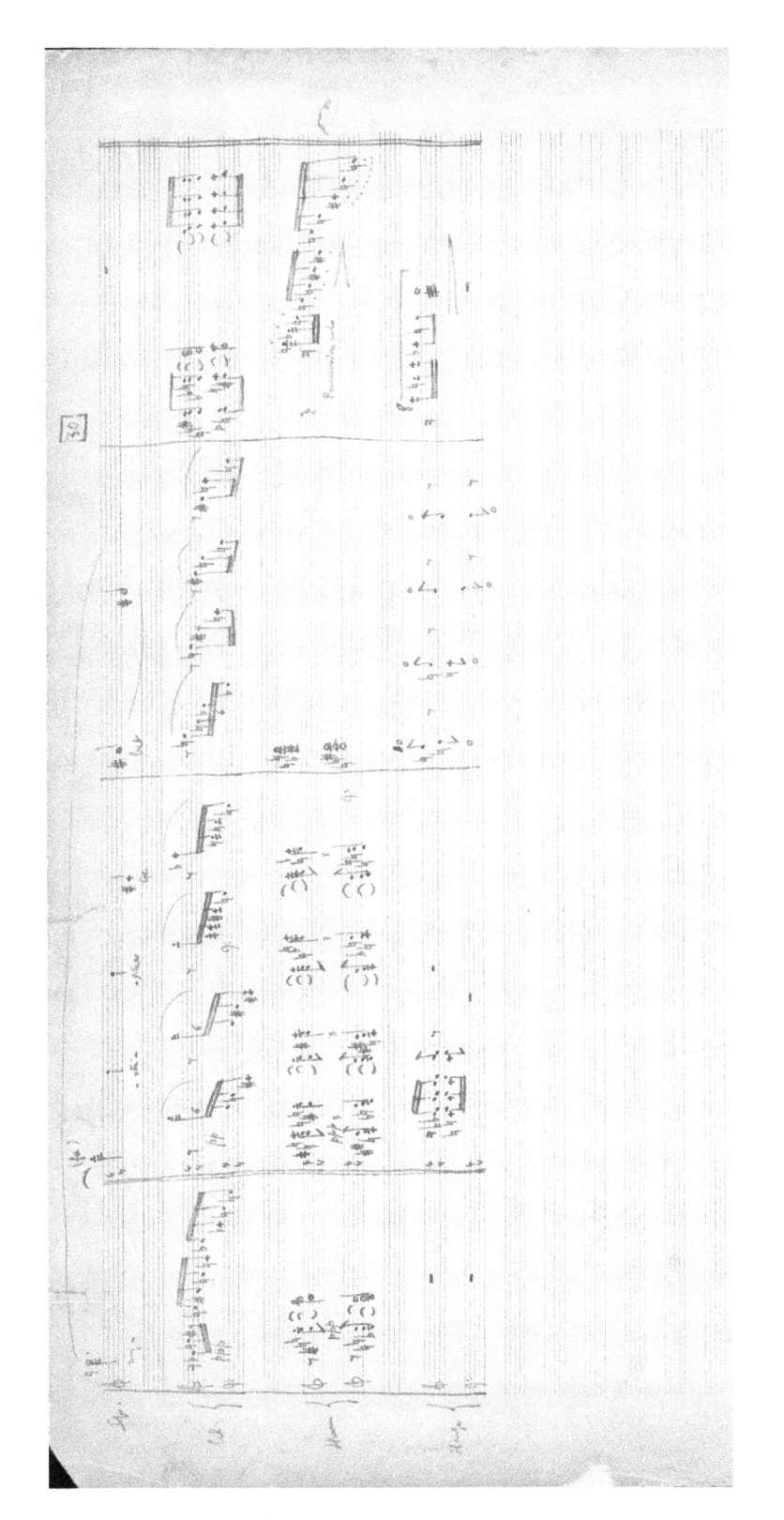

Fig. 4.1 Schoenberg, *Herzgewächse*: bars 26–30, hand copy by Boulez

Ex. 4.1 Boulez, *Le Visage nuptial*, first version, 'Conduite': bars 1–2

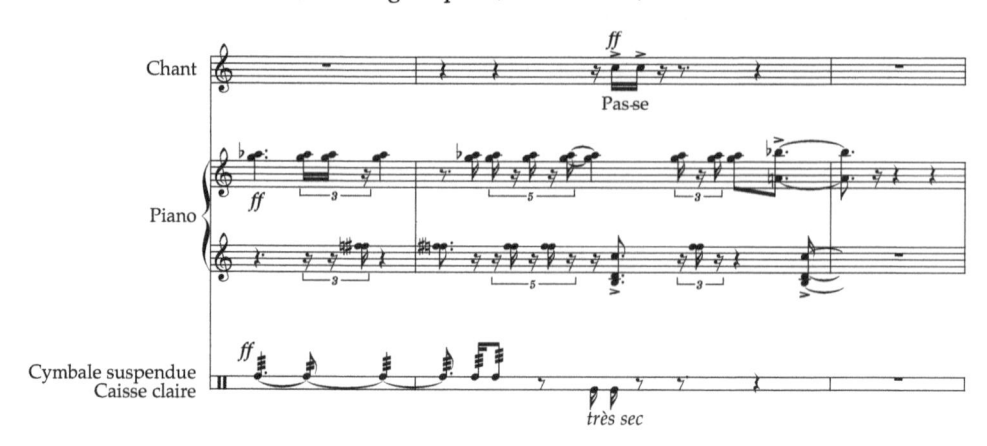

A particularly knotty passage in 'Conduite' appears at bars 18–19, when the vocalist sings the words 'À leur quintessence' above the treble stave with the ondes Martenot at the same loud dynamic providing 'contradictory' notes a semitone away. The parts are therefore not only independent contrapuntal lines, but also clash strongly with each other. But the singer and ondes are expected to drop the dynamic level to *piano* in bar 19, though at this point the vocal line actually rises to B natural above the treble stave (Ex. 4.2).

Ex. 4.2 Boulez, *Le Visage nuptial*, first version, 'Conduite': bars 18–19

Boulez uses contrasting registers or textures for the ondes Martenot parts in different movements, for instance using one instrument in the extreme treble register and one in the extreme bass in the second movement, 'Gravité (L'Emmuré)', and also precisely indicating the different sonorities or playing techniques required. One good example of this in 'Gravité' is the second ondes part, which is often notated with an expanding or contracting wiggly or spiral line, annotated thus by Boulez: 'Ce signe servira à indiquer une légère pulsation de la touche et un petit agrandissement du vibrato. Le signe contraire indiquera l'exécution contraire' (This sign indicates a slight pressure on the key and a small increase in vibrato. The opposite sign indicates the opposite performance direction). Therefore, the expanding wiggly line indicates an increase in vibrato, and a diminishing wiggly or spiral line, the opposite. Boulez adds a further instruction to the performer, this time a warning: 'Surtout, ne pas exagérer la pulsation et jouer avec beaucoup de finesse' (Above all, do not exaggerate the pressure and play with a lot of finesse); Fig. 4.2 illustrates all of this in the opening bars of the movement. The second ondes has almost exclusively this type of material in 'Gravité', with the first ondes operating in the same field as the voice in the same manner as in the first movement.

'Gravité' makes a particularly good contrast with 'Der kranke Mond', the seventh movement of *Pierrot lunaire*, which is scored for voice and flute. In Schoenberg's piece, the flute sometimes has a heterophonic relationship with the vocal line and sometimes seems to exist in a different universe, with completely contrasting material. Boulez's writing for voice and first ondes in 'Gravité' is more rigorous. One of the music examples in his 1948 article 'Propositions' is the opening of 'Gravité', which he uses to illustrate an irregular rhythmic canon, linking this technique with Messiaen.[28] While Boulez does not use this term, the Messiaen procedure he describes is 'agrandissement asymétrique' (asymmetrical expansion), where some rhythmic values in the canon remain unchanged from the first statement of the theme, some move from short to long and others from long to short. This material is combined with irregular strikes on both the high and low crotales, creating a quasi-ritualistic atmosphere which was surely inspired by the Balinese gamelan; these metallic interjections are greatly expanded in the final (1994) orchestral version of the work, which includes no fewer than eight pairs of crotales.

---

[28] Pierre Boulez, 'Propositions', *Polyphonie*, no. 2 (1948): pp. 65–74, at p. 69.

Fig. 4.2 Boulez, *Le Visage nuptial*, first version: opening of 'Gravité'

Bars 11–12 of 'Gravité', at the words 'Ô toi, la monotone absente', again demonstrate the voice and ondes in counterpoint, here with quartertone melodic inflections that further enhance the contradictory roles of each instrument. In Boulez's first orchestral revision, published in 1959, the role of the first ondes is taken by the chorus sopranos, and in the final (1994) published revision, the shape of the contrapuntal lines is retained but the quartertones are omitted. The second ondes concludes the movement on an extremely high E, with its sound reducing towards silence; in this last bar, Boulez also indicates a 'balafon (si possible)' doubling the pitch, the only moment in the piece where this instrument is required.

By far the longest movement is the central one, 'Le Visage nuptial', and its title shared with the group of poems suggests that it is also central to the meaning of the collection. Char's long poem is set without cuts by Boulez, using a wide variety of vocal techniques, including a psalmodic intonation reminiscent of many Messiaen vocal works (for instance, the second of his *Trois petites liturgies*). This type of vocal line, here hovering around middle C and C sharp, opens the movement, accompanied only by three timpani – two small and one regular-sized – though unusually, Boulez does not indicate specific pitches, but high, medium and low sounds. The rest of the first verse is composed with a Sprechstimme vocal line, until the climactic final phrase where it is given an expansive, florid gesture: 'J'aime' (Ex. 4.3). This highly melismatic vocal writing is rare in the first version of *Le Visage nuptial*, appearing only at points of high emotional intensity: there is a similar ecstatic melisma at the end of 'Conduite' on the words 'Ô Bien-aimée' (O beloved). There is a sense of urgency in this movement, of extreme expression using different vocal techniques ranging from speaking to crying out. This passionate force is most easily achieved with the single vocalist of the 1946 version, though it is notable that in the first revision, the two vocalists (soprano and alto) are often used on their own or in rhythmic unison with each other and sometimes also in unison with the choral sopranos and altos. In the revision, comprehension of the text is therefore privileged, though it inevitably lacks the intimacy of the chamber ensemble of 1946.

Ex. 4.3 Boulez, *Le Visage nuptial*, first version, 'Le Visage nuptial': 'J'aime'

The fourth movement, 'Évadné', scored for voice and piano, stands out for several reasons.[29] First, the vocal line is directed to be 'Presque parlé. Absolument sans nuances, mais en observant les accents' (Almost spoken. Absolutely without nuances, but observing the accentuation), and in a fainter script Boulez underlines 'Pas de hauteurs' (No pitches). So while the vocal line is written with pitches on a stave, these pitches are not intended to be sung. The voice declaims the text in regular quavers, and an accentuation which is often counter to natural speech patterns is indicated (the regular quaver rhythm already removes the vocal line from natural declamation, producing a distancing, ritualistic effect). For example, the first line is to be declaimed, with accents underlined noted: 'L'été et notre vie étions d'un seul tenant.' How this might be performed is an intriguing question, and in the second version of *Le Visage nuptial*, Boulez notates it using a stem with a downward arrow in place of a notehead; he has moved more explicitly to pitched speaking. And for the final revision, the unusual accentuation is retained, but this time the psalmodic chanting is to be sung rather than spoken, showing that Boulez ultimately rejected the experimental vocal production of the first version. But the abrupt shift from third to fourth movement, from ecstatic, sometimes melismatic vocal writing to ritualistic chanting, is an explicit illustration of the mood shift in Char's poems from passionately expressed love to disillusion, from the relationship narrated in the present tense to the past tense.

Added to this unnatural word stress pattern, the balance between the voice and piano in 'Évadné' is the inverse of usual practice, as Boulez indicates 'La voix doit être nettement à l'arrière-plan' (The voice must be clearly in the background).[30] The piano opens with an ascending flourish using all twelve pitches in the order E flat, F sharp, B, F, E, C sharp, B flat, A, D, G, C, A flat; the serial nature of the writing is evident

---

[29] None of Schoenberg's *Pierrot lunaire* movements are for voice and piano; the only one for voice and solo instrument is the seventh, 'Der kranke Mond'.

[30] On the score of the second version, Boulez notes, 'Les voix doivent se situer sur un autre plan que la sonorité d'orchestre' (The voices must be on a different level from the orchestral sonority).

as the movement concludes with a piano gesture which reverses the order of the initial twelve pitches, though the piece ends with a low A (after the E flat which ends the retrograded series).

'Post-scriptum' is a brief, very slow, pared-back concluding movement where the instrumentalists are directed to follow the vocal line, which has moved back to the foreground. Boulez writes a note to the performers at the base of the first page about the asterisks which litter the score: 'Ces silences sont mis pour exécuter plus facilement les rythmes en suivant le chant' (These silences are marked so the rhythms may be executed more easily, following the voice). But his other note is even more striking: 'Essayez de donner à cette mélodie un éclairage sur-réel' (Try to give this song a surreal light). In 'Post-scriptum' Char uses the formal mode of address 'vous', though the previous poems address the lover with the intimate 'tu'.

The extreme mood of this poem, one of loss and desolation, is mirrored in Boulez's extreme use of register and timbre. As in 'Gravité', the writing features quartertones, the piano again being absent from the ensemble. Boulez underlines the structure of the four-stanza poem by giving a specific musical character to each one. The ondes open the setting in an exceptionally low register, and the two small timpani interject frequently, often alternating two pitches a quartertone apart in an irregular rhythm. A five-bar timpani solo in irregular rhythm concludes the first quatrain, and Boulez punctuates the end of the next, two-line verse with a suspended cymbal marked 'son soufré'. Its 'sulphurous' sound is coupled with the ondes in an extremely high register, alternating two pitches a quartertone apart in a similar manner to the timpani interjections. More than any other work, the 1946 version of *Le Visage nuptial* shows that the ondes Martenot appealed to Boulez because of its ability to express extremes: dynamic contrasts, pitch bends, exceptionally high or low pitches and glissandi beyond anything that had previously been imagined, as well as striking new electronic timbres. Then the first line of the poem is reprised, with the vocal line intensified and at a much louder dynamic level – 'Écartez-vous de moi qui patiente sans bouche' (Step away from me, who is waiting without a mouth), marked by Boulez 'Très violent (mais sans presser)' (Very violent but without rushing) (Ex. 4.4).

Ex. 4.4 Boulez, *Le Visage nuptial*, first version,
'Post-scriptum': 'Écartez-vous de moi'

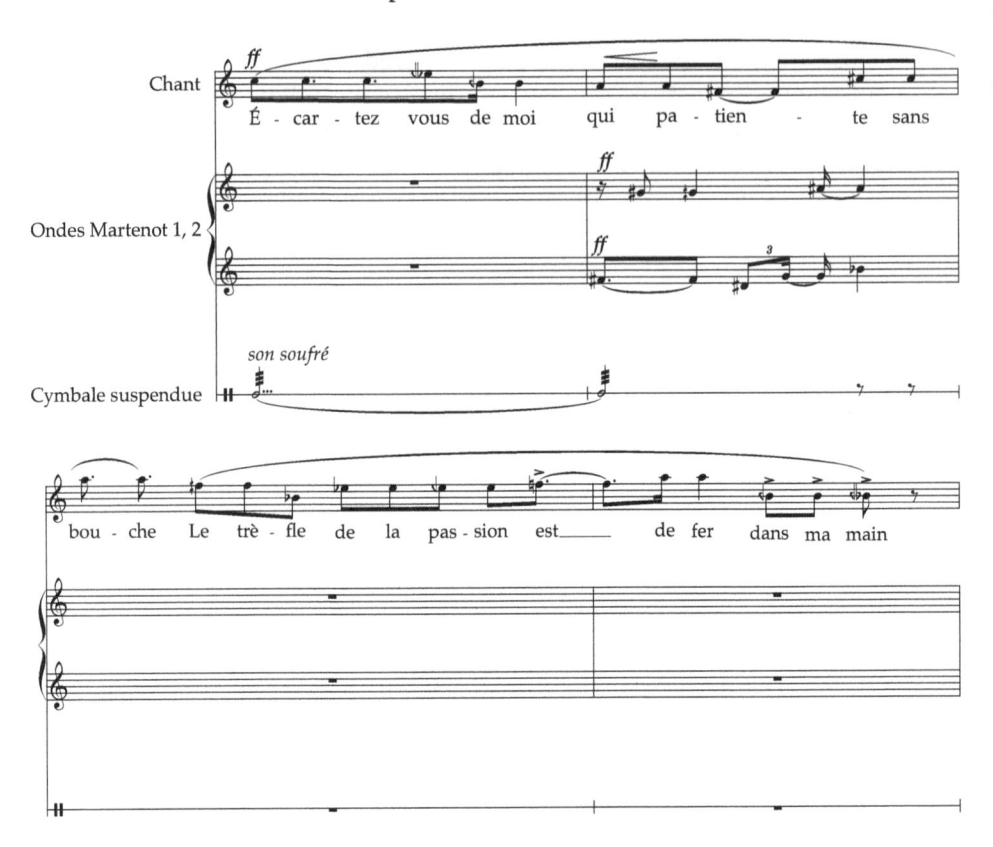

The final word of the poem, 'aigri' (bitter), is the only word in this movement marked 'parlé' (spoken): this is in the extreme low register for the singer, F sharp below middle C, and the note stem is overlaid with a cross, indicating Sprechstimme. The ondes conclude the piece, their sound gradually fading out ('de plus en plus imperceptible') followed by the mysterious timpani oscillation, this time between B quartertone flat and C 'Plus clair, mais plus lointain que la 1ère fois' (Clearer, but more distant than the first time). This heartrending movement concludes a love story that progressed from first meeting ('Conduite') through the awakening of feelings ('Gravité') to love's fulfilment ('Le Visage nuptial'); by 'Évadné', disillusionment has set in, and 'Post-scriptum' looks back on the end of the affair.

The publisher's programme note for *Le Visage nuptial* states that the 'first version [...] benefited from a (partial?) private first performance in Paris in 1947 and would soon be greatly filled out.'[31] Surprisingly little specific detail is available about the early performance history of the work, and none at all about this supposed 'private' performance. The only documented performance of this first version happened at the Triptyque contemporary music concert series in Paris late in 1947, with Mady Sauvageot as singer. Boulez himself told Meïmoun that only 'the first of the two pieces, due to lack of rehearsal time' was given,[32] but the first version of *Le Visage nuptial* has five movements and is not explicitly divided into two parts. Material in the Paul Sacher Stiftung may shed some light on this remark, as only two movements of one of their copies, 'Évadné' and 'Post-scriptum', feature what look like performance annotations. From the fifth bar, the score of 'Évadné' includes handwritten indications of the number of semiquaver beats in the piano part, and these numbers and lines are not in Boulez's hand. As these subdivisions would be useful for the pianist in parsing the score (they do not map onto the phrasing or accentuation of the vocal part), it is reasonable to surmise that these are annotations made by a performer. In addition, a score of 'Post-scriptum' has Ginette Martenot's name on the top left-hand corner of the first page and the name of the first ondes is circled throughout, so we can assume that she played this part. Again, there are annotations on this score which are not in Boulez's hand.[33] It therefore appears that 'Évadné' and 'Post-scriptum' were prepared for performance, and perhaps only one of the movements was actually included in the concert.

Suzanne Demarquez, a regular reviewer of Triptyque contemporary music concerts for *La Revue musicale*, was present at this premiere, which was given under the auspices of a new concert organisation called Contact. The concert 'was one of the events of the season in Paris and attracted a large audience.'[34] The main draw was the second Paris performance of Bartók's Sonata for Two Pianos and Percussion (1937) performed by a predominantly Hungarian ensemble. Demarquez does not provide a complete list of works performed in the rest of the concert, but she wrote: 'Two young Schoenberg adepts, Yvette Grimaud and Pierre Boulez, performed works in which piano, ondes Martenot and percussion interact more or less felicitously, also displaying a constant searching for

[31] Anonymous author, programme note on *Wise Music Classical* website: https://www.wisemusicclassical.com/work/49985/ [accessed June 2023].

[32] François Meïmoun, interview with Pierre Boulez, https://www.musicologie.org/publirem/entretien_avec_pierre_boulez.html [accessed June 2023].

[33] Paul Sacher Stiftung, Boulez collection, 577-0964-7, 577-0970 and 577-1009.

[34] Suzanne Demarquez, 'Le Triptyque', *La Revue musicale*, no. 208 (1948): pp. 22–3, at p. 22: '[…] a été un des événements de la Saison de Paris et avait attiré une foule considérable'.

something new for which [the composers] should be congratulated.'[35] The only work from this part of the concert specifically named by Demarquez is Luc-André Marcel's *Livre des eaux* (1947) for two pianos, ondes, vibraphone and percussion. Marcel was not, it appears, someone with whom Boulez was likely to find common ground. Presenting himself as an isolated figure, Marcel wrote in an article published in *Polyphonie*: 'I say that serialism represents one of the most acute *sado-masochistic* crises of the twentieth century' (emphasis his).[36]

What Demarquez's assessment does demonstrate is that a Boulez world premiere was not, in 1947, considered noteworthy enough to merit a reviewer's focus, and she also fails to mention Grimaud as a composer. Boulez told Meïmoun that '[Grimaud] had composed some pieces which contained quartertones, works that she copied for me and showed me the way.'[37] It is probable that her *AUM sur le nom de Jean-Claude Touche en 1/4 de ton non tempérés* (1945) for ondes Martenot, voice and two percussionists playing Chinese bells was performed on the same programme;[38] this is one of her three pieces for ondes Martenot, voice and percussion that were performed at the ISCM festival in Palermo in 1948.[39] The ensemble of Grimaud's work is strikingly similar to that of Boulez's first version of *Le Visage nuptial*, and it is a great pity that no score or recording of this work appears to have survived.

Boulez's publisher's programme note also uses the interesting phrase 'a scale model' about the first version of *Le Visage nuptial*, suggesting that the 1946 original both articulates the definitive form and already represents the essential kernel of the work – what Boulez might have called, paraphrasing Breton, its 'unshatterable kernel of darkness'. This is

35 Demarquez, 'Le Triptyque', p. 23: 'Deux jeunes adeptes schoenbergiennes, Yvette Grimaud et Pierre Boulez, ont fait entendre des pages où voix, piano, ondes et percussion s'enchevêtrent avec plus ou moins de bonheur mais aussi une constance dans la recherche de l'inédit dont il est juste de les féliciter.'

36 Luc-André Marcel, 'Lettres d'un solitaire sur le sujet du concert', *Polyphonie*, no. 5 (1949): pp. 3–29, at p. 8: 'Je dis que le dodécaphonisme représente une des crises *sado-masochistes* les plus aiguës du vingtième siècle.'

37 Meïmoun, interview with Boulez: 'Elle [Grimaud] avait composé des œuvres qui contenaient des quarts de ton, œuvres dont elle m'avait fait copie et qui me guidèrent dans cette voie.'

38 Jeanne Loriod, *Technique de l'onde électronique type Martenot*, 3 vols (Paris: Leduc, 1999); vol. 3, p. 34 lists some works by Grimaud that include the ondes Martenot, and as Loriod states that *AUM* was premiered in the Triptyque concert series, one can assume it was heard during the 1947 event alongside the extract of *Le Visage nuptial*.

39 Anonymous, 'The I.S.C.M. Festival at Palermo', *Musical Times*, vol. 89 no. 1270 (December 1948): p. 381. The article states that Grimaud's work features the 'ondes Martinet'.

the case because, according to an interview Boulez gave *Le Monde* which was published on 12 July 1990, '*Le Visage nuptial* clarifies the narration of [the] poem, models itself entirely on the form, and is literally organised according to it. The music invents itself in parallel with the text, following it in its twists and turns, from encounter to renunciation.'[40]

Boulez made two significant revisions to *Le Visage nuptial*, in 1951–3 and 1994, transforming it into a large orchestral work. The Bibliothèque Nationale de France's manuscript of the first version of 'Gravité' is interesting because Boulez faintly writes notes to himself for a possible expansion. Pencil indications for both 'Une Sopr.[ano] + Alto solo', which first appear at the major dynamic climax of the movement at bar 26, show that Boulez was already thinking about how to divide the taxing vocal line between two female singers, and elsewhere he gives indications for both solo and choral vocal parts.

It is clear that the first version of *Le Visage nuptial* was the source for subsequent revisions. What is particularly curious is that Boulez retained quartertones in 'Gravité' and 'Post-scriptum' – the two movements in the first version that could employ quartertones because they omitted the piano – for the first orchestral version, but the other three movements use the chromatic scale only. He therefore retained this inconsistency of harmonic language even though the original reason for it was no longer valid, and even though the 1951–3 orchestration ditches the two ondes Martenot. This inconsistency was not ironed out until the 1994 version, which omits quartertones altogether. In an BBC Radio 3 interval conversation that was broadcast in 1989, Boulez said his first version was 'very austere' and 'too strict' in style; he felt that Char's poems needed a setting with 'more instruments and more body'.[41] However, elsewhere he stated that when revising the work, he 'wanted to find again the flesh that this work had in 1946, and that I dried out in 1952 with too many theoretical argumentations …'.[42] Perhaps he meant that the 1946 version is austere in its texture, if not in his response to Char's passionate poetry.

The second version of *Le Visage nuptial* transfers the instrumental parts to a large orchestra and divides the extremely challenging and wide-ranging vocal line between two soloists – a soprano and contralto

---

[40] Cited in anonymous author, programme note on *Wise Music Classical* website: https://www.wisemusicclassical.com/work/49985/ [accessed June 2023].

[41] Pierre Boulez, interview with Martin Cotton broadcast during interval of Paris Festival d'Automne performance with BBC Symphony Orchestra, BBC Radio 3, 17 November 1989 (recording housed in the British Library).

[42] Cited in anonymous author, programme note on *Wise Music Classical* website: https://www.wisemusicclassical.com/work/49985/ [accessed June 2023].

– and female chorus. Much of the material for ondes Martenot is also transferred to a vocal part: for instance, the second ondes in 'Gravité', notated with an expanding and contracting wiggly line, becomes at the start of the movement a low sustained hum for the alto chorus. However, its enormous orchestra and frequently subdivided choral parts, if anything, augment the exceptional challenge this piece represents to performers, and the use of two voices plus chorus distances the piece from the intimate, personal emotions of Char's poetry. The 1951–3 version also suffers, as Boulez himself acknowledged, from his lack of experience as an orchestrator. His 1994 revision has greater orchestral clarity – Boulez told Martin Cotton that 'the lines of the first version are more present' in this version – and he removed the quartertones because they were 'not possible with a big mass of people [...], or they are so performed by chance that I had better rework them'. He compensated for the absence of quartertones with richer polyphony.[43]

Peter O'Hagan, for one, believes that the 1994 revision to *Le Visage nuptial* resulted in some lessening of its emotional impact: 'There is a great gain in both clarity of texture and exquisite detail of orchestral writing in the 1994 revision, but arguably some dilution of the starkness of emotional loss, expressed with almost unbearable poignancy in the final movement of the 1951–3 version. Rarely was Boulez to express himself with such directness in his later music [...]'.[44] But, even though most of the word setting and pitch content of the first version is retained in the later orchestrations, they cannot compete with the intense intimacy of the original 1946 composition.

Le Soleil des eaux

René Char's play *Le Soleil des eaux. Spectacle pour une toile de pêcheurs* (The sun of the waters. Spectacle for a backdrop of fishermen; 1946) has a topic that strongly resonates with today's environmental concerns, even though the action takes place in summer 1904. Set in the small town of Saint-Laurent on the banks of the Crillonne river in Provence, the play tells the story of the townsfolk, almost all of whom are involved in the fishing industry; their livelihood is being destroyed by factory waste leeching into the river. A love story involving the characters Francis, a fisherman who leads the protest against the factory, and Solange, daughter of the factory foreman, forms a side plot. The conflict between

---

[43] Boulez, interview with Cotton.
[44] Peter O'Hagan, 'Boulez and the foundation of IRCAM', in Richard Langham Smith and Caroline Potter (eds.), *French Music since Berlioz* (Aldershot: Ashgate, 2006), pp. 303–30, at p. 308.

local workers who depend on the river and the factory owners who are concerned solely with profit is at the heart of the play, and Char's published notes indicate that many of the characters are based on real people (indeed, he received correspondence after the broadcast from people who said they knew some of the characters).[45] *Le Soleil des eaux* could therefore be viewed as a very modern combination of theatre and quasi-documentary reportage.

The location of Char's play is one he knew intimately. He was born in l'Isle-sur-Sorgue, and after World War II he returned to the area of his birth to dedicate himself to poetry. Having been involved in the Resistance during the war, in its aftermath Char felt the need to move towards a simpler, more accessible poetic language;[46] his 'chansons' (literally 'songs') of the late 1940s, including the texts later set by Boulez, are emblematic of this more direct style. One of Char's sources of inspiration was friends from the region who continued a performing tradition that dates back to the troubadours of the medieval period. In his commentary on the play, Char wrote:

> In the evenings they read aloud, often adding material and miming the events. Between them, they perform the play [...]. They had asked me to write something for them that would be a play without exactly being a play, in the course of which they could easily veer off and touch on quite familiar memories, but mainly something that would be like life multiplied two or three times, not more, exploring the secrets of the landscape as well as the need for rebellion, whether victorious or in defeat, but never in vain.[47]

The text of *Le Soleil des eaux* was developed, in rather Boulezian fashion, in several different iterations. The first version was broadcast on 29 April 1948 by French Radio (la Radiodiffusion Française) as a play produced by André Trutat with incidental music by Boulez conducted by André Girard. The text of this play, with watercolour illustrations by Georges Braque, was first published by Henri Matarasso in a limited

---

[45] See René Char, 'Pourquoi du "Soleil des eaux"? Correspondance', in *Œuvres complètes* (Paris: Gallimard, 1983), pp. 1061–2.

[46] See Christine Dupouy, *René Char* (Paris: Belfond, 1987), p. 247.

[47] Char, 'Pourquoi du "Soleil des eaux"', p. 1056: 'Ils se font le soir la lecture à haute voix, *lecture à laquelle souvent ils ajoutent*, et en miment les péripéties. Entre eux, c'est *se jouer la pièce*. [...] Ils m'avaient demandé d'écrire pour eux quelque chose qui fût du théâtre sans en être précisément, dans la trame de quoi ils pussent aisément se glisser et toucher des souvenirs assez proches, mais principalement quelque chose qui fût de la vie deux ou trois fois multipliée, pas plus, et s'étalant sur les secrets du paysage autant que sur la nécessité de la révolte, victorieuse ou défaite, jamais vaine.' Emphasis in the text.

edition of 200 copies in 1949, and then appeared with Gallimard in 1951. There was also talk of a film starring Jean Vilar, though this project proved impractical and was shelved;[48] a Char text published as part of the preface of the Matarasso edition is bluntly titled 'ÉCHEC D'UN FILM' (failure of a film). It is clear that Char regretted that, for financial reasons, the film could not be made. Radio France reprised the radio play in 1967, though not with Boulez's music.

René Char gave Boulez two poems at the time he composed the incidental music, neither of which appear in the published version of his play. These texts prompted the composer to recontextualise some of his radio work; Boulez told Martin Cotton that otherwise 'this incidental music will be lost [...] I could take these poems and put the incidental music around them.'[49] Gerald Bennett notes that a first revision was made in October 1948.[50] This short cantata, which is under ten minutes long, is based on the poems 'Complainte du lézard amoureux' and 'La Sorgue (Chanson pour Yvonne)'; the first of these was included in the radio play after scene 14 (this is the end of no. 10 of the orchestral score),[51] with minor differences in the text and music of both versions, and 'La Sorgue' is the second poem in Char's collection *La Fontaine narrative* (1947). While the nature theme, especially its multiple references to a river, connects 'La Sorgue' to the radio play *Le Soleil des eaux*, this poem did not appear in the broadcast. The cantata version was premiered in Paris on 18 July 1950, conducted by Roger Désormière with Irène Joachim, Joseph Peyron and Pierre Mollet as the soprano, tenor and bass soloists; a third version was made in 1958, expanding the orchestra and adding a chorus, and in 1965 Boulez made his final revision for soprano solo, chorus and orchestra.

The French scholar Benoît Tarjabayle demonstrated in a master's thesis completed in 1995 that the cantata version of *Le Soleil des eaux* draws extensively on material from the radio incidental music.[52]

[48] See Edouard Launet and René Solis, 'René Char renaît', *Libération* (5 July 2007), https://www.liberation.fr/cahier-special/2007/07/05/rene-char-renait_97619 [accessed June 2023].

[49] Boulez, interview with Cotton.

[50] Gerald Bennett, 'The early works', in William Glock (ed.), *Pierre Boulez: A Symposium* (London: Eulenburg, 1986), pp. 41–84, at p. 75.

[51] Catherine Steinegger (*Pierre Boulez et le théâtre*, Liège: Mardaga, 2012) writes (p. 140): 'Dans le texte dramatique, ce poème ['Complainte du lézard amoureux'] est placé après la scène XIV consacré au couple Apollon et Marie-Thérèse.'

[52] Benoît Tarjabayle, 'René Char, Pierre Boulez: *Le Soleil des eaux*. Étude critique et analytique', 2 vols., mémoire de maîtrise, Université de Paris-Sorbonne (Paris IV), 1995. While this analysis is not without flaws, it is an impressive achievement and by far the most detailed study of the work.

Tarjabayle's thesis, like much existing work on Boulez, focuses largely on the composer's serial manipulations: for instance, he points out that the work is based on three partly related twelve-note series which were first used in the radio incidental music and re-employed in the cantata. Boulez's recycling of musical material from one version to the next underlines that he considered this to be a developing single work – a work in progress – even though there are significant differences in Char's textual material for the two versions. The published play has twenty-six named characters and is divided into forty short scenes (a later version has forty-two), and only one of the texts set by Boulez in his cantata version appears in the radio version of the work.

Boulez's incidental music is more than three times longer than his later concert piece for voices and orchestra titled *Le Soleil des eaux*.[53] This incidental music is divided into thirty-one short sections, and it is not obvious how these link to the dialogue as there are no verbal cues on the orchestral score. There is a good deal of reuse of material within the score (for example, the sixth and fifteenth sections are almost identical), and the orchestral texture is for the most part less dense than in the cantata version. Boulez writes for an orchestra with double woodwind, with one flute doubling on piccolo, the first clarinet also playing E flat clarinet, and the second oboe and second clarinet doubling on cor anglais and bass clarinet respectively. Three horns in F, two trumpets (the first doubling on piccolo trumpet), a trombone, a tuba, harp, percussion and string section complete the orchestral forces. Only in places do we see the overlapping contrapuntal intricacy of the *Soleil des eaux* concert piece we now know; while the cantata version reuses a lot of the material of the radio version, it is often reorchestrated and complexifying detail is added.

One important consistent feature of the different versions of *Le Soleil des eaux* is the use of three twelve-note rows, the most important of which comprises the pitches E, B flat, D, F sharp, A, F, B, E flat, G, A flat, C, C sharp. For instance, these pitches, in that order, are the opening notes of the unaccompanied setting of 'Complainte du lézard amoureux' (Ex. 4.5), which is the musical centre of the action of the radio play. This intimate moment, which appears at the end of the tenth section of the orchestral score (pp. 60–1), is framed by orchestral passages which, in a manner already typical of Boulez, might use the row in a fragmentary manner. One example of this appears eight bars before the start of 'Complainte du lézard

---

[53] The complete score, which is in a copyist's hand, is now housed in the Paul Sacher Stiftung, Boulez collection, microfilm 578.

Ex. 4.5 Boulez, *Le Soleil des eaux*: 'Complainte du lézard amoureux', opening

amoureux' (p. 58 of the score), where the flute and harp have a solo consisting of the opening of the row, and this important moment initiates a slight quickening of the tempo. There are many similar examples elsewhere in the orchestral score. G. W. Hopkins, in an article introducing the British premiere of the concert version, noted that 'The opening series is not used in a Schoenbergian way, but is subjected to various permutations.'[54] Boulez might also introduce a note 'foreign' to a twelve-tone sequence which then initiates a new statement of the row, and he frequently uses fragments of the core tone row. 'Complainte du lézard amoureux' is incorporated with only minor textual changes, including one additional verse, in the cantata, but while the radio version of the setting was sung from beginning to end without a break, in the concert piece Boulez breaks up the verses with orchestral interludes.

One of the most curious sections of the radio incidental music happens about a third of the way through, on pp. 49–50 of the orchestral score. Here, a soprano and alto chorus enters, and its music, which has no text, forms the conclusion of section 6 of Boulez's score and the entirety of section 7 (the first eleven bars are given as Ex. 4.6). While no verbal cues are present on the score, this twenty-six-bar wordless vocal section would work very well with Char's scene 8, in which Solange and Francis are in a cedar wood, alone for the first time. The only dialogue in this scene is Solange whispering 'Il n'y avait que de toi' (There was only you), and the presence of a silent bar in this passage (bar 19 out of 26) leaves space for Solange's words. Sometimes in rhythmic unison and sometimes in counterpoint, the voices' yearning sevenths create an emotionally intense, expressionist mood. This material stands apart harmonically, too, from the major-third-focused tone row that forms the material of 'Complainte du lézard amoureux'; it is based on a different series (G, F sharp, E flat, D, A flat, D flat, C, B, B flat, E, F, A) which subsequently became the prime series of

---

[54] G. W. Hopkins, 'Boulez's "Le Soleil des eaux"', *Tempo*, no. 68 (Spring 1964): pp. 35–7, at p. 36.

Ex. 4.6 Boulez, *Le Soleil des eaux*, first version: soprano/alto duet, bars 1–11

'La Sorgue'.[55] (For this second movement of the cantata version, the musical source material therefore predated Boulez's acquaintance with the text.) Perhaps the most interesting aspect of this wordless vocal section is its early evidence of Boulez using voices as part of an instrumental texture, not only as a vehicle for communicating words, seen most notably in the final movement of *Le Marteau sans maître*. This section also shows his willingness to be impractical, as French Radio would have needed to employ a female chorus only for this twenty-six-bar section.

This first large-scale orchestral score by Boulez incorporated material from other, smaller-scale pieces which he subsequently withdrew. Gerald Bennett identified that some of the score recycles a *Passacaille-variations* (1948) for two pianos. He writes 'For the incidental music to Char's drama, besides writing a good deal that was new, Boulez had used bits and pieces of the February 1948 movement quite out of context but in an order appropriate to the dramatic development of the play'.[56] This *Passacaille-variations*, dedicated to Andrée

[55] See Tarjabayle, '*Le Soleil des eaux*' for more detail on this, especially p. 85 and vol. 2, example 4.
[56] Bennett, 'The early works', p. 66.

Vaurabourg-Honegger, started life as the first movement of a Sonata for two pianos (1948) which, continuing the theme of recycling, itself drew on a three-movement Quartet for ondes Martenot which also remained unpublished. [57]

The 1948 radio broadcast of the play *Le Soleil des eaux* was the first opportunity for a wider listening public to encounter Boulez's music. François Ségo's review of the production was mixed; focusing on Char's text, he wrote that the thirty-one scenes were 'too brief, too fragmentary' and overall the work was 'far too long for what the author had to say'. Finally, he mentioned that *Le Soleil des eaux* was

> accompanied by music by Pierre Boulez. Accompanied is not the right word because the composer took pains to add, in a sense, an extra character to the text, to integrate it into the play rather than illustrate it. Perhaps, bound by the text, he was not able to express himself fully; one can, in any event, expect much of him in this medium and in others. [58]

Boulez's revision of the work turned it into a concert piece. He told Benoît Tarjabayle in 1994 about his decision to expand 'Complainte du lézard amoureux': 'rather than prolonging it artificially, [I wanted to] underline the structure of the poem using extracts of the incidental music.'[59] This is demonstrated, for instance, when Boulez cannibalises the fifth and sixth sections of the radio incidental music to form most of the interludes that appear between the verses of the poem. While 'La Sorgue' was not part of the original radio play at all, Boulez also reuses material from his score as the basis for this setting. For example, the opening bars of this movement are taken from the eighteenth number, and he reuses number 29, marked 'sourdement agité' (dully agitated), extensively in the second half of 'La Sorgue', adding subdivisions to the string parts but retaining most of the pitch and rhythmic content. Surviving working manuscripts show Boulez explicitly using numbers

57 O'Hagan, 'Boulez and the foundation of IRCAM', p. 308.

58 François Ségo, 'A la radio: une tentative paysanne' [review of *Le Soleil des eaux*], *Les Lettres françaises* (6 May 1948): p. 6: 'une série de scènes trop brèves, trop hachées [...] c'est, en somme, beaucoup trop long pour ce que l'auteur avait à dire [...]. *Soleil des eaux* était accompagné d'une musique de Pierre Boulez. Accompagné n'est certes pas le mot, car le musicien, ici, s'est efforcé d'ajouter, en quelque sorte, un nouveau personnage à la pièce, de l'y intégrer, et non de l'illustrer. Sans doute, lié par le texte, n'a-t-il pu donner toute sa mesure; on peut, en tout cas, beaucoup attendre de lui en ce domaine et en d'autres.'

59 Tarjabayle, '*Le Soleil des eaux*', p. 11; interview on 11 May 1994: 'plutôt que de faire un prolongement artificiel, de souligner l'articulation des strophes par des extraits de la musique de scène'.

relating to sections of the radio version to remind himself of the material he wanted to reuse in the cantata.

As in *Le Visage nuptial*, the wide range of vocal expression is a salient feature of this second version of *Le Soleil des eaux*, particularly in 'La Sorgue'. Tarjabayle's important interview with Boulez reveals that the composer aimed for two vocally contrasting movements: 'For the first movement I had a solo soprano, I thought for the second there ought to be something more collective – that is, polyphonic – to contrast, where the voices would be part of the orchestral texture.'[60] In the first version of this two-movement work, Boulez uses soprano, tenor and bass soloists, and evidence from manuscript sketches now housed in the Paul Sacher Stiftung suggests that Boulez's original conception of 'La Sorgue' was for an entirely sung text (that is, with no other types of vocal expression such as speaking or Sprechstimme). A later orchestral sketch, dated 31 October 1948, is much closer to the vocal writing in the cantata version, where Boulez often uses unpitched but precisely rhythmically notated chanting.[61] This ensures the text is clearly audible, but the chanting generally appears in counterpoint with elaborately embellished vocal lines where the musical rather than the textual value predominates. Hopkins interestingly considers this a 'surrealistic effect':

> It is, above all, the use of declamation, in addition to normal singing, which creates the surrealistic effect. The effect of Sprechstimme – as in *Pierrot Lunaire*, *Wozzeck* and *A Survivor from Warsaw* – always appears to tend towards the anti-realistic, and it is notable that this technique has done much of its best work in the service of expressionistic music; this is because it heightens the artificiality (and perhaps even the absurdity) of the relationship of words to music. Boulez has seized on this effect and used it in a thoroughly appropriate context. The insistent chanting of the word 'rivière' throughout this movement ['La Sorgue'] is haunting, as are some of the individual effects.[62]

The concert premiere of the two-movement *Le Soleil des eaux* was conducted by the work's dedicatee Roger Désormière at the Théâtre des Champs-Élysées in Paris on 18 July 1950. Only one critic from the major daily newspapers appears to have been present, as only one review survives, by Clarendon (Bernard Gavoty), published in *Le Figaro* on 3 August 1950. Gavoty addresses the distinguished singers as 'unfortunate

---

60 Tarjabayle, '*Le Soleil des eaux*', p. 18: 'J'avais pour le premier mouvement une soprano solo, j'ai pensé qu'il faudrait pour le deuxième, quelque chose de plus collectif, c'est-à-dire, polyphonique, pour contraster, où les voix seraient incluses dans la texture orchestrale.'

61 Paul Sacher Stiftung, Boulez collection, Mappe A Dossier 4f,1 and 4f,2b2.

62 Hopkins, 'Boulez's "Le Soleil des eaux"', p. 36.

victims of a capricious tyrant' who had to deal with 'unsingable scores', though the same reviewer surprisingly claims he was also 'intrigued' by Boulez's Second Piano Sonata when it was performed earlier that year.[63] But the concert was recorded and is now available on CD, and not only is this a remarkably detailed and accurate performance, but the audience did not seem to share Gavoty's reservations, as enthusiastic applause is audible after the end of the piece.[64]

Peyser's excitable claim 'The escape from death – or from the love affair – apparently precipitated a burst of prodigious talent'[65] is not entirely borne out in reality. The first versions of the two Char settings and Second Piano Sonata were followed by a period of experimentation, revision and new projects including a string quartet (*Livre pour quatuor*) and the totally serial *Polyphonie X*. However, these projects proved problematic: the quartet went through a number of revisions and was not released in almost completed form until 2012, and while the premiere of *Polyphonie X* was recorded in 1951, it was soon withdrawn.[66] No new completed compositions appeared until the first book of *Structures* for two pianos (1951–2). After Boulez's remarkable formative years, it is as if he had burned himself out creatively. What is even more significant is the presence in Boulez's later music of ideas and concepts that interested him in the late 1940s; even specific musical themes were given very different life in the decades that followed. The next chapter shows just how persistent was this creative core of his identity.

---

[63] Cited in Dominique Jameux, *Boulez* (Paris: Fayard, 1984), pp. 59–60: 'Victimes infortunées d'un tyran capricieux [...] vos partitions résolument inchantables [...] La [deuxième] Sonate de Pierre Boulez nous avait intrigués cet hiver [...].'

[64] See *Roger Désormière: Orchestre national de la RTF*, INA, mémoire vive IMV041 (2001).

[65] Peyser, *Boulez: Composer, Conductor, Enigma*, pp. 33–4.

[66] The piece was revived for two performances in Lucerne and Donaueschingen in 2021 by the Lucerne Festival Contemporary Orchestra conducted by Baldur Brönnimann; see https://www.lucernefestival.ch/en/magazine/lfco-bei-den-donaueschinger-musiktagen-2021/128 [accessed June 2023].

5

THE CHARM OF NUMBERS: CONTINUING THREADS IN BOULEZ'S LATER MUSIC

BOULEZ'S EXTRAORDINARY FORMATIVE PHASE was followed by a period when he completed very few works. After the Second Piano Sonata – explicitly an annihilation of the classical sonata model – and his Char settings, which Paul Griffiths so aptly describes as 'confirmation that this last destruction proceeded through love',[1] how was Boulez to emerge from the wreckage? What would remain?

It is perhaps not surprising that this extremely intense compositional phase should have been followed by one of consolidation, though there are missing pieces in this jigsaw; for instance, Boulez started sketching a *Symphonie-concertante* for piano and orchestra in 1947 but lost the score. And even in the earliest stages of his career, Boulez's penchant for revising works was evident, and both *Le Visage nuptial* and *Le Soleil des eaux* would not reach their final forms for many years. What is more interesting is that Boulez's works of the 1940s served as repositories of musical ideas for new compositions almost until the end of his life. For Susan Bradshaw, 'it is from the mid-1970s that he seems more and more to have opted for the art of recomposition at the expense of composition',[2] and the *Notations* in particular were reimagined in multiple guises, from the reuse of an individual theme to the recasting of some of these tiny piano pieces as much longer works for huge orchestra. His frequent reuse of the seven-note motif from the seventh *Notation*, as well as his subsequent recycling of a six-note motif based on the name of the philanthropist and conductor Paul Sacher, show that these ideas had the function of a fetish for Boulez. His continual obsession with these found objects is the main focus of this chapter.

[1]   Paul Griffiths, *Boulez* (Oxford: Oxford University Press, 1978), p. 16.
[2]   Susan Bradshaw, 'Comparing notes', *Musical Times*, vol. 137 no. 1844 (1996): pp. 5–12, at p. 5.

Boulez's relative lack of musical productivity immediately after his Second Piano Sonata also had roots in his work as musical director of the Renaud–Barrault company, not only because these duties left him with less time to focus on composition, but also because his tours with the company prompted him to reassess his earlier enthusiasms. His shifting attitude to Artaud's 'collective hysteria' is exhibited in a letter written in 1950 to Pierre Souvtchinsky from Buenos Aires at the end of a tour with the Renaud–Barrault company. He recalled seeing a Brazilian macumba (traditional sacred rite), recalling

> some impressive hysterical states, but the rites and cults that are addressed to God, to the devil, to the phallus or to the virgin, are always ineffectual rites and cults for their own ends; I am more and more convinced that Artaud was on completely the wrong track and that the *Coup de dés* contains the true magic, which leaves no room, even for hysteria, hysteria being one of the most passive states, despite the paradox that implies.[3]

The reference to the *Coup de dés* is to Mallarmé's startling typographical poem *Un coup de dés jamais n'abolira le hasard* (A throw of dice will never abolish chance; 1897), and Boulez's letter underscores his fundamental intellectual pivot away from Artaud and towards Mallarmé. Mallarmé's importance to Boulez from the late 1940s to the end of his life has been explored by many authors, and a detailed assessment is beyond the scope of this book. However, the paradox expressed in the title of Mallarmé's innovative poem is an angle under which Boulez continued to explore his surrealist-inflected notion of chance.

This shift towards Mallarmé is first apparent in the title of Boulez's string quartet, *Livre pour quatuor* (Book for string quartet, begun in 1948), an obvious reference to the poet's all-encompassing *Livre*, the hypothetical 'book' which represents the totality of an artist's work. Some of the quartet's material is drawn from twelve-note series employed in the Second Piano Sonata, but the overall structure of the work is quite unlike that of the sonata. Boulez initially conceived of a work in six

---

[3]   Cited in Edward Campbell, 'Pierre Boulez: composer, traveller, correspondent', in Edward Campbell and Peter O'Hagan (eds.), *Pierre Boulez Studies* (Cambridge: Cambridge University Press, 2016), pp. 3–24, at p. 7: 'Nous avons vu une macumba brésilienne; quelques états hystériques impressionnants mais les rites et les cultes, qui s'adressent à Dieu, au diable, au phallus ou à la vierge, ce sont toujours des rites et des cultes impuissants dans leur propre dénouement; je suis de plus en plus convaincu qu'Artaud était en pleine fausse piste et que le Coup de Dés recèle la vraie magie, qui ne donne aucune prise, même à l'hystérie, l'hystérie étant un des états les plus passifs, en dépit du paradoxe que cela implique.' I am grateful to Peter O'Hagan for locating the French original of this letter in the Bibliothèque Nationale de France.

sections whose individual elements are not movements but 'feuillets' (leaves) which were grouped in pairs, with the first and second, third and fifth, and fourth and sixth sections being twinned. These 'pages' or 'leaves' continue the book metaphor, though not in the sense that there is a story with a narrative that the reader/listener needs to follow from beginning to end. Although an initial version of sections 1–3 and 5 was completed in July 1949, *Livre pour quatuor* was not performed until 1955 at the Donaueschingen Festival, and then in fragmentary form, as only the first two sections were played. The quartet remained incomplete in its originally intended form – the fourth movement was never released – though Boulez's final revision of the remaining five movements was recorded by the Quatuor Diotima in 2012 under the composer's supervision.[4] Another work composed under Mallarmé's impact, the Third Piano Sonata (begun 1955), similarly was never finished in its originally conceived five-movement version.

Musically speaking, *Livre pour quatuor* represents another pivot, from Schoenberg to Webern, and its often spare yet contrapuntally intense musical texture, using a wide variety of string playing techniques, is very distant from the violent episodes of the Second Piano Sonata. It is as if there is a distinct break between the emotional world of the expressionist Schoenberg/Artaud early work and the Webern/Mallarmé universe of pieces from *Livre pour quatuor*. And this renewal of Boulez's style went hand in hand with a new theory of structure derived from Mallarmé, that of the 'work in progress', where a single piece is not an isolated work but part of a large, overarching oeuvre, and at the same time this single piece in itself might embody only a fragment of the composer's original plan.

Boulez most lucidly explored his Mallarméan notion of the work as fragment in 'La Mémoire, l'écriture et la forme', the final published section of *Leçons de musique*. Here, he distinguishes two different notions, one which is either orientated ('orientée'), where the fragments must be listened to in a set order, or non-orientated or 'floating' ('non-orientée', 'flottante'), where the order of the sections of a work is not fixed. The conclusion of this article – a conclusion that, unsurprisingly, can only be provisional according to Boulez – reads:

> [T]he work can only be the fragment of an imagined whole. If the work were considered as a totality, this could only be a skilfully constructed illusion, one which, like light through a prism, is split into its constituent fragments which as the work moves forward through time, take on the

---

[4] Quatuor Diotima, *Pierre Boulez: Livre pour quatuor révisé*, Megadisc Classics MDC 7796 (2015).

appearance of the whole. But, as in some novels by Kafka whose ending is uncertain or even unfinished, the work as such – beyond the linguistic narrative functions which it has obeyed for a long time – can only be unfinished, a fragment of an unreal, hypothetical totality. As [musical] language no longer has any constraints, particularly not cadential constraints, any end can only artificially plug a whole, which absolutely contradicts this notion of an end or completion.[5]

If an individual work is indeed but a fragment of a whole that can exist only in theory, it was also true for Boulez that individual ideas could take on new life when recycled in new contexts. *Notations* proved particularly fertile: Theo Hirsbrunner's 1986 article in *Melos*, the first detailed study of the work, details multiple links between the twelve short pieces and subsequent works, most notably the reworking of *Notations* 5 and 6 in 'Le Vierge, le vivace et le bel aujourd'hui' (1957), Boulez's first *Improvisation sur Mallarmé* that became part of the cycle *Pli selon pli*.[6] Tobias Bleek, writing some years later, mentions that this passage had an intermediate form as music for a radio play composed in 1957.[7] This larger-scale recycling is not unusual in Boulez, and some small fragments gained multiple new leases of life as recontextualised found objects, which more or less explicitly had a talismanic value.

In conversation with Peter O'Hagan in 2013, Boulez acknowledged O'Hagan's point that the seven-note theme of the seventh piece of his set of piano *Notations* relates to the theme of a series of works titled *...explosante-fixe...*. Boulez's very interesting response was:

> It could be once I was looking at the old manuscripts, and I picked it up. You know that with Surrealism, one has spoken very much of *objets trouvés* – one takes something you meet by chance. I myself have *objets*

[5] Pierre Boulez, 'L'Œuvre: tout ou fragment', in *Leçons de musique (Points de repère III)*, ed. Jean-Jacques Nattiez (Paris: Christian Bourgois, 2005), pp. 671–713, at p. 713: 'l'œuvre ne peut être que le fragment d'un tout imaginaire. L'œuvre considérée comme tout ne serait qu'une illusion habilement construite, mais comme la lumière à travers le prisme, se décompose en constituants fragmentaires, qui dans une continuité temporelle, reprennent l'apparence du tout. Mais, comme dans certaines nouvelles de Kafka à la fin incertaine, voire inaboutie, l'œuvre en tant que telle – hors des fonctions narratives du langage auxquelles elle a longuement obéi – ne pourrait être qu'inachevée, fragment d'un tout irréel, hypothétique. Le langage n'ayant plus de contraintes, y compris, et surtout, les contraintes cadentielles, toute fin ne pourrait qu'artificiellement bloquer un tout qui contredit absolument cette notion de fin, d'achèvement.'

[6] Theo Hirsbrunner, 'Pierre Boulez: *Notations* (1945)', *Melos*, vol. 2 (1986): pp. 2–20.

[7] Tobias Bleek, 'Pierre Boulez: *Douze Notations*', https://explorethescore.org/pierre-boulez-douze-notations-history-and-context-musical-metamorphoses.html [accessed June 2023].

trouvés but in my own production, and sometimes when I look at old works, I think, 'Oh, I have not done anything with that – I must begin' – and it comes as I turn the pages of a work and suddenly find something of interest to me. It's a mixture of chance and a will to explore and work on things.[8]

The notion of a theme that functions as a 'found object' to be employed subsequently in different contexts forms a continuing thread in Boulez's oeuvre and is the clearest demonstration that this overtly surrealist concept was at the heart of his creative life. Two of these found objects will be explored here: the seven-note theme of the seventh *Notation*, and the SACHER theme, more literally a 'found object' as it was provided to Boulez by a third party.

Two *objets trouvés*

1. Magic numbers: from *Notation 7* to *Mémoriale ... explosante-fixe... Originel*

Breton's suggestive fragmentary phrase 'explosante-fixe' was used by Boulez in the title of a series of works composed between 1972 and 1993. First, Boulez provided a tribute to Stravinsky for the British contemporary music journal *Tempo* in 1972 as one of a commissioned set of compositions in homage to the composer who had died the previous year. This is more a construction kit than a fully realised composition; a seven-note idea (E flat – G – D – A flat – B flat – A natural – E natural), labelled 'Originel', is surrounded by six transformations labelled 'Transitoires', and the notated music is accompanied by six pages of instructions which need to be followed in order to turn this raw material into a musical work. The seven-note idea is identical to the seven-note theme of *Notation 7*. Boulez's dedication at the top right-hand corner of the score reads like a magic spell:

À fin – d'évoquer | Igor Stravinsky
de conjurer | son absence

[In order – to evoke | Igor Stravinsky
to conjure up | his absence]

It is significant that E flat (specifically, the E flat above middle C on the piano) is the first note of 'Originel', and the 'Transitoire' sections constantly return to this pitch. This note had a symbolic value because in German musical notation, E flat is Es (pronounced S); this oblique reference to Stravinsky's

---

8   Peter O'Hagan, *Boulez and the Piano* (Abingdon: Routledge, 2017), p. 329.

165

initial is the only explicit connection between *...explosante-fixe...* and Stravinsky and is the instigator of the spell being conjured up.

Let us return to the context of the composition of *Notation* 7, as recounted by Boulez in an interview with Tobias Bleek: 'This piece recalls Asian music. I was listening to a lot of non-European music at the time. Once I heard a dirge sung to save the soul of a man who had drowned.'[9] The tempo marking of the piece, 'Hiératique' (Hieratic), underlines the background idea of a religious ceremony of unspecified, but non-European, origin. If, in 1945 when it was composed, the theme of *Notation* 7 was Boulez's equivalent of a musical charm to save the soul of a recently departed man, surely it retained this meaning when reused many years later. This 'charm' signification is even stronger when one considers the other contextual influence on *Notation* 7: the opening bar of Jolivet's *Mana* (1935), a piano suite whose title openly connects its musical substance with a mystical force, as we saw in Chapter 2.

Boulez told Joan Peyser a story about his choice of the flute as soloist for *...explosante-fixe...*:

> I began to think about the work in August 1971, soon after receiving the commission. That month I visited a castle in Scotland that had once belonged to the Duchess of Argyll. The woman who invited my sister and me was an Austrian woman who lived in France, and she had with her a son who was not very oriented; he did not know what to do with his life. Since then he committed suicide. The young man played the flute as an amateur and he improvised in this empty eighteenth-century castle. It was quite impressive. I had the idea then of the work beginning with a flute solo.[10]

There is an unnerving coincidence between this anecdote about a young flautist's tragic death and *Mémoriale*, a subsequent version of the Stravinsky tribute which is dedicated to Lawrence Beauregard, who died in 1985 (several years after the publication of Peyser's book).

From the seven-note 'Originel' theme of the Stravinsky tribute – ultimately, from its root in *Notation* 7 – a long sequence of works emerged. First, a short piece titled *...explosante-fixe...* for violin, clarinet and trumpet was performed by the London Sinfonietta in St John's, Smith Square in London in June 1972 and soon withdrawn, but the following year, it was developed into a work for solo flute, clarinet, trumpet, harp, vibraphone, violin, viola, cello and electronics. Each soloist has its moment in the spotlight, with the flute both opening and closing the

9   http://www.explorethescore.org/pierre-boulez-douze-notations-boulez-video-interview.html [accessed June 2023], filmed in May 2012; English subtitles by Bleek.

10   Joan Peyser, *Boulez: Composer, Conductor, Enigma* (London: Cassell, 1977), p. 238.

piece; each uses the seven-note 'Originel' theme, ensuring a consistent harmonic identity throughout, though the soloists have some flexibility in their precise choice of tempo. (This version effectively has seven solo parts, as the harp and vibraphone are treated as a single unit.) The electronic element was provided by a halaphone, described by Harold C. Schonberg, who reviewed the work for the *New York Times*, as a piece of equipment that

> give[s] a composer a chance to experiment with a new kind of sound, and all kinds of ingenious effects are possible. For example, '...explosante/fixe ...' starts with a flute solo. Presently the flutist is in effect playing a duet with herself (it was Paula Robison at this concert), with her sound coming out in various parts of the hall in a different timbre and even a time delay (for this, an echo chamber).[11]

This version was performed five times, first in 1973 in New York, then in Rome, at the Proms in London, at the Donaueschingen Festival, and finally in Paris in 1974. The recorded Proms performance, which lasts around thirty-five minutes,[12] features material which will be familiar to listeners who know the final 1991–3 version of *...explosante-fixe...* and the shorter realisation of the material as *Mémoriale*, which will be discussed later. But the halaphone did not prove reliable, and Susan Bradshaw wrote, 'It was the all-too-audible failure of electronic control over musical events at a Proms performance in August 1973 that decided Boulez to abandon any attempt to finalise his chamber ensemble version.'[13] Bradshaw's valuable commentary on this unpublished version tells us that this *...explosante-fixe...* was

> a purely linear construct, in which each instrumental part followed its own individually-paced route through the transitional material [the 'Transitoire' sections], with the players cueing each other on entry until the flute (the first to start and the last to end) reached a properly harmonious conclusion on the E flat tonic of the Stravinsky matrix.[14]

Boulez described this structure as 'not complete chance, but prepared chance':[15] the music is fully notated, but the speed of the journey

---

[11] Harold C. Schonberg, 'Music: now we have the halaphone', *New York Times* (7 January 1973): p. 65.

[12] This recording, made on 17 August 1973, is housed in the British Library Sound Archive (P939).

[13] Bradshaw, 'Comparing notes', p. 8.

[14] Bradshaw, 'Comparing notes', p. 12.

[15] Pierre Boulez, *Par volonté et par hasard: entretiens avec Célestin Deliège* (Paris: Seuil, 1975), pp. 137–8: '[...] non pas de hasard complet, mais de hasard préparé [...].'

through the musical material is left up to the performers' judgement. It seems that in 1973, there was too much tension between explosion and stability in this work, and, thanks to unreliable technology, it was too heavily balanced towards uncontrollable explosion.

Over the next two decades, ...*explosante-fixe*... proliferated beyond the bounds of a chamber work, culminating in a piece composed in 1991–3 for three flutes and large orchestra lasting half an hour, and this exploits only a small part of the 'Transitoire' material. But before this version was finalised, Boulez used the seven-note *Notation* 7 theme again in two fully notated works. First, *Rituel in memoriam Bruno Maderna* (1974–5) was dedicated to the Italian composer and conductor (1920–73), who was a great champion of contemporary music. *Rituel* was composed remarkably quickly and premiered in London on 2 April 1975. The instrumental ensemble is divided into eight groups of different sizes, all but one of which features a percussionist, and Boulez indicates specific stage positions for each group on his score.

Reusing the *Notation* 7 theme in *Rituel* reinforces still more the theme's indelible associations with mourning and tribute. The seven-note theme forms the basis of the musical material in *Rituel*, and Bradshaw underlines the primordial importance of the number seven: 'so absolute is the Rule of Seven that it permeates every level of the organisation: from the smallest particular detail of pitch and duration, including the number of instruments and instrumental groups, to the number and length of the sections whose sum is the eventual form of the work.'[16] This is indeed the case, although Boulez disguises the symbolism by pointing out that the piece is 'for orchestra in eight groups': at the same time, there are seven groups each with between one and seven instruments, and a larger ensemble of 14 (2 × 7) brass players linked to a group comprising seven gongs and seven tam-tams. In this sense, *Rituel* parallels Messiaen's much larger orchestral and choral work *La Transfiguration de Notre Seigneur Jésus-Christ* (1965–9), which is based on the same number: for instance, there are seven soloists and fourteen movements in Messiaen's work (and seven words in the title).

Brice Tissier sees in *Rituel* a wider use of the magic number, which most interestingly he connects with Artaud's numerical symbolism, as illustrated in the author's letters and more tellingly in the 'Tutuguri' section of *Pour en finir avec le jugement de Dieu*.[17] Written in the wake

---

[16]   Susan Bradshaw, 'The instrumental and vocal music', in William Glock (ed.), *Pierre Boulez: A Symposium* (London: Eulenburg, 1986), pp. 127–229, at p. 217.

[17]   Brice Tissier, 'Pierre Boulez et le *Théâtre de la cruauté* d'Antonin Artaud: de *Pelléas* à *Rituel, in memoriam Bruno Maderna*', Intersections, vol. 28 no. 2 (2008): pp. 31–50, at pp. 44–45.

of Artaud's journey to Mexico and participation in a drug-fuelled ritual, 'Tutuguri' also makes extensive reference to musical instruments ('Sur le déchirement d'un tambour et d'une trompette longue', On the ripping of a tambour and a long trumpet note), and Artaud's recorded performance is self-accompanied by wild improvised percussion interjections. The ritual as described by Artaud is fuelled by a combination of raw essences and numerical symbolism:

> The Rite is that the new sun passes through seven points before
> bursting in the orifice of the earth.
> And there are six men, one for each sun, and a seventh man who is the
> sun in all its
> rawness
> dressed in black, with red skin.
> Now, this seventh man
> is a horse,
> a horse led by a man.
> But it's the horse who is the sun
> and not the man.[18]

To return to *Rituel*, Boulez's score preface presents the work as a musical ritual ceremony. This preface is more extensive than the heading of his Stravinsky tribute and more precise in its description of the structure of the ritual:

> Perpetual alternation:
> Suite of verses and responses for an
> imaginary ceremony.
>
> Ceremony of remembrance – whence these
> recurrent patterns, changing in profile
> and perspective.
>
> Ceremony of extinction, ritual
> of death and survival:
> thus the images are engraved
> on the musical memory –
> present/absent, in uncertainty.[19]

---

[18] Antonin Artaud, *Pour en finir avec le jugement de Dieu* (1948): "Le Rite est que le nouveau soleil passe par sept points avant d'éclater à l'orifice de la terre. / Et il y a six hommes, un pour chaque soleil, et un septième homme qui est le soleil tout / cru / habillé de noir et de chair rouge. / Or, ce septième homme / est un cheval, / un cheval avec un homme qui le mène. / Mais c'est le cheval qui est le soleil / et non l'homme."

[19] Score preface on Universal Edition website, https://www.universaledition.com/ pierre-boulez-88/works/rituel-in-memoriam-bruno-maderna-4426 [accessed June 2023], translation modified: 'L'alternance se perpétue: / Suite de versets

In *Rituel*, Boulez alternates between odd- and even-numbered sections (seven of each) whose musical material is chordal and conducted in the odd-numbered sections, and heterophonic and freer in tempo in the even-numbered ones. The fifteenth section is itself comprised of seven sections and forms the final third of the work. Each of the odd-numbered sections starts with a gong stroke and concludes with a unison E flat (the 'S' that was symbolic of Stravinsky). Boulez uses the terms 'répons' and 'versets' ('responses' and 'verses') for the odd- and even-numbered sections, giving Christian religious labels to his imagined ceremony. The constant reiteration and proliferation of the seven-note theme and the alternation of chordal and heterophonic material form the 'recurrent patterns, changing in profile and perspective'. Boulez sums up the piece in strikingly surrealist terms: the musical ritual breaks down the either/or binaries of 'death and survival' and 'present/absent', fusing them as long as the work is 'engraved on the musical memory' into a simultaneous both/and.

It is unclear whether Boulez's preface was a post hoc rationalisation of the work's structure and function, or whether this verbal plan was his starting point. Julian Anderson suggests that another musical tribute might be central to *Rituel*: one to André Jolivet, who died in 1974, one year after Maderna. Anderson connects the title with Jolivet's orchestral *Cinq danses rituelles* (1939), a work Boulez analysed as a student, and more importantly, he believes that

> the musical material suggests Maderna not at all and Jolivet's music from the 1930s much more. [...] The opening monody shows so many of the typical incantatory features – repeated pivot notes, juxtaposition of extremes of long and short note values, a hypnotically stark use of repetitive, untuned, exotic percussion (a tabla) etc. – that one is instantly put in mind of Messiaen [...], Varèse [...] and Jolivet.[20]

But most of all, it is striking that Boulez uses a number that has spiritual connotations at the heart of the construction of *Rituel*. It would be easy to dismiss the spiritual dimension of Boulez's work by pointing to his biography, especially his distancing as an adult from the Catholic religious education of his youth. It is also undeniable that the Catholic dimension of contemporary music in Boulez's France was synonymous

---

et répons pour une cérémonie imaginaire. / Cérémonie de souvenir – d'où ces nombreux <u>retours</u> sur les mêmes formules, tout en changeant profils et perspectives. / Cérémonie de l'extinction, rituel de la disparition et de la survivance: ainsi s'impriment les images dans la mémoire musicale – présente/absente, dans la doute.'

20 Julian Anderson, 'Jolivet and the *style incantatoire*', in Caroline Rae (ed.), *André Jolivet: Music, Art and Literature* (Abingdon: Routledge, 2019), pp. 15–40, at p. 33.

with Messiaen. One could understand any composer wanting to avoid invidious comparisons with a contemporary, particularly when this overbearing figure is a former teacher. But the titles, dedications and programme notes Boulez provided for his works show that the spiritual aspect of his music was in fact hidden in plain sight.

We might also recall that another source of the *Notation* 7 theme was the opening of Jolivet's *Mana*, and might go still further by investigating the sources of Jolivet's fascination with magic in a musical context. Jolivet was influenced by Jules Combarieu's 1909 book *La Musique et la magie* and by his contemporary Hélène de Callias, whose *Magie sonore* (1938) draws on Combarieu while further elucidating his ideas. Callias summarises that 'magic formulae in sound are produced by three principal powers: numerical symbolism; repetition; cosmic appropriation.'[21] Three is indeed a magic number, particularly in European civilisation, as Callias explains:

> Number one represents, symbolically, primordial force which is not yet revealed to us; in religions, God. Number two represents God's actions in the world, and also good and evil, light and shadow, the active and the passive.
>
> Between one and two can be created a link which is the third; in physics, there are two poles, positive and negative, and between these poles, the neutral. There are also two columns united by a vaulting arch.
>
> Number three is thus perfectly constituted by the two poles of which it is the centre, or the culmination depending on its usage; it is then symbolised by the triangle.[22]

And what Callias terms 'the triple incantation' is a feature of both sacred and secular ritual.[23] Boulez may or may not have been familiar with Combarieu's or Callias's writings, but he was certainly familiar with Jolivet, and whatever it might have symbolised for him, the number three is another fetish figure in his work.

---

[21] Hélène de Callias, *Magie sonore* (Paris: Librairie Vega, 1938), p. 57: '[…] les formules de magie sonore propagées par trois puissances principales: le symbolisme des nombres; la répétition; les appropriations cosmiques'.

[22] Callias, *Magie sonore*, p. 57: "le nombre un représente, en symbolisme, la force primordiale non encore révélée: dans les religions, Dieu; le nombre deux, Dieu œuvrant dans le monde; aussi le bien et le mal, la lumière et l'ombre, l'actif et le passif. Entre un et deux, il se crée un trait d'union qui est le ternaire; en physique, il y a deux pôles: le positif et le négatif; puis entre ces deux pôles: le neutre. Ce sont aussi les deux colonnes unies par l'arc de voute. Le nombre trois est donc parfaitement constitué par les deux pôles dont il est le milieu, ou le point culminant selon son appropriation; il est alors symbolisé par le triangle."

[23] Callias, *Magie sonore*, p. 61.

The topics of tribute, litany and ceremony are at least as prominent in *Mémoriale ...explosante-fixe... Originel* (1985), a chamber work for flute and ensemble which is another fully scored realisation of the *Tempo* construction kit, this time with the number three as its primary numerical obsession. As this is a short and relatively accessible work, I propose to explore it in detail to show how magic, memory and incantation are at the heart of Boulez's mature work. There is also an intriguing suggestion that Boulez might have backed away from the more or less explicit expression of these topics in his revised version of the score.

The threefold title of *Mémoriale ...explosante-fixe... Originel* is a useful starting point for an analysis of the piece. *Mémoriale* was written in memory of the Canadian flautist Lawrence Beauregard (1956–85), a member of the Ensemble Intercontemporain, which Boulez had founded in 1977; the dedication 'En souvenir de Lawrence Beauregard (4/9/85)', referencing the date of his death, is present at the end of the first published edition of the piece. Beauregard's premature death from cancer was a severe blow to Boulez; Dominique Jameux wrote that 'Boulez had liked and respected him greatly, and their close creative collaboration was evidenced by the projected new version of ...*explosante-fixe*...'[24] Boulez used material from the ...*explosante-fixe*... work in progress, on which he had worked with Beauregard, to compose *Mémoriale*. The instrumental ensemble of *Mémoriale* includes a solo flute, an obvious reference to Beauregard. In addition, the eight other instruments (two horns, three violins, two violas and a cello) are clearly subservient to the soloist, as they almost exclusively double the flute, echo its ideas or play an accompanimental role.

Some features of the versions of ...*explosante-fixe*... which predate *Mémoriale* are equally relevant to the tribute to Beauregard. The 'Originel' row was also the starting point for *Mémoriale*, and in the 'Transitoire' sections of the *Tempo* construction kit, all twelve notes of the chromatic scale are used and they are each assigned a fixed register. The seven notes of 'Originel' always appear in the register of their first appearance, and Boulez added the other five notes of the chromatic scale to this set for *Mémoriale* (Ex. 5.1). While these precise pitches are not strictly adhered to for the entire work, Boulez's principle of fixed register is valid for perhaps 90 per cent of *Mémoriale*, and this limited pitch range and restricted tessitura contribute greatly to its veiled, elegiac quality. Boulez avoids both the rich low notes of the viola and cello and the shrill, penetrating higher register of the flute and violin. He frequently uses evanescent *sur le*

---

24 Dominique Jameux, *Boulez*; trans. Susan Bradshaw (London: Faber, 1991), p. 212.

Ex. 5.1 Fixed registers of the chromatic scale in Boulez's *Mémoriale*

touche and *sul ponticello* effects and harmonics in the string parts, and the dynamic level is generally low. In particular, Boulez ensures that the flute is at the same dynamic level as or louder than the rest of the ensemble. It is important to note that the twelve pitches of the chromatic scale are in no sense used serially as a tone row, with inversions or transpositions of the original sequence. Rather, the flute's melodic line often rotates obsessively around two or three pitches.

There are six types of section in *Mémoriale*, each with a specific tempo marking and identifiable characteristics, though there is no exact large-scale repetition (analogous to Boulez's practice in *Rituel*, whose preface refers to 'these recurrent patterns, changing in profile and perspective'). One of these sections is related to the 1973 version of *...explosante-fixe...* for flute, clarinet, trumpet, harp, vibraphone, violin, viola, cello and electronics. While this piece is not available for study, we can learn something about its form from Susan Bradshaw's article on Boulez's instrumental and vocal works. She states that 'the 'Originel' act[ed] as a coda to each instrumental part';[25] it appears six times, always ending with the focal note E flat. Boulez uses this idea in what Robert Piencikowski termed the refrain sections of *Mémoriale*[26] at figures 3, 6, 10, 14, 18 and 29 of the score. In these refrains, the flute is given a progressively increasing number of pitches from the 'Originel' row, culminating in a complete statement at figure 29, exactly as in Bradshaw's description of the 1973 version of *...explosante-fixe...* .

The specific characteristics of the five other sections are as follows:

A (Rapide, stable): with this musical material, a flute melisma is followed
by a sustained note – a Boulez fingerprint – and this sustained note
is usually doubled by one or more of the accompanying instruments.
It is typical of *Mémoriale* that if the other instruments do not double
the solo flute, they add a dissonant interval, or in Boulezian terms a
'contradictory note'. This process is apparent in the opening bar of
Mémoriale, where the second viola adds a C natural to the flute's C
sharp, and the cello contributes a D sharp.

[25] Bradshaw, 'The instrumental and vocal music', pp. 212–13.
[26] Robert Piencikowski, sleeve note for Erato 2292-45648-2 (1991), trans. Stewart
Spencer, p. 12.

B (Modéré, Modulé): The time signatures and tempi in these sections vary (hence the 'modulated' indication) but typically include a 10/16 bar. The flute line is staccato and repetitive, incantatory in feel, constantly returning to a focal pitch. As in the 'Rapide, stable' sections, each phrase comes to rest on a sustained note. The string accompaniment is often pizzicato, occasionally reminiscent of the harp or guitar. This is a section where the principle of fixed register is not always adhered to, as shown in figure 5 of the score. In the final bar of this section, the flute comes to rest on a trilled a', a pitch that was anticipated by the strings in their preceding bars, and the accompanying string chord includes pitches outside the fixed registers. This particular section accounts for an apparent anomaly in the refrain sections, as there are seven notes in the theme but only six refrains. One note is added to the refrains at each of its appearances, apart from at figure 6; the prominence given to the a' in the bars before figure 6 replaces its expected first appearance in the refrain.

C (Rapide, irrégulier, vacillant): In these 'fast, irregular, hesitant' sections, the rhythm of the solo flute is usually based on a triplet or quintuplet and can often be described as permutational; for instance, at figure 4 of the score, a pair of semiquavers is shifted progressively from the last quaver of a quintuplet unit to its first quaver. Heterophony is the characteristic texture, with the accompaniment being derived from the flute part, and as in other sections, the flute's phrases come to rest on a sustained pitch.

D (Lent. Libre, continu; Slow. Free, continuous) and E (En se raréfiant – Redevenant dense; Thinning out – Becoming dense again): As the two appearances of D sandwich the only appearance of E, these could be considered as a tripartite group, and they all have in common a cello pedal E flat. Here, the cello has the only regular rhythmic pulse in the piece, playing pizzicato on the first beat of the bar, moving gradually from the fingerboard to the normal playing position in the first D section, tremolo in section E, and moving progressively towards the bridge in the second D section. This focal E flat is also prominent in the flute part, which constantly gravitates to this pitch, and the flute's almost symmetrical arabesques culminate on a sustained pitch.

Each refrain features all nine instruments in a chordal texture, contrasting with the complex heterophony of the rest of the piece, and the tempo of the refrains is markedly slower than that of the other sections. Also, while the refrains all end on a unison E flat (the 'Es' of Stravinsky), they do not necessarily conform to the principle of fixed register, and it is in these sections that Boulez is most likely to depart from this principle. No note is harmonised in the same way twice, and the chordal density in the refrains ranges from three to eight pitches. There is a parallel here with Messiaen, specifically with 'Neumes rythmiques', the second of his *Quatre études de rythme* for piano (1949). Most of the nineteen building blocks of this piece (Messiaen's analogy is to the 'neumes' of Gregorian chant) end on the E above middle C, but this pitch is harmonised differently each time it appears. The Breton-derived subtitle *...explosante-fixe...* is an analogy for these paradoxical musical values of instability and stability, contrast and conformity; small wonder it was such a powerful metaphor for Boulez.

The sections vary in length, and they appear in the following order:

ABA (refrain) CB (refrain) C AC (refrain) A CB (refrain) C BA (refrain) B AC DED CAC B (refrain)

This illustrates that the sections are grouped in threes for much of the piece, with two of one particular type sandwiching a contrasting section, though as the refrains often cut across these groups and there is no exact repetition, the pattern is not easily perceivable by the listener. It is surely no accident that there are 10 × 3 sections in total, 2 × 3 types of section and 2 × 3 refrains, and the intriguing question of trinitarian symbolism is all the more pertinent when the first edition of the score is examined. There are 117 bars in the piece (39 × 3), 57 (19 × 3) indicated changes of tempo, and all the tempo markings are divisible by three. The number of instruments in the ensemble (three wind and six strings) and even the tripartite title of the work seem unlikely to be fortuitous in this context. In *Mémoriale*, this fixation with the number three ties in with the obsessional repetition of pitches and the multiple (and similarly obsessive) reflections of the flute line in the accompaniment. While the dedication at the head of the *Tempo* construction kit explicitly states that this piece is intended to 'evoke' Stravinsky and 'conjure up his absence', by analogy, *Mémoriale* was surely intended to evoke and conjure up Lawrence Beauregard. It appears that the flute – Beauregard's instrument – the *Notation 7* theme and the 'magic' number three are the core components of this particular spell.

In the revised version of the score, Boulez changed a number of these tempo markings and indications. The changes are noted in Table 5.1 (the 'Modulé' – modulated – sections all feature fluctuating tempi, and the table gives the initial metronome marking for this type of section).

What do all these changes signify? It would be easy to rationalise the changes in tempo as resulting from practical performance experience that was absent when the first edition was published. In the revised version, the tempi no longer adhere to the original 'rule' that they should be divisible by three. Wearing his conductor hat, Boulez may well have discovered that some of the initial tempi did not work effectively in practice, and this lived experience of the piece has ultimately overridden the theoretical (and magical) conception of the original. Boulez's

Table 5.1 Boulez, *Mémoriale*: comparison of tempo indications in the original and revised versions of the published score

Section	Tempo indication: first edition	Tempo indication: revised edition
A	Rapide, stable: crotchet = 120	Modéré, stable: crotchet = 84
B	Modéré, Modulé: crotchet = 90	Assez rapide, Modulé: crotchet = 92
C	Rapide, irrégulier, vacillant: crotchet = 120/132	Un peu vif (crotchet = 98/102), irrégulier, vacillant
D	Lent. Libre, continu: crotchet = 108/120	Assez lent: crotchet = 72/78. Libre, continu
E	En se raréfiant – Redevenant dense: crotchet 120 → 96	En se raréfiant – Redevenant dense: crotchet 78 → 60
Refrain	Lent, souple: crotchet = 60	Lent, calme: crotchet = 56

deletion of the tribute to Lawrence Beauregard in the new edition raises other questions. Did the composer want to hide the personal impulse behind the piece, and is there any connection between this concealment of the original dedication and the removal of part of the 'magic' use of the number three to 'evoke' Beauregard and 'conjure up' his absence?

2. The SACHER hexachord

Another talismanic *objet trouvé* for Boulez was the SACHER hexachord (E flat [S] – A – C – B flat [H] – E – D [Ré]), referencing the highly musical surname of his supporter and close friend, the Swiss conductor and philanthropist Paul Sacher (1906–98). Sacher came across Boulez's name as early as 1946 in conversation with his fellow Swiss Arthur Honegger; when he asked 'if he knew of any interesting young composers, Honegger initially replied in the negative. The following day, after reconsidering, he added: "There is one talented fellow among Vaura's [Honegger's wife, Andrée Vaurabourg-Honegger] young rogues: his name is Pierre Boulez."'[27]

This musical cipher is a 'found object' because Boulez and eleven other composers were commissioned by Mstislav Rostropovich to write a piece for cello based on the SACHER hexachord in celebration of Sacher's 70th birthday. Boulez somewhat extended the terms of the commission in his

[27] Robert Piencikowski, 'Pierre Boulez and Paul Sacher: chronicle of a friendship', in Felix Meyer (ed.), *Settling New Scores: Music Manuscripts from the Paul Sacher Foundation* (Mainz: Schott, 1998), pp. 82–5, at p. 82.

Messagesquisse (Message-sketch; 1976–7), as it is composed for the solo cellist Rostropovich and an ensemble of six other cellos.

Boulez's foreword to the published score (1977) is unusually personal in tone:

> Messages are often secretly hidden
> Music has this advantage:
> It dispenses with words,
> The messages are essentially personal,
>
> decoded by everyone according to the time.
> A cipher – symbolic (reduced)
> Notes – symbolic (multiplied)
> Rhythms – symbolic (split up)
> in order to add a certain number of messages, diverse, divergent,
> in order thus to let some emotions to pass by, certainly not symbolic
>   ones. [...]
>
> This manuscript
> Dear Paul
> Is just as much testimony as it is a message ...
> Testimony to the cordial bonds made over all the years
>   by you to me
>   With deep and faithful affection.
>   Pierre Boulez[28]

Boulez's affection for Sacher was evident for all to see at Sacher's funeral service. The conductor Michael Haefliger, who was also present, recalls that Boulez gave the address and 'He simply broke off in the middle and left the stage because he was unable to continue. He and his discipline and rationality disguise an incredibly emotional person.'[29] His reuse of the SACHER hexachord in multiple contexts can be seen, in part, as a manifestation of his affection for Sacher. I will briefly mention each of these pieces, pausing en route to consider how aspects of these works represent continuing threads in Boulez's oeuvre.

Répons, a major work composed using the contemporary resources of IRCAM, the institute founded by Boulez in Paris that aimed to bring together musicians and cutting-edge technology, might be dedicated to the publisher Alfred Schlee for his 80th birthday, but the musical material is again based on the SACHER hexachord. The work, for soloists,

[28] https://www.universaledition.com/pierre-boulez-88/works/messagesquisse-3625 [accessed June 2023].

[29] Michael Haefliger, interview with Wolfgang Schaufler, trans. Rosemary Bridger-Lippe, for *Musiksalon* (August 2014), http://musiksalon.universaledition.com/en/article/michael-haefliger-on-pierre-boulez [accessed June 2023].

ensemble and live electronics, was started in 1981 and moved through various iterations and durations, the first of which was premiered in 1985. All the versions have the same core musical material, showing that Boulez's penchant for proliferation might have no end, and all have six soloists: two pianos, harp, cimbalom, vibraphone, and one performer playing glockenspiel and xylophone. The sound is manipulated in real time and projected through six loudspeakers. Six is therefore the central 'magic number' of *Répons*, though its title and structure align it more with *Rituel*. We should recall that in his preface to *Rituel*, Boulez used the terms 'répons' and 'versets' for the two different types of material. As the score preface to *Répons* puts it, 'The title of this work refers to the responsorial form of Gregorian chant in which a solo singer alternates with a choir.'[30]

This alternation is translated in Boulezian secular terms to a series of relationships: that of solo plus ensemble, of the live soloist plus the manipulation of this sound in real time by electronic means, and musically, as a constant interplay between isolated and fast-moving material. As the chamber ensemble and conductor are intended to be in the centre of the performing space and the soloists and loudspeakers on the edges of the space, surrounding the audience, the audience's relationship to the performers is also far more immersive and mobile than for conventional concert works where the listeners face the front. The 1980s might be distant in time from Boulez's formative years, but his desire to create 'sonic sorcery' and 'music that is alive – in the sense that it obliges listeners to be involved'[31] is something he was already concerned about four decades earlier.

In the same year that the first version of *Répons* was finished, Boulez composed *Dérive* (1984), another homage to a contemporary music patron to whom he was close and another work with a title that has six letters. The dedicatee of *Dérive* is William Glock, who in his roles as BBC Controller of Music from 1959 to 1972 and director of the Bath Festival from 1976 to 1984 was a strong supporter of Boulez. Indeed, *Dérive* was completed in Bath in June 1984. The work is based on a set of six chords which, like the pitches in *Mémoriale*, each tend to keep their registral identity; the first is the SACHER hexachord and the others are derived from it, all being transposed variants constructed on the central pitch E flat, 'Es' here standing for Sacher rather than Stravinsky (Ex. 5.2).

---

[30] https://www.universaledition.com/pierre-boulez-88/works/repons-4375 [accessed June 2023].

[31] 'l'envoûtement par le son [...] la musique vivante – dans le sens où elle oblige les auditeurs à participer [...]'. From Boulez's first draft of 'Propositions' (1948), Paul Sacher Stiftung, Boulez collection, microfilm 025.1.854.

Ex. 5.2 Boulez, *Dérive*, set of six chords

The title *Dérive* is multiply suggestive. Most literally, it indicates that the piece is 'derivative', in this case of the *objet trouvé* SACHER hexachord. The website of Boulez's publisher Universal Edition explains more precisely that 'The "derivative" is also a sequence of variations "on the name Sacher." Six chords build a circular rotation, which mimic the structure of the piece, but also soften it.'[32] This is an admirably concise explanation of the musical origins and construction of the piece, but the title also has other meanings. 'Drift' is another possible English translation of 'dérive', or literally one could render it 'away from the shore' (dé – rive). Jonathan Goldman notes that chords 2–6 are generated from the SACHER hexachord 'rotated through cyclic permutations [...] of the initial interval series', though the fifth chord features an A natural rather than the A flat that an exact intervallic rotation would produce – Goldman aptly describes this as '"drifting" away from the original plan – one of those accidents [...] which make the realization more interesting than the idea.'[33] As in *Mémoriale*, Boulez was happy to diverge from his self-imposed 'rule'.

'Derivative' and 'drift' are meanings of *Dérive* that work in English, but perhaps its French signification is the most important of all. In a French literary context contemporaneous with Boulez, the term immediately evokes the work of the Situationist International, whose instigator, Guy Debord (1931–94), devised in the 1960s 'the technique of the dérive, the day- or week-long "drift" through everyday life, a kind of roving research along the margins of dominant culture'.[34] It is inconceivable that Boulez was unaware of this particular meaning of 'dérive'.

This 'dérive' has many antecedents in French literature, from the nineteenth-century Baudelairean flâneur to Breton's seemingly random walks around Paris leading to chance encounters which turn out to be

[32] Anonymous author, https://www.universaledition.com/pierre-boulez-88/works/derive-1-1953 [accessed June 2023].

[33] Jonathan Goldman, *The Musical Language of Pierre Boulez: Writings and Compositions* (Cambridge: Cambridge University Press, 2011), p. 119.

[34] Edward Ball, 'The Great Sideshow of the Situationist International', *Yale French Studies*, vol. 73 (1987): pp. 21–37, at p. 31.

no coincidence. In this sense, Hal Foster is correct to say that 'surrealist precedents did inspire situationist practices of *dérive* and *détournement*.'[35] While Boulez's use of *Dérive* as a title may specifically refer to his 'derivation' of the piece from the SACHER hexachord he had previously used, I believe that the Situationist concept of *dérive* is especially relevant not only to the compositional process, which circles around the SACHER hexachord and its derivations, but also to the listener. The notion of wandering aurally through Boulez's musical landscape is potentially a very rich metaphor. Frequently, critics refer to Boulez's music as a labyrinth, and it seems to me that *dérive* would be a more culturally apposite metaphor for this elaborate, mysterious musical journey which is quite unlike the experience of listening to Western tonal goal-directed classical music.

Yet another literary analogue for this wandering journey is the work of Michel Butor, which interested Boulez in the 1950s and 60s. In his article 'Sonate, que me veux-tu?' about his Third Piano Sonata, Boulez explicitly draws an analogy between the 'Constellation' section of the third formant of this sonata, 'Constellation-miroir', and

> the plan of an unknown town (such as plays an important part in Michel Butor's *L'Emploi du temps*). The actual route taken is left to the initiative of the performer, who has to pick his way through a close network of paths. This form, which is both fixed and mobile, is thus situated at the centre of the work as pivot, or centre of gravity.[36]

('Fixed and mobile': both/and again.) For Butor, as for Italo Calvino in his 1972 novella *Invisible Cities*, Venice was the ideal model, its labyrinthine streets an irresistible invitation to *dérive*. Butor wrote an article 'Mallarmé selon Boulez' for *Melos* in 1961[37] and was close to Boulez at the time, though they never worked together and Butor's closest musical collaborator was the Belgian composer Henri Pousseur.

In 1994, Boulez wrote a short piano work, *Incises*, which he composed as a test piece for the Umberto Micheli piano competition. His explanation of the title on the published score places the work, once again, in a religious context:

> INCISE, a rhythmic unit of several notes analogous to a motif. The term is utilised especially by the Gregorian theory of Solesmes as an intermediate

---

[35] Hal Foster, *Compulsive Beauty* (Cambridge, MA: MIT Press, 1993), p. xvi.

[36] Pierre Boulez, 'Sonate, que me veux-tu?', *Méditations*, 7 (1964), pp. 61–75; in English, trans. Martin Cooper in *Orientations*, ed. Jean-Jacques Nattiez (London: Faber, 1986), pp. 143–54; this quotation at p. 151.

[37] Michel Butor, 'Mallarmé selon Boulez', *Melos*, vol. 28 (1961): pp. 356–9.

subdivision between the basic rhythm and the body of a phrase. Other theoreticians, such as M. Lussy, define it as a rhythmic group.[38]

The following year, he published a spin-off fragment of this piece, two lines with the tempo marking 'Très lent', as part of a Festschrift in honour of the distinguished ethnomusicologist Simha Arom, a long-time friend.[39] Again, the musical material of this fragment is based on the SACHER hexachord. It seems that Boulez's two musical *objets trouvés* had quite different meanings: works based on the seven-note figure derived from *Notation* 7 were all tributes to the recently departed, while the SACHER hexachord was used for pieces written as homages to living people. It is possible that the title represents an additional homage to Arom, as the term 'incise' – referring to an incision or engraving – might have been inspired by an article written by Arom in 1969 on the notation of monody, where he uses the terms 'incise' and 'chute' to denote the start and end of a melodic line.[40]

Boulez's *sur Incises* for three pianos, three harps and three percussionists (1996–8) was dedicated to Sacher for his 90th birthday; here we have the SACHER hexachord brought home, as it were, being the basis of a work written for the original source of the fetish object. On the surface, this piece for 3 × 3 performers is another manifestation of the composer's trinitarian obsession, though Peter O'Hagan's detailed analysis has revealed that the music is also another example of the importance of the number seven. For example, the second part of the work starts with a sequence of fourteen chords, as does the climax of the Prestissimo section, and a development section is based on seven variations based on a series of seven chords and seven rhythmic values. Likewise, the codetta is based on seven chords, each with seven pitches.[41]

sur Incises represents a reimagining of the sound world that was so characteristic of Boulez's formative years: in the mid-1940s, he and his classmates performed many works for multiple keyboards (though Boulez has never used Wyschnegradsky's quartertone keyboard tuning), and one is also reminded of the original *Visage nuptial* ensemble combining piano, ondes Martenot and percussion, a combination also used by contemporaries including Yvette Grimaud. It is as if the harp now

---

[38] Cited in O'Hagan, *Boulez and the Piano*, p. 288.

[39] O'Hagan, *Boulez and the Piano*, p. 297. Boulez's contribution appeared in Emmanuelle Olivier et al. (eds.), *Ndroje balendro: musiques, terrains et disciplines. Textes offertes à Simha Arom* (Paris: Peeters, 1995), p. 239.

[40] Simha Arom, 'Essai d'une notation des monodies à des fins d'analyse', *Revue de musicologie*, vol. 55 no. 2 (1969): pp. 172–216.

[41] Peter O'Hagan, *Pierre Boulez: sur Incises* (Geneva: Contrechamps, 2021), pp. 222–3.

performs the 'intermediary' role between percussion and piano that in Boulez's formative years was assigned to the ondes Martenot. There is still a clear non-Western inspiration behind this sonic universe, not only because the extensive percussion instrumentation of *sur Incises* includes steel pans. The many fast toccata sections with an obsessive quality also hark back to the exceptionally mobile piano writing of the first two sonatas.

Works by Boulez with no connection to a talismanic musical 'found object' might also have a 'magic number' at their centre. One example of this is *Domaines* for clarinet and six ensembles (1961–8), where the magic number is six. Paul Griffiths writes that this 'sixness' 'extends to more than the constitution of groups and the number of antiphonies in each part. The work's plan suggests a prefiguring of *Rituel*, with six rather than seven being the magic number: there are six sections (here termed 'cahiers', notebooks) and six mirror versions, each containing six fragments of music that can be read either horizontally or vertically. The solo 'cahiers' (which can each be played alone as a solo work) each have six elements which may be linked in different orders, and the music abounds in rhythmic and pitch configurations of six.[42] The performer first lays the six cahiers in an order of their choosing, followed by the six mirror sections.[43]

Coda

The popular view of Boulez tends to be that he is a mathematical composer, an opinion that surely has roots in his use of serial compositional methods, perhaps also in his biography as he studied mathematics to a high level at school. But closer investigation shows that it is not mathematics that is the key to his art, but number; not only calculation, but also magic; both serialism and surrealism. This conclusion should not come as a surprise, given that Boulez himself was always at pains to emphasise his distaste for a mechanical approach to serialism. In 1952, he wrote in 'Éventuellement', an article that both sums up his current aesthetic and points to future possibilities:

> From everything I have written about the discovery of a serial universe, it transpires quite clearly that creation cannot be defined simply as a mechanical realisation of a starting point. The sort of assurance this

[42] Griffiths, *Boulez*, p. 51.
[43] See Roger Heaton's article: https://www.rogerheaton.uk/boulez-domaines [accessed June 2023] and his 'The contemporary clarinet', in Colin Lawson (ed.), *The Cambridge Companion to the Clarinet* (Cambridge: Cambridge University Press, 1995), pp. 163–83.

mechanism provides cannot satisfy, because the act of writing would then be nothing but a conditioned reflex with no more importance than a carefully presented accountancy ledger, even one that has been kept in minutest detail. Composition cannot take on the appearance of an elegant list of expenditure, however ingenious, without being condemned as inane and pointless.

From this initial material, which I have studied in detail, the unpredictable emerges. There is freedom within and between all these serial structures; they only appear rigid to people who are unaware of this freedom or who deny it, being prisoners of a daily routine and of a conservative mindset that wants what we have learned from the past to be untouchable.

After this theoretical essay, which many might consider to be the extolling of intellectualism over instinct, I come to a conclusion. Once more, the unexpected; *creativity only happens when the unforeseen becomes a necessity.*[44]

For Boulez, there was ultimately no contradiction between intellectualism and instinct, or between explosion and stasis, as both are necessary ingredients of creativity. As early as 1946, in letters to André Souris, Boulez made clear that he detested those serial composers who relied on constructivist principles at the expense of every other aspect of their music. His statement in 'Éventuellement' is certainly more extended and sophisticated, but his underlying belief is the same. Constructivism in music needs to be coupled with a violent, shocking,

---

[44] Pierre Boulez, 'Éventuellement', first published in *La Revue musicale*, no. 212 (1952): pp. 117–48, and later in *Points de repère*, 2nd edition (Paris: Christian Bourgois, 1985), pp. 263–95; English trans. by Stephen Walsh, 'Possibly ...', in Boulez, *Stocktakings from an Apprenticeship* (Oxford: Clarendon Press, 1991), pp. 111–40, at p. 133 (translation modified): "De tout ce que nous avons écrit à propos de la découverte d'un monde sériel, il transparaît assez clairement que nous refusons de définir la création comme la seule mise en œuvre de ces structures de départ: une assurance ainsi acquise ne saurait nous satisfaire, par l'aspect de réflexe conditionné que prendrait alors l'acte d'écrire, geste qui n'aurait guère plus d'importance qu'une comptabilité soigneusement tenue ou même minutieusement mise au point. La composition ne saurait revêtir l'aspect d'une économie distributive élégante, voire ingénieuse, sans se voir condamnée à l'inanité et à la gratuité. A partir de ces données, que nous avons étudiées en détail, l'imprévisible surgit. Nous avons vu le libre jeu que laissent à l'intérieur d'elles-mêmes et entre elles toutes ces organisations sérielles, qui n'apparaissent rigides qu'à ceux qui les ignorent ou les refusent systématiquement, prisonniers d'une routine quelque peu séculaire et d'un préjugé conservateur qui veut que soient intangibles les acquisitions du passé. Après cet essai de théorie, qui aura apparu à beaucoup comme la glorification de l'intellectualisme contre l'instinct, nous conclurons. L'inattendu, encore: *il n'y a de création que dans l'imprévisible devenant nécessité.*"

life-giving property, and for Boulez, this was explicitly or implicitly a ritualistic property.

The fundamental surrealist concepts of the found object, objective chance, and the unification of apparent opposites are apparent in Boulez's first mature compositions and were vital continuing threads in his work. His post-1950 compositions show that found objects – principally his seven-note theme from the seventh *Notation*, and the SACHER hexachord – have infinite, unquenchable possibilities. Indeed, he told Deliège 'I have a probably innate sense for what I would term the proliferation of materials.'[45] For Boulez, a musical idea could only ever be the starting point of a *dérive* through different musical landscapes, a fragment of a composer's creative activity.

Above all, the sensual, emotional side of Boulez's art is one that has been severely underplayed. In a talk she gave in 1985, Susan Bradshaw drew attention to Boulez's belief that listeners want to 'lose yourself in a work of art' – as in a labyrinth or a random walk. Bradshaw claimed that Boulez is a 'contradictory character' because 'his music is so tightly put together' and yet he also asks listeners to 'lose themselves'[46] but in reality there is no contradiction between the two positions. Boulez's entire oeuvre epitomises the union of control and chance, construction and freedom, rationalism and emotionalism: both/and, not either/or.

---

[45] Boulez, *Par volonté et par hasard*, p. 14: 'j'ai un sens probablement inné pour ce que j'appellerai la prolifération des matériaux'.

[46] Susan Bradshaw, 'In search of Pierre Boulez', talk given at the National Sound Archive, 26 March 1985, now housed in the British Library (B627/1).

SELECT BIBLIOGRAPHY

Abolgassemi, Maxime. '*La beauté sera CONVULSIVE (André Breton)*: conférence prononcée au lycée Chateaubriand de Rennes le mardi 21 octobre 2008'. http://www.abolgassemi.fr/index.php/page1-2/conference-sur-la-beaute-convulsive/ [accessed June 2023]

Abolgassemi, Maxime. 'Hasard objectif et mémoire involontaire'. *Poétique*, no. 159 (2009): pp. 299–310

Allet, Natacha and Christy Wampole. 'Myth and Legend in Artaud's Theater'. *Yale French Studies*, 111 (2007): pp. 143–56

Anderson, Julian. 'Jolivet and the *style incantatoire*: aspects of a hybrid tradition'. In Caroline Rae (ed.), *André Jolivet: Music, Art and Literature*. Abingdon: Routledge, 2019, pp. 15–40

Andreyev, Samuel. 'Pierre Boulez' Deuxième Sonate' [video analysis]. https://www.youtube.com/watch?v=8giW4XdcV-M [accessed June 2023]

Arfouilloux, Sébastien. 'Surréalisme et musique: les écrits d'André Souris'. *Textyles*, vol. 26–7 (2005): pp. 87–93

Arfouilloux, Sébastien. *Que la nuit tombe sur l'orchestre. Surréalisme et musique*. Paris: Fayard, 2009

Arom, Simha. 'Essai d'une notation des monodies à des fins d'analyse'. *Revue de musicologie*, vol. 55 no. 2 (1969): pp. 172–216

Artaud, Antonin. *Le Théâtre et son double* (1938; reprinted Paris: Gallimard, Folio edition, 1964)

Artaud, Antonin. 'To end god's judgment', trans. and preface by Victor Corti. *The Tulane Drama Review*, vol. 9 no. 3 (1965): pp. 56–98

Asimov, Peter. 'Une invention "essentiellement française": seeing and hearing the Ondes martenot in 1937'. *Musique, images, instruments*, vol. 17 (2018): pp. 107–26

Atkin, Will. 'Crystalline thought: alchemy and "visionary mineralogy" in the writings of André Breton'. *Immediations*, vol. 4 no. 1 (2016). https://courtauld.ac.uk/research/publications/immediations/immediations-2016-volume-4-number-1/article-immediations-2016-volume-4-number-1/will-atkin-immediations-2016 [accessed June 2023]

Aubin, David. 'The withering immortality of Nicolas Bourbaki: a cultural connector at the confluence of mathematics, structuralism and the Oulipo in France'. *Science in Context*, vol. 10 no. 2 (1997): pp. 297–342

Balmer, Yves, Thomas Lacôte and Christopher Brent Murray. *Le Modèle et l'invention: Messiaen et la technique de l'emprunt*. Lyon: Symétrie, 2017

Barbedette, Sarah (ed.). *Pierre Boulez* [exhibition catalogue]. Paris: Actes Sud, 2015

Barrault, Jean-Louis. 'Travailler avec Boulez'. *Cahiers Renaud-Barrault, no. 41* (December 1963). Reprinted in *Résonance*, no. 8 (March 1995). http://articles.ircam.fr/textes/Barrault95a/index.html [accessed June 2023]

Bassetto, Luisa. 'Marginalia, ou *l'opéra-fantôme* de Pierre Boulez'. In Pascal Decroupet and Jean-Louis Leleu (eds.), *Pierre Boulez: techniques d'écriture et enjeux esthétiques*. Geneva: Contrechamps, 2006, pp. 255–98

Bassetto, Luisa. 'Ritratto del compositore come apprendista etnologo. Pierre Boulez prima dell'incontro con André Schaeffner'. *Musicalia*, vol. 7 (2010): pp. 61–82

Bataille, Georges. *The Sacred Conspiracy*, ed. Alastair Brotchie and Marina Galletti. London: Atlas Press, 2018

Bauduin, Tessel M. *Surrealism and the Occult: Occultism and Western Esotericism in the Work and Movement of André Breton*. Amsterdam: Amsterdam University Press, 2014

Bennett, Richard Rodney. Interview with Pierre Boulez. Broadcast on BBC Radio 3, 20 January 1986

Bleek, Tobias. 'Pierre Boulez: *Douze Notations*'. *Explore the Score*. http://www.explorethescore.org/pierre-boulez-douze-notations-history-and-context-composing-within-narrow-confines.html [accessed June 2023]

Bohn, Willard. 'From surrealism to surrealism: Apollinaire and Breton'. *The Journal of Aesthetics and Art Criticism*, vol. 36 no. 2 (1977): pp. 197–210

Boivin, Jean. *La Classe de Messiaen*. Paris: Christian Bourgois, 1995

Bonnefoy, Yves. 'Le Surréalisme et la musique'. *Inharmoniques*, vol. 5 (1989): pp. 142–8

Boulez, Pierre. *Conversations with Célestin Deliège*. London: Eulenburg, 1976. Originally published in French as *Par volonté et par hasard: Entretiens avec Célestin Deliège*. Paris: Seuil, 1975

Boulez, Pierre. *Entretiens avec Michel Archimbaud*. Folio Essais. Paris: Gallimard, 2016

Boulez, Pierre. *Leçons de musique (Points de repère III)*, ed. Jean-Jacques Nattiez .Paris: Christian Bourgois, 2005

Boulez, Pierre. *Orientations*, ed. Jean-Jacques Nattiez and trans. Martin Cooper. London: Faber, 1986

Boulez, Pierre. *Penser la musique aujourd'hui*. Paris: Denoël/Gonthier, 1963

Boulez, Pierre. *Points de repère*, 2nd edition. Paris: Christian Bourgois, 1985

Boulez, Pierre. 'Prenons garde à la démagogie'. Interview with Richard Millet. *Revue des deux mondes* (2001), no. 1, pp. 28–34

Boulez, Pierre. 'Propositions', *Polyphonie*, no. 2 (1948): pp. 65–74

Boulez, Pierre. *Regards sur autrui*, ed. Jean-Jacques Nattiez and Sophie Galaise. Paris: Bourgois, 2005

Boulez, Pierre. *Stocktakings from an Apprenticeship*, trans. Stephen Walsh. Oxford: Clarendon Press, 1991. First published in French as *Relevés d'apprenti*, ed. Paule Thévenin. Paris: Seuil, 1966

Bradshaw, Susan. 'Pierre Boulez at 65'. *Musical Times*, vol. 131 no. 1765 (1990): pp. 127–8

Bradshaw, Susan. 'Comparing notes'. *Musical Times*, vol. 137 no. 1844 (1996): pp. 5–12

Bradshaw, Susan, 'The instrumental and vocal music'. In William Glock (ed.), *Pierre Boulez: A Symposium*. London: Eulenburg, 1986, pp. 127–229

Breatnach, Mary. *Boulez and Mallarmé: A Study in Poetic Influence*. Aldershot: Scolar, 1996

Breton, André. *L'Amour fou*. Paris: Gallimard, 1937. Originally titled 'La beauté convulsive', *Minotaure*, no. 5 (May 1934): pp. 8–16

Breton, André. *L'Art magique*, Formes de l'art. Paris: Club Français du Livre, 1957

Breton, André. 'Le Message automatique'. *Minotaure, no.* 3–4 (December 1933): pp. 55–65. See Breton, *Œuvres complètes* (Paris: Gallimard, 1928), vol. 2, pp. 375–94

Breton, André. *Les Vases communicants*. 1933; Paris: Gallimard, 1955

Breton, André. *Nadja*. Paris: Gallimard, 1928; revised edition, 1964

Cadieu, Martine. *A l'écoute des compositeurs*. Paris: Minerve, 1992

Campbell, Edward. *Boulez, Music and Philosophy*. Cambridge: Cambridge University Press, 2010

Campbell, Edward and Peter O'Hagan (eds.). *Pierre Boulez Studies*. Cambridge: Cambridge University Press, 2016

Carrouges, Michel. *André Breton et les données fondamentales du surréalisme*. Paris: Gallimard, 1950

Charles, Daniel. *For the Birds: Conversations with John Cage*. Boston and London: Marion Boyars, 1981

Clifford, James. 'On ethnographic surrealism'. *Comparative Studies in Society and History*, vol. 23 no. 4 (October 1981): pp. 539–564. Reprinted in Clifford, *The Predicament of Culture: Twentieth-Century Ethnography, Literature, and Art*. Cambridge, MA: Harvard University Press, 1988: pp. 117–51

Coult, Tom. 'Pierre Boulez's *sur Incises*: refraction, crystallisation and the absent idea(l)'. *Tempo*, vol. 67 no. 264 (April 2013): pp. 2–21

Dunbar, Rudolph and Felix Aprahamian. 'The news from Paris'. *Tempo*, no. 9 (December 1944): pp. 15–17

Foster, Hal. *Compulsive Beauty*. Cambridge, MA: MIT Press, 1993

Gable, David. 'Boulez's two cultures: the post-war European synthesis and tradition'. *Journal of the American Musicological Society*, vol. 43 no. 3 (1990): pp. 426–456

Gable, David. 'Ramifying connections: an interview with Pierre Boulez'. *Journal of Musicology*, vol. 4 no. 1 (1985–6): pp. 105–13

Gärtner, Susanne. *Werkstatt-Spuren: Die Sonatine von Pierre Boulez*. Bern: Peter Lang, 2008

Glock, William (ed.). *Pierre Boulez: A Symposium*. London: Eulenburg, 1986

Goeyvaerts, Karel. 'Paris – Darmstadt 1947–1956: excerpt from the autobiographical portrait. *Revue belge de Musicologie / Belgisch Tijdschrift voor Muziekwetenschap*, vol. 48 (1994): pp. 35–54

Goldman, Jonathan. 'Charting *Mémoriale*: paradigmatic analysis and harmonic schemata in Boulez's *...explosante-fixe...*' *Music Analysis*, 27 no. 2–3 (2008): pp. 217–52

Goldman, Jonathan. *The Musical Language of Pierre Boulez: Writings and Compositions.* Cambridge: Cambridge University Press, 2011

Goléa, Antoine. *Rencontres avec Pierre Boulez.* Paris: Julliard, 1958

Goléa, Antoine. 'French music since 1945', trans. Lucile H. Brockway. *Musical Quarterly*, vol. 51 no. 1 (1965): pp. 22–37

Griffiths, Paul. *Boulez.* Oxford: Oxford University Press, 1978

Griffiths, Paul. 'Poèmes and Haïkaï: a note on Messiaen's development'. *Musical Times*, vol. 112 no. 1543 (September 1971): pp. 851–2

Griffiths, Paul. *The Sea on Fire: Jean Barraqué.* Rochester: University of Rochester Press, 2003

Guldbrandsen, Erling E. 'Pierre Boulez in interview, 1996: (II) serialism revisited'. *Tempo*, vol. 65 no. 256 (April 2011): pp. 18–24

Heaton, Roger. 'The contemporary clarinet'. In Colin Lawson (ed.), *The Cambridge Companion to the Clarinet.* Cambridge: Cambridge University Press, 1995, pp. 163–83

Henderson, Robert. '*Le Soleil des eaux*'. *Musical Times*, vol. 106 no. 1471 (September 1965): pp. 673–74

Hertz, Uri. 'Artaud in Mexico'. *Fragmentos*, no. 25 (2003): pp. 11–17

Hill, Peter and Nigel Simeone. *Messiaen.* New Haven: Yale University Press, 2005

Hirsbrunner, Theo. 'Die surrealisistiche Komponente in Pierre Boulez' *Le Marteau sans maître*'. *Neue Zeitschrift für Musik*, vol. 135 no. 7 (July 1974): pp. 420–5.

Hirsbrunner, Theo. 'Pierre Boulez: *Notations* (1945)'. *Melos*, vol. 2 (1986): pp. 2–20.

Hopkins, G. W. 'Boulez's "Le Soleil des eaux"'. *Tempo*, 68 (Spring 1964): pp. 35–7

Hopkins, G. W. 'Portrait of Debussy. 10: Debussy and Boulez'. *Musical Times*, vol. 109 no. 1506 (August 1968): pp. 710–14

James, Alison. *Constraining Chance: Georges Perec and the Oulipo.* Evanston, IL: Northwestern University Press, 2009

Jameux, Dominique. *Boulez.* Paris: Fayard, 1984

Jameux, Dominique. *Boulez*, trans. Susan Bradshaw. London: Faber, 1991

Jolivet-Erlih, Christine (ed.). *André Jolivet: écrits*, 2 vols. Paris: Delatour, 2006

Joos, Maxime. 'Variations esthétiques (Schloezer, Boulez, Schaeffner)'. *Revue de musicologie*, vol. 91 no. 2 (2005): pp. 401–24

Kayas, Lucie. *André Jolivet.* Paris: Fayard, 2005

Kuczyńska, Agnieszka. 'Surréalisme en 1947 – occultism and the post-war marginalisation of surrealism'. *Art Inquiry*, vol. 16 (2014): pp. 87–99

Labussière, Annie and Jean-Marc Chouvel. 'Pierre Boulez: Mémoriale (... explosante-fixe... – Originel)'. *Musurgia*, vol. 4 no. 1, Dossiers d'analyse (1997): pp. 42–66

Lacôte, Thomas. 'Le Puzzle et les cubes de bois'. 22 November 2020. https://phtoggos.wordpress.com/2020/11/22/le-puzzle-et-les-cubes-de-bois-g-perec-a-schonberg-et-quelques-autres/ [accessed June 2023]

Lamont, Rosette C. and Jean Louis Barrault. 'Entretien avec Jean Louis Barrault'. *The French Review*, vol. 45 no. 1 (1971): pp. 31–6

Laurendeau, Jean. *Maurice Martenot, luthier de l'électronique*. Montréal: Dervy-Livres, 1990

Le Marrec, David. 'Boulez après les Folies Bergère: Agamemnon de Pierre Boulez'. 24 April 2015. http://operacritiques.free.fr/css/index.php?2015/04/24/2666-inedit-agamemnon-de-pierre-boulez-l-orestie-eschyle-jean-louis-barrault-madeleine-renaud-1955-bordeaux-marigny [accessed June 2023]

Leibowitz, René. *Introduction à la musique de douze sons*. Paris: L'Arche, 1949

Leiris, Michel. 'Quant à Arnold Schoenberg'. In *Brisées*. Paris: Mercure de France, 1966, pp. 20–4

Mariën, Marcel. *L'activité surréaliste en Belgique*. Brussels: Lebeer-Hossmann, 1979

Meïmoun, François. 'Entretien avec Pierre Boulez'. https://www.musicologie.org/publirem/entretien_avec_pierre_boulez.html [accessed June 2023]

Meïmoun, François. *Entretien avec Pierre Boulez: la naissance d'un compositeur*. Paris: Aedam Musicae, 2010

Meïmoun, François. *La Construction du langage musical de Pierre Boulez: la Première Sonate pour piano*. Thesis submitted to EHESS, Paris, 2018. Published as a book, Paris: Aedam Musicae, 2019.

Mendelssohn, Edmund. 'Ontological appropriation: Boulez and Artaud'. *Twentieth-Century Music*, vol. 18 no. 2 (2021): pp. 281–310

Merlin, Christian. *Pierre Boulez*. Paris: Fayard, 2019

Murray, Christopher Brent and Yves Balmer. 'Pierre Boulez and Olivier Messiaen's harmony class'. In Paolo dal Molin (ed.), *Immagini di gioventù. Saggi sulla formazione e le prime opere di Pierre Boulez, Musicalia*, vol. 7 (2014): pp. 31–59

Myers, Rollo. 'Some reflections on French music today'. *Musical Times*, vol. 88 no. 1247 (1947): pp. 18–19

Nattiez, Jean-Jacques (ed.). *Pierre Boulez/John Cage: correspondance*. Paris: Christian Bourgois, 1991

Nattiez, Jean-Jacques (ed.) and Robert Samuels (trans.). *The Boulez–Cage Correspondence*. Cambridge: Cambridge University Press, 1993

Née, Patrick. 'Le "hasard objectif": une allégorèse problématique'. *Revue d'histoire littéraire de la France*, vol. 108 (2008): pp. 133–57

Nichols, Roger. *From Berlioz to Boulez*. London: Kahn & Averill, 2022

Nicholson, Melanie. 'Surrealism's "found object": the enigmatic Mexico of Artaud and Breton'. *Journal of European Studies*, vol. 43 no. 1 (2013): pp. 27–43

Nougé, Paul. *La Conférence de Charleroi*. Brussels: Le Miroir Infidèle, 1946

O'Hagan, Peter. 'Boulez and the foundation of IRCAM'. In Richard Langham Smith and Caroline Potter (eds.), *French Music since Berlioz*. Aldershot: Ashgate, 2006, pp. 303–30

O'Hagan, Peter. *Pierre Boulez and the Piano*. Abingdon: Routledge, 2017

O'Hagan, Peter. *Pierre Boulez: sur Incises*. Geneva: Contrechamps, 2021

Pawlik, Joanna. 'Artaud in performance: dissident surrealism and the postwar American avant-garde'. *Papers of Surrealism*, no. 8 (2010): pp. 1–25

Pereira de Tugny, Rosângela. *Pierre Boulez, André Schaeffner: correspondance 1954-–1970*. Paris: Fayard, 1998

Peyser, Joan. *Boulez: Composer, Conductor, Enigma*. London: Cassell, 1977

Peyser, Joan. *To Boulez and Beyond: Music in Europe since the Rite of Spring*, revised edition. Lanham, MD: Scarecrow Press, 2007

Piencikowski, Robert. 'Pierre Boulez and Paul Sacher: chronicle of a friendship'. In Felix Meyer (ed.), *Settling New Scores: Music Manuscripts from the Paul Sacher Foundation*. Mainz: Schott, 1998, pp. 82–5

Potter, Caroline. 'Pierre Boulez, surrealist'. *Gli spazi della musica* vol. 7 (2018), http://www.ojs.unito.it/index.php/spazidellamusica [accessed June 2023]

Price, Sally and Jean Jamin. 'Conversation with Michel Leiris'. *Current Anthropology*, vol. 29 no. 1 (February 1988): pp. 157–74

Programme note for Pierre Boulez, *Le Visage nuptial*. *Wise Music Classical*. https://www.wisemusicclassical.com/work/49985/ [accessed June 2023]

Rae, Caroline (ed.). *André Jolivet: Music, Art and Literature*. Abingdon: Routledge, 2019

Roueff, Olivier. 'L'Ethnologie musicale selon André Schaeffner, entre musée et performance'. *Revue d'Histoire des Sciences Humaines*, vol. 1 no. 14 (2006): pp. 71–100

Rubio, Emmanuel. 'Christian Dotremont, entre surréalismes belge et français'. *Europe*, vol. 83 no. 912 (2005): pp. 197–206

Salem, Joseph. 'Boulez's *Kunstlerroman*: using *blocs sonore* to overcome anxieties and influence in *Le Marteau sans maître*'. *Journal of the American Musicological Society*, vol. 71 no. 1 (2018): pp. 109–54

Samuel, Claude. Interview with Olivier Messiaen. *Messiaen Edition*, 18 CD box set, Warner Classics 2564 62162-2 (2005); trans. Stuart Walters in CD booklet, pp. 109–35

Savarese, Nicola. '1931: Antonin Artaud sees Balinese theatre at the Paris Colonial Exposition', trans. Richard Fowler. *The Drama Review*, vol. 45 no. 3 (2001): pp. 51–77

Sholl, Robert. 'Love, mad love, and the "*point sublime*": the surrealist poetics of Messiaen's *Harawi*'. In Robert Sholl (ed.), *Messiaen Studies*. Cambridge: Cambridge University Press, 2007, pp. 34–62

Siguret, Françoise. 'Boulez/Mallarmé/Boulez: pour une nouvelle poétique musicale'. *Études françaises*, vol. 17 no. 3–4 (1981): 97–109

Simeone, Nigel. 'Messiaen and the *Concerts de la Pléiade*: "a kind of clandestine revenge against the occupation"'. *Music and Letters*, vol. 81 no. 4 (2000): pp. 551–84

Simeone, Nigel. 'Music at the 1937 Paris Exposition: the science of enchantment'. *Musical Times*, vol. 143 no. 1878 (2002): pp. 9–17

Smigel, Eric. 'Recital hall of cruelty: Antonin Artaud, David Tudor, and the 1950s avant-garde'. *Perspectives of New Music*, vol. 45 no. 2 (2007), pp. 171–202

Souris, André. *Conditions de la musique et autres écrits*. Brussels: Editions de l'Université de Bruxelles/CNRS, 1976

Souris, André. *La Lyre à double tranchant: écrits sur la musique et le surréalisme*, ed. Robert Wangermée. Liège: Mardaga, 2000

Sprout, Leslie A. 'The 1945 Stravinsky debates: Nigg, Messiaen, and the early Cold War in France'. *Journal of Musicology*, vol. 26 no. 1 (2009): pp. 85–131.

Stacey, Peter F. *Boulez and the Modern Concept*. Aldershot: Scolar Press, 1987

Steinegger, Catherine. *Pierre Boulez et le théâtre*. Liège: Mardaga, 2012

Steinegger, Catherine. 'Pierre Boulez et Paul Claudel'. *Bulletin de la Société Paul Claudel*, no. 202 (2018). http://www.paul-claudel.net/bulletin/bulletin-de-la-societe-paul-claudel-n%C2%B0202 [accessed June 2023]

Strinz, Werner. '"Il y a un couteau que je n'oublie pas": Antonin Artaud et Pierre Boulez'. In Florence Fix, Pascal Lécroart and Frédérique Toudoire-Surlapierre (eds.), *Musique de scène, musique en scène*. Paris: L'Harmattan/Orizons, 2012, pp. 21–33

Tarjabayle, Benoît. 'René Char, Pierre Boulez: *Le Soleil des eaux*. Étude critique et analytique'. 2 vols. Mémoire de maîtrise, Université de Paris-Sorbonne (Paris IV), 1995

Thomas, Gavin. 'Work not in progress'. *Musical Times*, vol. 136 no. 1827 (May 1995): pp. 225–29

Tissier, Brice. 'Pierre Boulez et le *Théâtre de la cruauté* d'Antonin Artaud: de *Pelléas* à *Rituel, in memoriam Bruno Maderna*'. *Intersections*, vol. 28 no. 2 (2008): pp. 31–50

Troche, Sarah. *Le hasard comme méthode*. Rennes: Presses Universitaires de Rennes, 2015

Walters, David. 'The aesthetics of Pierre Boulez'. PhD thesis, Durham University, 2003. Available at Durham E-Theses Online: http://etheses.dur.ac.uk/3093/

Wangermée, Robert. *André Souris et le complexe d'Orphée: entre surréalisme et musique sérielle*. Liège: Mardaga, 1995

Worton, Michael. 'Archipel & Labyrinthe: l'importance de la poésie de René Char pour la musique de Pierre Boulez'. *Interférences*, vol. 13 (January–June 1981): pp. 57–69

Zenck, Martin. 'Die unveröffentlichte Bühnenmusik von Pierre Boulez zu Nietzsches/Barraults philosophischer Prosa-Dichtung "Ainsi parlait Zarathoustra" (1974)'. *Die Musikforschung*, vol. 57 no. 3 (2004): pp. 234–48

Zenck, Martin. 'Pierre Boulez' "Orestie" (1955–1995). Das unveröffentlichte Manuskript der szenischen Musik zu Jean-Louis Barraults Inszenierung der Trilogie im Théâtre Marigny'. *Archiv für Musikwissenschaft*, vol. 60 no. 4: (2003): pp. 303–32

INDEX

PIERRE BOULEZ